52 WEEKEND ADVENTURES *in* NORTHERN CALIFORNIA

TOM STIENSTRA

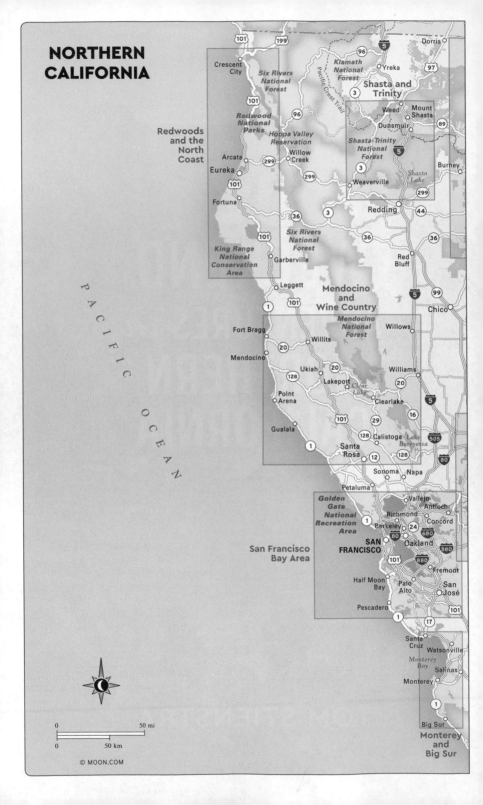

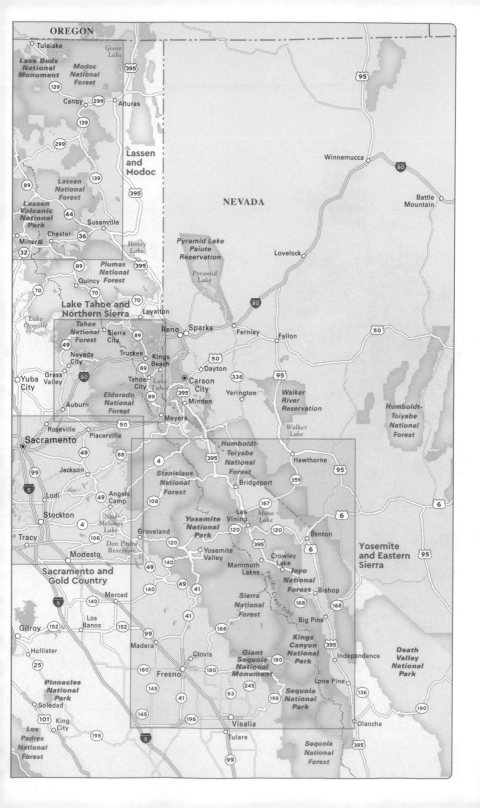

WHERE ARE YOU GOING NEXT?

*W*hen I first began writing, I started receiving letters from people asking me to plan their weekend trips: the best hikes, campgrounds, lakes, rivers, fishing spots, to see wildlife . . . it has never stopped. Often they ask, "Where are you going next?"

The answers are now in your hands: My favorite destinations—52 in all, one for each weekend of the year, from Mount Whitney to the Oregon border; from the California coast to the High Sierra.

To make each trip work, I've revealed my favorite places for getaways and adventures, as well as my favorite places to eat and sleep. I've also added personal insights. Find just the right rock to stand on for a view, the right lure for that elusive big fish, and all the places where I felt like I could stop the world for a while and take in the power of place.

My mission in this book is to shape a great trip for anybody who wants to get out there. This collection of information is based solely on my personal travels, with feedback from field scouts. It's not available as a whole anywhere else.

These are the places I love. Over the years, I've found that all anybody needs is something great to look forward to. This book provides that.

As for this coming weekend, let me ask you: Where are you going next?

WHAT SETS YOU FREE?
HIKE. BIKE. CAMP. FISH. BOAT. EXPLORE.

◁ *view of Half Dome from Glacier Point*

CONTENTS

REDWOODS AND THE NORTH COAST 23

SHASTA AND TRINITY 47

∽ A PERSONAL NOTE ∽

*O*n top of Mount Whitney, I took a seat on a rock cornice, peered across 100 miles of alpine peaks, ridges and canyons, and felt free in the world. A light breeze swept up the canyon. The air tasted thin, cool and sweet.

I felt this dreamlike sense of the past, as if the ghosts of John Muir, William Brewer, and Joe Walker were guiding me. As I took in the scope of the landscape, I also sensed the answer for my life was out there. I felt this calling to venture to every lake, river, and mountain, to every park, national forest, and wilderness, to see it all and write about it, and to live a life where I would always feel this way: free in the world.

Many know something of this sensation. We get there on different paths, but arrive at the same place. It was the only way I could find my place in the world.

One night at a gas station, at one of the many jobs I worked to pay my way through college, a guy asked me for change. As I opened the till, he got behind me and then hit me in the back of my head with a hatchet. The paramedics got there before I could bleed out; they saved my life. When I got out of the hospital, it felt like I was cast in a movie that was set in the wrong time, that I didn't belong in the present day, but in the 1830s, out there with mountain man Joe Walker, camping at the Forks of the Kern.

In a crowd, a building, a city, in traffic, everything felt miscast. Yet in the outdoors, everything was right, even perfect. It wasn't long before I found myself roaming across the land with my dog, Rebel. I often teamed up with my best friend, Jeffrey Patty (nicknamed Foonski) and his dog, Sam. I eventually discovered that Jeff was recovering from a car accident where he nearly died from head trauma. Back in the day, we had no idea that we had severe PTSD; our dogs were like service animals. Later, my big brother Bob (nicknamed Rambob), six years my senior and imprinted by severe trauma from combat in Vietnam, also found a place with us on the trail. Michael Furniss also joined us. In a society where few understand PTSD, we were misfits, yet on the trail, brothers.

Among us, we've never talked much about our near-death encounters, but on a subliminal level, they connected us. For each of us, when we were out there, hiking, fishing, boating, biking, tracking wildlife... all was right with the world.

I remember how I felt that day on top of Whitney and the lesson that came to me. It can speak to anybody. The outdoors can set you free.

—*Tom Stienstra*

Mountain climb: Mount Shasta

Mountain climb for youngsters: Lassen Peak, Lassen Volcanic National Park

Sierra panorama: Mitchell Peak, Jennie Lakes Wilderness

Most difficult permit: Mount Whitney from Whitney Portal, first weekend of August, 2 percent odds in preseason lottery

Lake view: Mount Tallac, Desolation Wilderness

Most unique payoff: Sierra Buttes Lookout, Tahoe National Forest

▽ *(top left) Lassen Peak trail; (top right) Mount Shasta summit;*
(bottom) Mount Whitney

Most dramatic easy hike with a view: Glacier Point to Pohono Trail, Yosemite National Park

Prettiest wilderness lakes: Shadow, Garnet, Minaret, Ediza; Ansel Adams Wilderness

Chain of lakes: Meeks Creek Trail to Genevieve, Crag, Hidden, Shadow, Stony Ridge, and Rubicon Lakes, Lake Tahoe Basin

Sierra trailhead: Tuolumne Meadows, Yosemite National Park

Hikers' boat shuttle: Echo Lakes to trailhead for PCT/Desolation Wilderness

Overnight backpack for kids: Deadfall Lakes, Trinity Divide, Shasta-Trinity National Forest

Complete mountain resort: Convict Lake Resort

Drive-to view: Glacier Point, Yosemite National Park

Prettiest lake trail: Wapama Falls, Hetch Hetchy Reservoir, Yosemite National Park

Trailhead for fishing: Agnew Meadows to River Trail on upper San Joaquin River

Snowshoe trek: Badger Pass to Dewey Point, Yosemite National Park

▽ *view near Glacier Point*

BEST OF THE REDWOODS

Most overlooked, pristine redwoods: Boy Scout Tree Trail, Jedediah Smith Redwoods State Park

Most species champion trees: James Irvine Trail, Prairie Creek Redwoods State Park

Redwood hike behind locked gate: Tall Trees Trail, Redwood National Park

▽ *Stout Grove*

Prettiest ferns: Fern Canyon, Prairie Creek Redwoods State Park
Kayaking: Big River Lagoon/Mendocino Bay, Mendocino coast
RV sites: Seacliff State Beach, Monterey Bay
Coastal campsite: Wildcat, Point Reyes National Seashore
Coastal waterfall: McWay Falls, Julia Pfeiffer Burns State Park
Scuba diving: Point Lobos Marine Reserve
Protected coastal preserve: Salt Point State Park
Most underrated trail for difficulty: Lost Coast Trail, Mattole Trailhead

▽ *(top left) Salt Point State Park; (top right) Big River Lagoon;*
(bottom) McWay Falls Overlook

BEST OF THE BAY AREA

Prettiest scope of view: East Peak, Mount Tamalpais State Park

Urban view: Mount Livermore (at night), Angel Island State Park

All-round park: Del Valle Regional Park (hiking, biking, boating, swimming, fishing, camping, backpacking, wildlife viewing, wilderness access)

Short backpack trip: Skyline-to-the-Sea Trail, Big Basin Redwoods State Park

Bike and hike: Skyline-to-the-Sea Trail out of Rancho del Oso, coastal access to Big Basin Redwoods State Park

Island campsites: Angel Island State Park

Route for continuous views: Perimeter Road, Angel Island State Park

Day hike for early spring: Montara Mountain, San Pedro County Park

▽ *(top left) Berry Creek Falls; (top right) spur on Perimeter Road on Angel Island; (bottom) my wife Denese taking in the view from the east flank of Mount Tamalpais*

BEST OF THE RIVERS

Water sports: San Joaquin River Delta

Prettiest one-mile canyon: Berry Creek, Big Basin Redwoods State Park

Prettiest river walk: McCloud River from Lower Falls to Middle and Upper Falls and on to Lakim Dam

All-round white-water rafting: South Fork American River

Class V white-water rafting: Clavey Falls, Tuolumne River

Most technical kayak run: Cherry Valley, upper Tuolumne River

▽ *(top left) San Joaquin Delta; (top right) South Fork American River; (bottom) McCloud River*

Widest array of campgrounds and cabins: Shasta Lake

Campground for quiet at night: Pardee Recreation Area

Prettiest site, boat-in camping: Emerald Bay State Park, Lake Tahoe

Prettiest lake for tent cabins: Mary Smith Campground, Lewiston Lake

Free loaner kayaks/boats: Independence Lake

Lake-based region for families: Union Valley Reservoir, Crystal Basin Recreation Area

Boat-to/hike-to waterfall: Bullards Bar Reservoir

Family destination: Historic Camp Richardson Resort, South Lake Tahoe

▽ *Emerald Bay State Park*

BEST FISHING

Largest trout: Lake Almanor
Most trout: Sacramento River, Redding to Anderson
Largest bass: Clear Lake
Most bass: Shasta Lake
Prospects for long-term future: Los Vaqueros Reservoir

▽ *(top left) my son Jeremy at Shasta Lake; (top right) Lake Almanor;*
(bottom) striped bass at Los Vaqueros

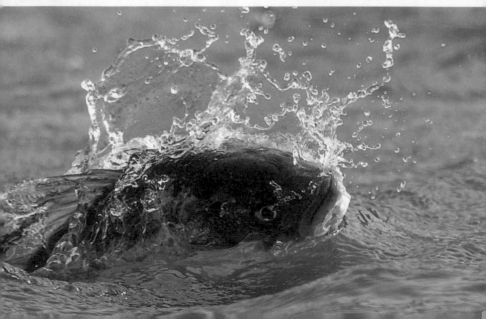

BEST SURPRISES

Most unique destination: Bumpass Hell geothermal area, Lassen Volcanic National Park

Most ironic sense of history: Captain Jack's Stronghold, Lava Beds National Monument

Waterfall, highest volume subliminal flow: Burney Falls, McArthur-Burney Falls Memorial State Park

Gold rush history: South Fork American River, Marshall Gold Discovery State Historic Park, Coloma

▽ *Bumpass Hell geothermal area*

BEST WILDLIFE SPOTS

Elk: Point Reyes National Seashore
Bear: Sequoia National Park
Deer: Lava Beds National Monument (in early winter)
Wild horses: Devil's Garden, Modoc Plateau
Sea otter viewing: Elkhorn Slough by kayak
Humpback whales: Monterey Bay
California condor: Big Sur/Ventana Wilderness
Raptors/eagles: Los Vaqueros watershed by boat

▽ *(top left) Tule elk at Point Reyes; (top right) wild horses in Devil's Garden; (bottom) humpback whale in Monterey Bay*

Tallest tree in world: Hyperion, 380.3 feet, Redwood Empire

Largest tree in world by volume: General Sherman, 275 feet tall, 36 feet diameter, 102.6 feet circumference, Sequoia National Park

North America's highest continuous trail: John Muir Trail

Tallest waterfall in North America: Yosemite Falls, 2,425 feet in three decks, Yosemite Valley

Largest single piece of granite in North America: El Capitan, 7,569 feet

Tallest single-strand waterfall in North America: Ribbon Fall, 1,634 feet, Yosemite Valley

Highest point in continental United States: Mount Whitney, 14,505 feet

Rainiest spot in continental United States: Camp 6 Weather Station, 257 inches in 1983, near Jedediah Smith Redwoods State Park

Largest natural freshwater lake inside state borders: Clear Lake

Longest continuous trail in state: 1,700 miles, Pacific Crest Trail

▽ *Mount Whitney*

Chapter 1

REDWOODS AND THE NORTH COAST

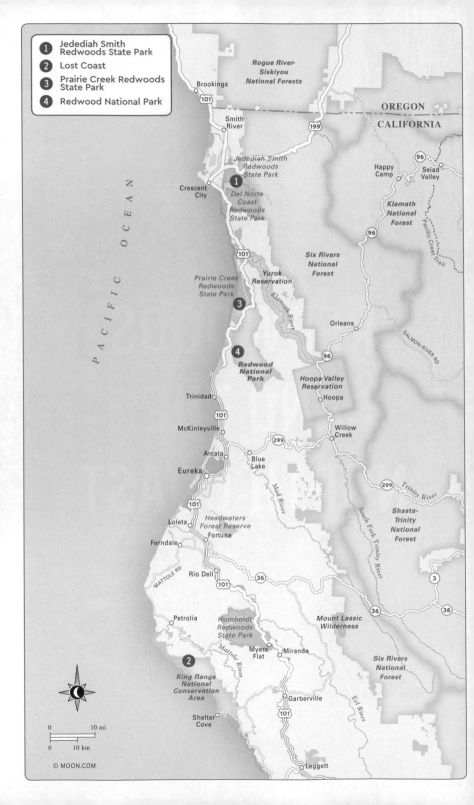

❶ Jedediah Smith Redwoods State Park

707/465-7335 | Crescent City | www.parks.ca.gov

Venturing into Jedediah Smith Redwoods State Park is like taking a trip back in time. The historic park showcases giant coast redwoods and the pristine Smith River, the crown jewel of America's last free-flowing, undammed rivers. There are two sides to Jed Smith, with park sections on each side of the Smith River.

On the north side of the river, just off U.S. 199, is the popular state park campground with a short trail to the river, a put-in for drift boats, and a good fishing hole (fish for steelhead in winter). In summer, a temporary bridge provides access to the Stout Memorial Grove (named after the giant Stout Tree). The pretty River Trail is popular among campers; it ventures through forest, across U.S. 199, and hooks up with the Simpson-Reed Interpretive Trail for an easy one-mile loop.

The south side of the river is a world apart. East of Hiouchi, on U.S. 199, turn right on South Fork Road and cross two bridges to Howland Hill Road, then bear right. Howland Hill Road leads to a staging area for the Stout Memorial Grove and trailheads for the Boy Scout Tree Trail and to Fern Falls.

With a little bit of effort, you can explore one of my favorite spots on the planet. Turn left on South Fork Road instead to head deep into the Six Rivers National Forest and the trailhead for the South Kelsey Trail. This gorgeous hike along the headwaters of the South Fork Smith River leads to the Buck Creek Cabin, a winter shelter close to where pretty Buck Creek pours into the South Fork Smith.

You'll never forget how this place changes your outlook.

▽ *trail to Stout Memorial Grove*

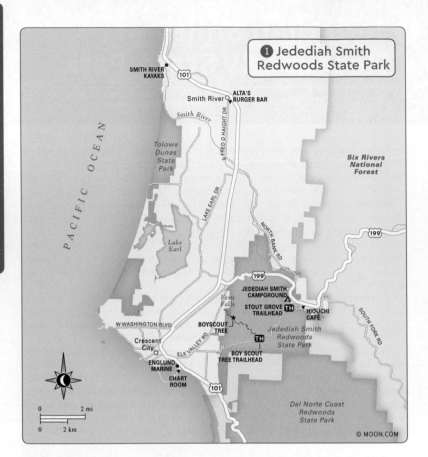

① Jedediah Smith Redwoods State Park

© MOON.COM

BEST HIKE: BOY SCOUT TREE TRAIL

The **Boy Scout Tree Trail** (5.5 miles round-trip, 4 hours) is a soft dirt path—often sprinkled with redwood needles—that allows hikers to venture deep into an old-growth redwood forest, complete with a giant fern understory and high-limbed canopy. This is an easy hike, nearly flat and with only small hills. You just walk into the forest, and a few hours later, walk out. Those few hours can change how you feel about the world.

The trailhead is on the north side of Howland Hill Road. The Boy Scout Tree Trail leads 2.8 miles to **Fern Falls,** a small cascade of silver water over black rock. This is one of the area's better hikes in winter.

The centerpiece of this hike is supposed to be the **Boy Scout Tree,** a big redwood that splits into two trees from a single trunk, located 2.5 miles in. Most people look for it and never find it. (Look for an unmarked spur trail that leads to it—that's right, no sign.) It's not the Boy Scout Tree that is unforgettable, you will discover, but rather how the scope of the experience here can transform your outlook. The beauty is pure and untouched.

FISHING THE SMITH RIVER

The Smith River is a fountain of pure water, undammed and unbridled, running sapphire-blue and free through granite canyons. The river grows California's biggest salmon and steelhead, which arrive at the Smith every fall and

△ *Armand Castagna on the Smith River*

winter, respectively, to beguile and excite anglers. Most who fish come for the steelhead, which arrive mid-January-March. During summer months, a decent fishery for sea-run cutthroat trout (in the lower river) is also provided. The most favored stretch is to put in with a drift boat at the Forks River Access and then make the trip down to the **Ruby van Deventer County Park** or to the popular take-out below the U.S. 101 bridge. Some of the best stretches are adjacent to Jedediah Smith Redwoods State Park, including **White Horse** and **Covered Bridge.** Covered Bridge can be accessed from the bank. There is also a good put-in spot at the park for river access in a drift boat, canoe, or raft.

I caught my life-best 18-pounder from the bank at Jed Smith. Another time, I calculated all the factors—river height (8.5 feet), rain (incoming storm, river coming up), tides (high tide would allow big fish to enter from ocean), and timing (second week of January)—for the best chance at a 20-pounder. Turned out that just downstream in a drift boat right in front of mine was a woman from Chico on her first steelhead trip. She got to

White Horse shortly before me and was the first boat through the hole at dawn. She caught that 20-pounder, the first steelhead of her life, right in front of me.

Fishing and outdoor supplies are available from **Englund Marine** (191 Citizens Dock Rd., Crescent City, 707/464-3230). Rent kayaks from **Smith River Kayaks** (12580 Hwy. 101 N, Smith River, 707/328-2022, www.smithriverkayaks.net).

BEST OVERNIGHT: JEDEDIAH SMITH CAMPGROUND

Jedediah Smith Campground (707/464-6101, www.parks.ca.gov) has camp-sites and cabins sprinkled amid a grove of pretty redwoods, with some sites set near the Smith River. There are 89 sites for tents or RVs and trailers, five hike-in/bike-in sites, and four camping cabins (with electricity, heat, and lighting). Picnic tables, fire grills, and food lockers are provided. Drinking water, coin/token showers, flush toilets, and a dump station are available. In the summer, interpretive

△ *rafters along the Smith River*

programs are offered. Some facilities (including the cabins) are wheelchair-accessible. Leashed pets are permitted in the campground only.

Reservations (800/444-7275, www.reservecalifornia.com, fee) are accepted May-early September and are strongly advised for summer weekends (the campground always fills on three-day holidays). Sites are first-come, first-served October-mid-May. Open year-round.

WHERE TO EAT

The best breakfast near Jed Smith is at the **Hiouchi Café** (2095 Hwy. 199, Hiouchi, 707/458-3445, 6am-2pm Sat.-Thurs., 6am-8pm Fri.), located one mile east of the state park entrance. They open early (even in winter) to accommodate anglers who want to hit the Smith River by dawn.

For the best dinner, I usually drive north to Oregon for seafood in Brookings Harbor at the **The Hungry Clam** (16350 Lower Harbor Rd., Brookings, OR, 541/469-2526) or **Catalyst Seafood** (16182 Lower Harbor Rd., Brookings, OR, 541/813-2422). The best burger in the area is at **Alta's Burger**

Bar (109 S. Fred D. Haight Dr., Smith River, 707/487-9191, 6am-4pm Tues.-Sat., 6am-2pm Sun.).

On the way into the park, campers can pick up supplies at a 24-hour **Safeway** (475 M St., 707/465-3353) in Crescent City.

DRIVING DIRECTIONS

From Crescent City, take U.S. 101 north for four miles to the junction with U.S. 199. Bear right on U.S. 199 and drive five miles to the well-signed park entrance on the right. Turn right and drive a short distance to the park entrance kiosk.

To reach the trailhead for the Boy Scout Tree, drive one mile east of Hiouchi on U.S. 199, then turn right on South Fork Road. Cross two bridges to a T intersection. Bear right on Howland Hill Road (South Fork Road is on the left) and drive to the trailhead.

There are two visitors centers: The **Jedediah Smith Visitor Center** (Hwy. 99, Hiouchi, 707/458-3496, 9am-5pm daily late May-Sept.) and the **Hiouchi Visitor Center** (Hwy. 99, Hiouchi, 707/458-3294, 9am-5pm daily spring-fall, 9am-4pm daily winter).

CAMPFIRE STORIES

*O*ne day in mid-January, it had rained so hard for so long, the Smith River was transformed into this muddy torrent. The water pounded down the gorge and climbed to the edge of the banks at Jed Smith and Cooper's Flat. At dawn at the campground, I climbed out of my tent and looked into the sky between the redwoods. It was raining so hard that if I opened my mouth, I could have drowned. What to do? After all, we were there for the steelhead. Instead, we drove past Hiouchi and turned right, over the bridges to South Fork Road, and cruised out to the route for the old G-O Road, which stands for Gasquet-Orleans Road (long closed as a through route). Here, with the rain still pounding, we found the trailhead for the Old Kelsey Trail. We salvaged the day by hiking 1.5 miles along the South Fork Smith River, where we ducked out of the rain, cooked a meal, and watched the floodwater at nearby Buck Creek roar by and pour into the South Fork Smith. It was one of the greatest easy rainy-day hikes, 3 miles out and back. For much of the way, the water streamed off my hat like a waterfall. It was another lesson that there is no such thing as bad weather, only bad gear—because in the middle of three inches of rain in 12 hours, this was a stellar day.

△ *Buck Creek Cabin on the Kelsey Trail*

② Lost Coast

707/986–5400 | King Range National Conservation Area | www.blm.gov

Once you come here, you'll understand why it is called the Lost Coast. This stretch of coastline features some of the most remote landscapes and beautiful beaches anywhere. The ocean views are spectacular, with miles and miles of scenery that will imprint on your mind forever. Other than country stores and the post office, there's not much out here and, except for the tides, nobody pays much attention to the time. You can take off your watch and leave the cell phone at home—it won't work here anyway.

Many visitors overlook the Lost Coast because of the slow and curvy drive required to get here. From Mattole Beach in the north down to Shelter Cove to the south, this coastal "island" is cordoned off from civilization by the Pacific ocean and the King Range National Conversation Area. Just three roads provide slow and curvy access from U.S. 101 to the coast: Mattole Road (south of Ferndale), Lighthouse Road to Mattole Campground, and Shelter Cove Road. There are no through-roads from north to south—only one long trail.

Hiking the Lost Coast Trail is one of the greatest treks on the Pacific coast. The experience is like being held in suspended animation. From the Mattole Campground south, the surroundings are peaceful and pristine with a striking lack of people. You emerge five days later at Shelter Cove, where a few small restaurants, hotels, and charter boats, a boat ramp, and all facilities are available, and where you will leave the Lost Coast behind.

If you yearn for a place where time doesn't matter, cell phones don't work, and nobody worries about social media, you can find it here. Whether you

▽ *hiking the Lost Coast Trail*

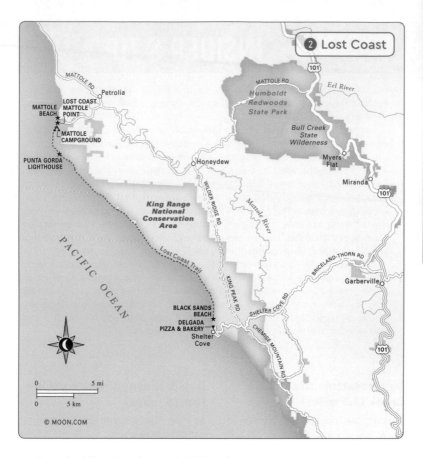

go for a day hike or backpack the full 25.7-mile route to Shelter Cove, you will find a world apart.

The best months to hike the Lost Coast Trail are September and October. November-March, the area gets hammered by heavy rain and high surf and the hiking is terrible—and often dangerous due to heavy rain and high surf. From April through August, the weather and tides are more benign. It is common for strong winds out of the northwest to hit the coast through early summer, which is why you always hike from north to south, so the wind is at your back. From late June through July and August, fog is common, though some days the sun might break through.

BEST ACTIVITY: LOST COAST TRAIL

The **Lost Coast Trail** (25.7 miles one-way, 5 days) is set on bluffs and beaches from the mouth of the Mattole River south to Shelter Cove. The full route spans 25.7 miles, best hiked from north to south so that the wind will be at your back (not in your face). Plan for five days to do it right.

To make this trip work, leave a vehicle at the end of the trail near Black Sands Beach. Then take another car (or a shuttle) to the trailhead at Mattole Campground. That way, a vehicle will be waiting for you when you finish the trip.

For this trip, it's imperative that you bring a **tide book.** (Pick one up at the Petrolia General Store.) At several spots along the trail, you can only pass during low tides.

At high tides in **winter,** you can face water-covered sections with sneaker waves that can carry you out to sea. In wet weather, landslides often cover the beach between Shipman and Buck Creeks. At times they are minor, but at other times, the slides can be significant. High tides and large swells wash against the base of these slides. During high tides and large swells, trying to pass through this landslide zone may be hazardous. Consult your tide book, keep an eye on ocean conditions, and plan to pass through this area at as low a tide as possible, particularly if ocean swells are large. In **summer,** the tides, weather, slides, and creeks are far more manageable, but you should still be cautious, always consulting your tide book.

Be aware: This is an extremely isolated area. In many parts, there is no trail, and there is a lot of boulder-hopping where it is possible to twist an ankle. You will also be walking across sand and cobblestones, which can be very tiring. In winter after heavy rain, several streams can be impassable.

Do not rush. Depend only on yourself. Come prepared for this trip and you will discover that is exactly how you want it.

Day 1: Mattole to Cooskie Creek (6.3 miles)

To start your trip, time the first day for a low tide at Punta Gorda. From Mattole Campground, hike south along the beach past Punta Gorda Lighthouse to Cooskie Creek. (**Note:** Do not take the Jeep Trail out of the campground, but rather start at the signed trailhead near the campground.)

On the beach near Punta Gorda, there is an impassable section at high tide that catches a lot of thru-hikers off guard and they can get stalled on the first day in. Cooskie Creek is right in the middle of an impassable high-tide zone, but there are lots of good campsites.

Here's how the rest of the trip breaks down:

Day 2: Cooskie Creek to Kinsey Creek (5.4 miles)

The section from Sea Lion Gulch to Randall Creek is susceptible to high tides.

Day 3: Kinsey Creek to Miller Flat (5 miles)

At Miller Flat, you will find the best camping area by far.

Day 4: Miller Flat to Gitchell Creek (5 miles)

The section from Big Flat to Gitchell Creek is susceptible to high tides.

Day 5: Gitchell Creek to Black Sands Beach (4 miles)

There are plenty of good places along the way to camp. At night, the rhythmic wave action will send you off to sleep. (When the ocean is rough, though, it can actually keep some people awake.) As for the physical test, the worst of it is along the sections where you must hike on sand. It feels like trudging through wet concrete. You can't fight it or get mad about it, though. That's like trying to fight an earthquake. Enjoy what the

△ *Black Sands Beach*

moment brings, and if you hit a stopper, just take a break for a while. After all, nobody is out here keeping track of you.

The trail surface, well, it often isn't much of a trail at all. Snug-fitting waterproof boots with good, gripping soles are a necessity. They should fit snugly for walking on soft sand and be waterproof for small creek crossings. Soles with good grip will help with scrambling over wet boulders.

A wilderness **permit** (www.recreation.gov) is required. Bear kegs are required for food storage. The **Petrolia General Store** (40 Sherman Rd., Petrolia, 707/629–3455) stocks tide books and rents bear-proof food canisters ($5).

BOATING THE MATTOLE RIVER

The Mattole River cuts a charmed path down the center of Honeydew Valley. The pretty stream is a winding ribbon capable of handling a tremendous volume of water in the winter months. In spring and early summer, when flows settle down, you can take a trip down a fairly benign stretch of water in a raft, canoe, or kayak. Put in at the

Honeydew Store (44670 Mattole Rd., Honeydew, 707/629–3310); there is no boat ramp. Then float and paddle your way to the take-out at the fire station, or make the 13-mile float to **A. W. Way County Park** (Miner Ln., Petrolia). Note that in the drier months, particularly late summer and fall, the river can be too low to run. It is usually runnable through June, and in wet years, sometimes well into July.

BEST OVERNIGHT: MATTOLE CAMPGROUND

Mattole Campground (www.blm.gov) is a small coastal camp set at the mouth of the Mattole River, right where it pours into the Pacific Ocean. It is beautiful and isolated with 14 sites for tents or RVs. Picnic tables and fire rings are provided. Drinking water and vault toilets are available. Some facilities are wheelchair-accessible. Leashed pets are permitted.

Reservations are not accepted; sites are first-come, first-served. Open year-round.

Another camping option is on the trail at Miller Flat.

△ *Mattole Beach*

WHERE TO EAT

When you get about five miles from finishing the Lost Coast Trail, well, that's when many start dreaming about the celebratory dinner in Shelter Cove, a rite of passage for all hikers. You will likely end up at **Delgada Pizza & Bakery** (205 Wave Dr., Shelter Cove, 707/986-7672, 4pm-9pm daily). While the curb appeal won't knock your socks off, the pizza is fresh, hot, and tasty, the beer is cold, the wine flows, and the service is friendly. You can eat outside, too.

The real question is: How far along on the trail do you start thinking about pizza? For those who have a favorite pizza here, the dreaming can begin weeks ahead of your trip.

DRIVING DIRECTIONS

Shuttle services are expensive and seem to go in and out of business. Try **Bill's Lost Coast Shuttle** (707/442-1983), **Lost Coast Adventure Tours** (707/986-9895, www.lostcoastadventures.com), or **Mendo Insider Tours** (707/962-4131, www.mendoinsidertours.com). For the latest information, contact the **Southern Humboldt Chamber of Commerce** (782 Redwood Dr., 707/923-2613) in Garberville.

To reach Mattole Beach: From U.S. 101 in Garberville, drive to exit 639B toward Redway. (**Tip:** Fill the gas tank in Garberville before continuing on.) Turn left on Redwood Drive and go 2.6 miles to Briceland Road. Turn left and drive 10 miles, then continue to Ettersburg/Honeydew Road and drive 5.8 miles to Wilder Ridge Road. Continue on Wilder Ridge Road and drive 13.5 miles to Mattole Road. Bear left on Mattole Road and drive 13.6 miles to Lighthouse Road. Turn left and drive 4.8 miles to the campground. The trailhead for the Lost Coast Trail is just past Mattole Campground. Allow 1.5 hours for the 42-mile drive.

To reach Shelter Cove: From U.S. 101, take the Redway/Garberville exit and follow signs to Shelter Cove. Allow 45 minutes for the 22-mile drive.

CAMPFIRE STORIES

We were soggy from rain and chilled from the cold like Antarctic glaciers. On the short drive from the end of the Lost Coast Trail at Black Sands Beach to Shelter Cove, our thighs, calves, and backs had tightened and stiffened. When we emerged from my truck, it felt like rigor had set in. In such a state, it seemed difficult to believe we had hiked the Lost Coast Trail, when it was all we could do to hobble in with the mobility of Frankenstein's monster and get a seat. Then magic happened. The first sip of beer. It was ice cold. Yes. It felt like every cell in my body had reawakened. Then the pizza. In our degenerative physical states, the first bite of that pizza tasted akin to what a death row inmate would order as the "last meal request."

△ hiking the Lost Coast Trail

③ Prairie Creek Redwoods State Park

707/488-2039 | Redwood National and State Parks, Orick | www.parks.ca.gov

You have the chance to experience the best of the best in the redwoods at Prairie Creek Redwoods State Park. After all, you deserve it, right?

Prairie Creek Redwoods State Park spans a vast landscape of 14,000 acres. It includes Fern Canyon, with its gorgeous walls of ferns, a thriving herd of Roosevelt elk, 10 miles of ocean frontage at Gold Beach, the James Irvine Trail (with four species of world-class conifers), and the drive up Cal Barrel Road for an overlook across mammoth redwoods. Take your pick.

Within the park are 75 miles of trails, a 19-mile bike loop, and a beautiful scenic drive past giant redwoods along the Newton B. Drury Scenic Parkway. Summer interpretive programs with guided walks and junior ranger programs are available through the visitors center. There's also two campgrounds—one set in the woods near Elk Meadow and another on Gold Beach near Fern Canyon—plus camping cabins and backcountry campsites.

The forest understory is dense due to moisture from coastal fog in summer and heavy rain in winter. The blooms of western azalea and rhododendron peak in May and June; these are best seen on the Rhododendron Trail. November-May, always bring your rain gear. Light weather fronts can skim across the coastal forests and produce fair amounts of rain even when the rest of inland California remains dry. Summer temperatures range 40–75°F, while winter temperatures range 35–55°F.

This is my favorite park in the Redwood Empire. Over the years, I have hiked every trail, stalked numerous elk, and marveled at the miniature waterfalls of Fern Canyon while knee-deep in the flowing stream. Every trip feels special and gives rise to life's cornerstone mystery: What will happen next?

▽ *bridge at Prairie Creek*

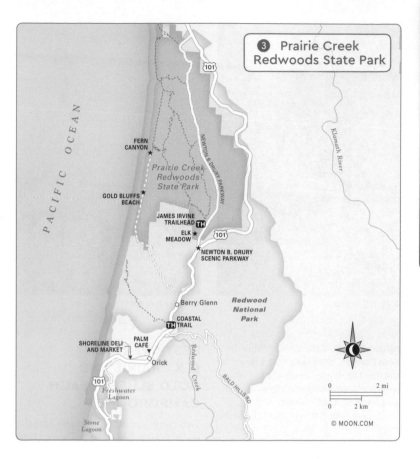

BEST ACTIVITY: COASTAL TRAIL/ FERN CANYON LOOP

You could search across the Pacific Coast and not find a better hike than this loop. The **Coastal Trail/Fern Canyon Loop** (8 miles, 3.5 hours) offers a good chance of seeing Roosevelt elk (see *Wildlife Watching*) on the route in to the trailhead. Then there's Fern Canyon, a coastal walk with the edge of the forest on your right and miles of spotless wilderness beach on your left, ending with a series of hidden waterfalls.

From the parking area, start by crossing the shallow Home Creek stream; most of the year, the cross-ing consists of a few rock hops (June-Sept., small temporary bridges are often provided). If the water level is higher, that's good news—it means the narrow waterfalls are running. Once you cross Home Creek, this hike becomes a near-level walk.

Follow the Coastal Trail for roughly 2.5 miles north, enjoying waterfalls, wilderness beach, ocean views, and coastal forest along the way. The stretch north along the Coastal Trail toward Ossagon Rock is some of the most pristine beach in California. For the Fern Canyon Loop, turn right on the West Ridge Trail and climb 1.8 miles amid towering Sitka spruce and Douglas fir to Friendship Ridge. Turn right again where the trail contours south for 3 miles through old-growth

△ Fern Canyon

△ Roosevelt elk

redwoods. You descend 1 mile into Fern Canyon, then take steps down to the floor of Home Creek where vertical fern walls, small streaming waterfalls, and a pretty creek await.

If it feels special here, that's because it is.

WILDLIFE WATCHING

Roosevelt elk wander freely throughout Prairie Creek Redwoods. They're often sighted at Elk Meadow, near the Elk Meadow Cabins, along Davison Road, and on the Friendship Ridge Trail. It's common to see sub-herds with about a half dozen elk. In the fall, big bulls sport giant antlers that just about poke holes in the clouds; you'll see them with harems of 12–15 females. In the late spring, you might spot cows with their calves.

Of course, always keep a safe distance of 25–100 yards from wildlife. If your behavior is affecting the behavior of an animal, you are too close. Bring a long camera lens, binoculars, or a spotting scope to keep your distance while still enjoying the elk and their nuances.

BEST OVERNIGHT: ELK PRAIRIE AND GOLD BLUFFS BEACH CAMPGROUNDS

Two campgrounds, plus cabin rentals, make Prairie Creek Redwoods State Park one of the best destinations for overnight stays in the redwoods. The park's best campground is **Elk Prairie,** located in forest near park headquarters and across from a meadow where Roosevelt elk are common. There are 75 sites for tents or RVs up to 27 feet and one hike-in site. Camping cabins are also available here. Several trailheads are nearby, including the trailhead for the James Irvine Trail, located across from the visitors center parking lot. The nearby **Elk Meadow Cabins** (P.O. Box 66, Orick 95555, 866/733-9637, http://elkmeadowcabins.com) are also a prime destination.

The other campground is **Gold Bluffs Beach.** The expanse of beach here is awesome, covering 10 miles of huge, pristine ocean frontage. These campsites are in a sandy, exposed

△ *Newton B. Drury Scenic Parkway*

area with windbreaks. You get a huge, expansive beach on one side and a backdrop of 100- to 200-foot cliffs on the other side. You can walk for miles on the beach, often without seeing another soul. The Fern Canyon Trail lies at the end of Davison Road. There are 26 sites for tents or RVs up to 24 feet (no hookups) and one backcountry site. Fire grills, food lockers, and picnic tables are provided. Drinking water and restrooms with flush toilets and showers are available. Leashed pets are permitted.

Reservations (www.reserve-california.com, fee) are accepted May-September; sites area first-come, first-served October-April. Open year-round, weather permitting.

WHERE TO EAT

On our way in to Prairie Creek Redwoods, we always stop in Orick at the **Shoreline Deli and Market** (120025 U.S. 101, Orick, 707/488–5761). For a remote little market, the deli sandwiches are decent, even great at times. This where the park rangers go, and they know best, right? You can also get bonus goodies for a day hike in the park. For a sit-down meal, better for breakfast than for dinner, the **Palm Café** (121130 Hwy. 101, Orick, 707/488–3381) is right

down the street. One dark spring night, after a dinner here, I put my beloved hat on top of Foonski's rig while we rearranged our gear, then drove off, leaving my hat on the roof. It took years to find another hat as good.

DRIVING DIRECTIONS

To reach Elk Meadow: From Eureka, take U.S. 101 north for 45 miles to Orick, and then continue north for 5 miles to the exit for the Newton B. Drury Scenic Parkway. Take that exit 0.2 mile to Newton B. Drury Scenic Parkway and continue north for 1.1 mile to the Prairie Creek Road and park entrance on the left. Turn left and drive 0.6 mile (you will pass the park's visitors center and headquarters on the right) to Elk Prairie Campground on the right.

To reach Gold Bluffs Beach: From Eureka, take U.S. 101 north for 45 miles to Orick, and then continue north for 2.8 miles to Davison Road on the left. Turn left on Davison and drive 5.6 miles to Gold Bluffs Beach Campground on the left, or continue 1.2 miles to the end of the road, Home Creek, and the trailhead for Fern Canyon and the Coastal Trail.

CAMPFIRE STORIES

*O*n the Friendship Ridge Trail, on the last leg of a loop hike at dusk, my pal Michael Furniss and I found ourselves staring into the bugged-out eyes of what appeared to be a 175-pound female elk, about 40 feet away. Suddenly the elk ran straight at us, a full-on, point-blank charge. To avoid her, we barreled over a fallen log on the right side of the trail and rolled down about 10 feet into a fern-covered gulch, then laughed like hell over what seemed a bizarre experience. Turns out 10 other hikers had been driven off the trail that day by small female elk. Turns out she had a calf. When she encountered hikers, her protective maternal instincts took over.

A half hour later, on the same trail, we ran into a giant bull, with antlers like the Hartford commercial and a harem of a dozen bulls. Even at 40 feet, he ignored us and we passed on the trail without an issue. You see, we were no threat at all.

The lesson here: The elk to be most wary of are not the big bulls with the giant racks, but the smaller females that guard their yearlings.

△ *along the trail*

④ Redwood National Park

707/465-7765 | Redwood National Park | www.nps.gov/redw

The redwood coast is world renowned. When visiting the redwoods, you are as likely to see someone from New York or Iowa or France as from Sacramento. Yet for many Californians, this region is off the radar. It is a long drive for most, with no direct route to reach it. But if you want to get away, this is the place to do it.

If it feels like life is passing by too fast, a hike through the redwoods has a way of slowing everything down to the pace of a walk. Most of the redwood hikes are easy, with no long climbs, traversing through forests or along streams or near the coast. The miles of secluded beaches and stretches of oceanfront with few people can stun those from a city used to crowds everywhere they turn. Best of all, the age, size, and feel of the mammoth old-growth redwoods puts our own time here on the planet in perspective.

Over the years, I have hiked every trail from Trinidad north to Crescent City. No matter your favorite landscape, whether woods or water or miles of open sea, you can slow down and find it here.

▽ *footbridge at Redwood National Park*

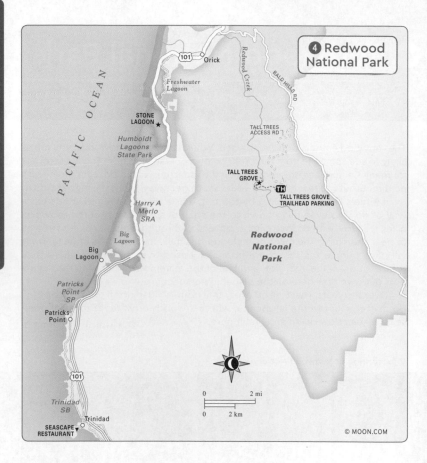

BEST HIKE:
TALL TREES TRAIL

The **Tall Trees Trail** (4 miles round-trip, 2.5 hours) is one of the signature walks on the Redwood Coast. The hike is an easy walk in the forest that leads to the Tall Trees Grove along Redwood Creek. The element that sets it apart (and keeps it off the tourist radar) is that a permit is required to drive to the trailhead, and only a limited number of cars are allowed per day. By limiting access, the park has created an oasis.

This is an easy walk into a grove of towering, ancient redwoods with cathedral-like beauty. The trail is shaded and surrounded by a lush fern understory as it descends 500 feet to Redwood Creek. Your mission here is

to reach the Tall Trees Grove, home of the Libby Tree. In the 1960s, the Libby Tree was believed to be the tallest tree in the world, and it helped lead to the creation of Redwood National Park. (After the top of the tree broke off in 1994, it became the 34th tallest tree.) Regardless, if you love big trees, this is a must-do hike.

Obtain a free permit at the **Kuchel Visitor Center** (U.S. 101, Orick, 707/465-7765, 9am-5pm daily spring-fall, 9am-4pm daily winter) after 9am on the day of your visit. The permit is actually the combination number for the locked gate on the drive in on C-Line Road. Once through the gate, it's another seven miles on a gravel road to the trailhead. Allow one hour for the drive.

△ *Redwood Creek*

△ *Tall Trees Grove*

BOATING AT STONE LAGOON

Stone Lagoon (Humboldt Lagoons State Park, 115336 U.S. 101 N, Trinidad, 707/677–3570, www.parks.ca.gov) is directly adjacent to U.S. 101, with a boat-in camp set in a cove out of sight of the highway. That makes it a secret spot for a lucky few. This is a great place to explore by canoe or kayak. Paddle upstream to the lagoon's inlet creek, then, after setting up camp, hike to a secluded sand spit and stretch of beachfront. The water is usually calm in the morning, but often gets choppy from afternoon winds. Translation: Get your paddling done early. There is also fishing for cutthroat trout. The marshland habitat is home to a wide range of flora, birds, and even elk.

Six primitive boat-in campsites are available. The best place to launch is directly behind the small **Stone Lagoon Visitor Center** (9am-6pm daily). Paddle directly across the lagoon, where you'll find boat-in campsites tucked into Ryan's Cove on the far side of the lagoon. The visitors center rents kayaks and paddleboards. Campsite registration is at Patrick's Point State Park (707/677–3570, www.parks.ca.gov), south of Stone Lagoon. Open late May-early September.

BEST OVERNIGHT: BACKCOUNTRY CAMPSITES

When visitors arrive from all over the world to see giant redwoods, it's common for the well-known campgrounds to fill. Lesser known are five trail camps that require anywhere from a short walk to a long hike to reach: DeMartin, Flint Ridge, Elam Creek, 44 Camp, and Redwood Creek. A free backcountry permit is required, available from the Kuchel Visitor Center.

DeMartin: Reaching the 10 sites requires a 3.5-mile hike, with some climbing and switchbacks. The trailhead is north of the Klamath River, on the east side of U.S. 101 at mile marker 15.7. Amenities include fire rings, food lockers, picnic tables, and a pit toilet. The elevation is 800 feet.

Flint Ridge: Reaching the eight sites requires an easy 0.25-mile walk from the Coastal Trail. Trailhead parking is at the end of Coastal Drive. Amenities include fire rings, food lockers, picnic tables, and a pit toilet. The elevation is 400 feet.

Elam Creek: Reaching the three sites requires a three-mile hike. From the Redwood Creek Trailhead, the moderate grade is routed through old-growth redwoods near Redwood Creek, which may be impassable.

INSIDER'S TIP

False Klamath Cove is one of the prettiest beaches anywhere on the Pacific Coast. The beach spans about a mile and is nestled in a half-moon cove. Stacks and outcrops pepper the inshore sea. It is gorgeous year-round and in all weather, but at dusk on a calm day it can take your breath away. A lot of things can make you scream and shout, but very few can make you quiet. False Klamath Cove is one of those things.

The turnoff for the parking area is at the north end of the beach off U.S. 101 (across from the turnoff to Wilson Creek Road).

Plan to camp June-September when bridges over Redwood Creek are in place. Amenities include fire rings, food lockers, picnic tables, and a pit toilet.

44 Camp: Reaching the four sites requires an eight-mile hike. From the Redwood Creek Trailhead, the hike is routed through old-growth redwoods near Redwood Creek. Amenities include fire rings, food lockers, picnic tables, and a pit toilet.

Redwood Creek: This is the centerpiece of the trail camps along Redwood Creek. Accessible via an eight-mile hike, these dispersed campsites are sprinkled along gravel bars on Redwood Creek. Trailhead parking is off Bald Hills Road. Open in summer only.

WHERE TO EAT

If you are looking for breakfast on the drive north, stop off at Trinidad and drive down to **Seascape Restaurant** (1 Bay St., next to the pier, Trinidad, 707/677-3762). They serve the best crab/shrimp omelets this side of heaven, as far as I can tell. For dinner, venture north into Crescent City. Just as you reach the harbor, look on the left for the **Chart Room** (130 Anchor Way, south end of harbor, Crescent City, 707/464-5993). Yeah, I know, first impressions: big parking lot, not the prettiest building, and this is where the

tourists go. But this is also the best seafood in town, plus you get a view of the harbor. From this lookout, I watched the 2011 tsunami destroy 35 boats and a bunch of docks in the harbor.

DRIVING DIRECTIONS

Redwood National Park is located along U.S. 101. The **Thomas H. Kuchel Visitor Center** (U.S. 101, Orick, 707/465-7765, 9am-5pm daily spring-fall, 9am-4pm daily winter) is 42 miles south of Crescent City and 20 miles north of Trinidad on U.S. 101. This is where you will pick up the permit for the Tall Trees Trail and the combination for the gate to the trailhead. Exit the visitors center, turn left (north) onto U.S. 101, and drive 3.1 miles to Bald Hills Road. Turn right and drive 7 miles to a locked gate (look for the Tall Tree Access sign). Unlock the gate and drive 6 miles to the parking area and trailhead.

To reach Stone Lagoon: From the Kuchel Visitor Center, take U.S. 101 south for 4.1 miles to the turnoff for the parking lot and visitors center. Boat access is on the left at the southern foot of the lagoon.

To reach False Klamath Cove: From the Kuchel Visitor Center, take U.S. 101 north for 30 miles. The parking turnoff and access are on the left (opposite Wilson Creek Road on the right).

CAMPFIRE STORIES

*A*t a visitors center for Redwood State and National Parks, a visitor ran in through the door, crying in hysterics. She was apparently devastated by something she had seen. A ranger took her aside to settle her down and hear the story. "I saw the most horrible thing," she wailed, "the most terrible thing I've ever seen that somebody has done." The tears were streaming down her face. The ranger edged closer to comfort her. Instead, she sobbed more deeply. "Tell me now, what did you see?" She talked in chopped words, trying to gather herself. "Along the highway out there, somebody killed some Irish setters, those beautiful red dogs, and just left them lying along the side of the road." She stopped to cry some more. "I love dogs, I love all animals. It's the worst thing I've ever seen." She agreed to show the ranger what she had seen. In his patrol vehicle, they drove out to U.S. 101, turned left, and drove up toward Bald Hills Road. "There's one, right up there!" As the ranger neared, he spotted one of the "dogs" lying along the road, and he pulled over to take a look.

It was a piece of redwood bark, one of several that had apparently fallen off a loaded logging truck while it was rumbling up the highway.

△ *campsite in Redwood National Park*

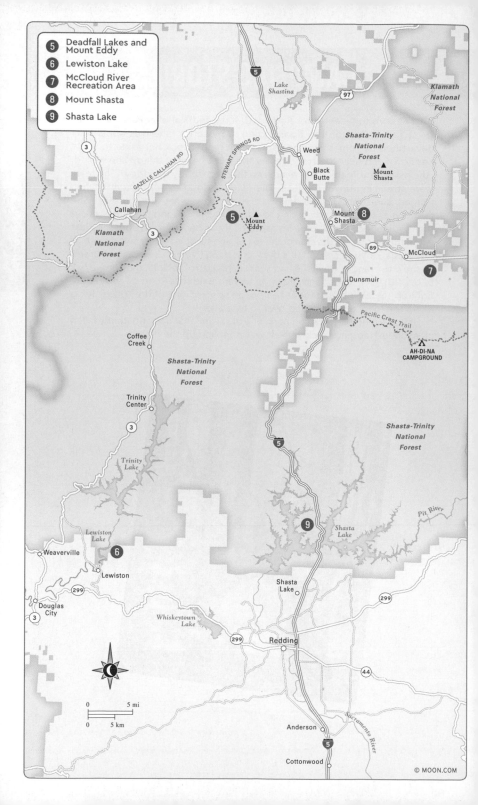

Klamath National Forest

3

Lake Shastina

97

Shasta-Trinity National Forest

Klamath National Forest

GAZELLE CALLAHAN RD

STEWART SPRINGS RD

Weed

Black Butte

▲ Mount Shasta

Callahan

3

Klamath National Forest

5   ▲ Mount Eddy

Mount Shasta   8

89

McCloud

7

Dunsmuir

Pacific Crest Trail

AH-DI-NA CAMPGROUND

Coffee Creek

Shasta-Trinity National Forest

Trinity Center

3

Shasta-Trinity National Forest

Trinity Lake

Pit River

Lewiston Lake

9

Shasta Lake

Weaverville

6

Lewiston

299

Shasta Lake

299

Douglas City

3

Whiskeytown Lake

299

Redding

44

0   5 mi

0   5 km

Anderson

Sacramento River

5

Cottonwood

© MOON.COM

~ Chapter 2 ~

SHASTA AND TRINITY

The first time you top the crest of 9,025-Mount Eddy, the view of 14,179-foot Mount Shasta hits you all at once—one of the greatest reveals in California. On the way up Mount Eddy, the hike passes a series of stellar springs and alpine lakes, with spots along the trail offering long-distance views of the Trinity Alps to the west. But there is no sign of Mount Shasta. As you venture up the trail and into the wildlands, there's a subliminal sense that the big view looms ahead. When it arrives all at once, it hits you right in the heart—a knockout punch.

Mount Eddy is located directly west of Mount Shasta; I-5 runs down the valley between the two. If you've ever cruised along I-5, you've probably already seen Mount Eddy, though it barely registers in the shadow of Mount Shasta.

The easy hike to Middle Deadfall Lake is one of the best (and easiest) backpack trips in California. This collection of small lakes provides excellent wilderness campsites, plus swimming and fishing. You can bring your dog.

Each summer, I carve out a day or two to hike to Deadfall Lakes and beyond to Mount Eddy. Along the easy, rhythmic walk, I breathe in the scent of pine duff in the air. At Middle Deadfall, the pristine cool water makes for great swimming that is alone worth the trip. Venture beyond, and atop the crest you will experience the magic moment of Mount Shasta and realize why you came this way.

The best time to hike to Mount Eddy is in early summer, June or early July. Mount Shasta will still have a coating of snow, and in a photo taken from Mount Eddy, it will look like a giant diamond poking a hole into the sky.

▽ *Mount Eddy summit*

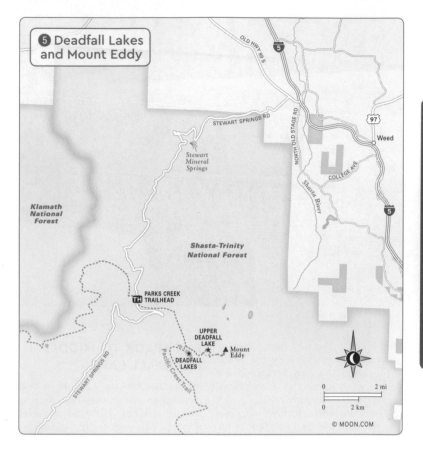

BEST ACTIVITY: MOUNT EDDY TRAIL

The hike to the top of **Mount Eddy** (10.3 miles round-trip, 5 hours) is one of the best one-day mountain climbs in California, with an elevation gain of 2,150 feet. Though you'll maintain a rhythmic pace for most of the trek, there are two steep sections, including a long stretch of switchbacks to the summit.

The launch point is the Parks Creek Trailhead (on Forest Road 42N17; parking area on the left), set on a ridge at an elevation of 6,830 feet in Shasta-Trinity National Forest.

The first destination is **Middle Deadfall Lake** (2.9 miles) featuring a 400-foot climb—easy and fun. The trail

pokes in and out of a mostly Douglas fir forest with occasional visits from golden-mantled ground squirrels. Off to the right is a great view of the Trinity Alps, topped by Thompson Peak; look ahead and you'll see the Deadfall Lakes Basin.

After rock-hopping over a small stream, you'll reach a junction with the **Mount Eddy Trail** on the left (the Pacific Crest Trail is to the right). Just beyond a short rise ahead is Middle Deadfall Lake.

To continue to Mount Eddy, turn left and start climbing 500 feet over the next mile, with one steep stretch to the first of the **Upper Deadfall Lakes.** The trail skirts two small lakes nestled in an alpine plateau, with the upper lake set against the back of

△ *Mount Eddy trail sign*

Mount Eddy. The trail then climbs a short distance to a saddle in the Trinity Divide ridge. The long-distance views to the west across the lakes below and beyond are breathtaking.

From the saddle, turn left to follow the trail as it climbs 1,200 feet in 1.5 miles with seven switchbacks up a barren slope.

Suddenly, just as you gain the top of Mount Eddy, the entire western exposure of Mount Shasta comes into view. From its 16-mile base, Mount Shasta rises high into a cobalt-blue sky, 11,000 feet above the surrounding valleys. The top of Mount Eddy is wide and slightly graded, with the remains of an old lookout scattered at the true summit.

On two different trips, I put logbooks into ziplock bags, tucked them into coffee cans, and placed them at the summit for people to record their observations. This proved to be popular: Folks expressed their feelings about the view, filling the logbooks with comments so fast that, after a few months, the filled logbooks were taken to the ranger station and never replaced.

BACKPACK TO MIDDLE DEADFALL LAKE

Middle Deadfall Lake is one of the best destinations for an easy backpacking trek in summer. The hike provides a great introduction to wilderness camping, with a series of lakeside campsites available at all the Deadfall Lakes. Most folks set up at Middle Deadfall Lake and use it as a base camp for a few days of fun, swimming, fishing, trekking, or climbing Mount Eddy.

From the **Parks Creek Trailhead** (Forest Road 42N17), follow the trail to Mount Eddy for 2.9 miles to Middle Deadfall Lake, the biggest of the three lakes. A series of popular campsites with good views are located near the foot of the lake, near the lake's outlet into Deadfall Creek. Several campsites are located along the perimeter of the shore within short range of the outlet. (The best campsite, which has shade, lake views, and good swimming, is at the head the lake. To find it, walk around the lake on an unsigned route near the lake's shore.)

△ *my son Kris and Buddy at Middle Deadfall Lake*

The water at Middle Deadfall Lake is cool and clean, making it a great hike-and-swim destination on hot summer days. While you're there, add in a picnic.

It takes about 1.5 hours to hike from the Parks Creek Trailhead on the PCT to Middle Deadfall. At the foot of the lake, look for a large rock and tree on the left, about 150 yards up the bank—this is the best swimming spot in the basin. Other good spots are across the lake near a small grove of trees and next to a campsite. The only thing to deter you from swimming is if there's a cold wind out of the north or occasional late afternoon thunderstorm activity (most common in June).

To the left, the trail climbs 500 feet to Upper Deadfall Lake, where the best campsites are found at the last of the small lakes you'll reach. A use trail leads to the left to sites on each side of the lake.

A campfire **permit** (www.prevent wildfireca.org, free) is required for overnight use. Parking and access are free.

BEST OVERNIGHT: STEWART MINERAL SPRINGS RESORT

This is not your parent's Best Western. **Stewart Mineral Springs** (4617 Stewart Springs Rd., Weed, 530/938-2222, www.stewartmineralsprings. com, 10am-6pm daily) is a retreat with woodsy cabins and apartments, mineral baths, and sauna and massage treatments. Parks Creek runs through the property, so you can jump from a sauna or a hot bath directly into the cold water, where the temperature change can be dramatic.

WHERE TO EAT

When locals talk about "The Goat," they're talking about **Bistro No. 107** (107 Chestnut St., Mt. Shasta, 530/918-5353, www.bistro107.com, 11am-9pm Mon. and Thurs.-Sat., noon-9pm Sun., shorter hours fall-spring) in downtown Mount Shasta. This small place features a menu that ranges from burgers to paninis and fire-dusted calamari to hot pastrami, plus garlic fries and craft beer. Outdoor seating is stellar in summer. (It used to officially be called "The Goat," and developed something of a cult following. The name was changed due to a trademark infringement, but the nickname stuck.)

DRIVING DIRECTIONS

From Redding, take I-5 north for 60 miles to the town of Mt. Shasta. Continue north for 12 miles and take exit 751 for Edgewood/Gazelle. At the stop sign at Edgewood, turn left and drive 0.2 mile to Old Highway 99. Turn right and drive 0.4 mile to Stewart Springs Road. Turn left and drive 3.9 miles to Forest Road 42N17 (Stewart Mineral Springs Resort is to the left). To reach the Parks Creek Trailhead, turn right, staying on Forest Road 42N17, and drive 9.2 miles to the trailhead parking area on the left.

CAMPFIRE STORIES

*O*n my first trek up Mount Eddy, I topped the crest at Upper Deadfall Lake then walked beyond to the last of the lakes when a flash of movement to the left caught my eye. I sat on a rock along the lake and took in Eddy's massive back wall. Then, to the left, I saw movement again and homed in. A large, brown, weasel-like critter emerged and strolled along the shore. A moment later, another appeared. For a few minutes they played tag, darting amid the rocks and chasing each other. They were fishers, a rare marten-like mammal. It was like witnessing a scene out of a PBS nature special. Then they were gone, vanished into the landscape.

△ *view of Shasta from Mount Eddy summit*

➏ Lewiston Lake

530/623-2121 | Shasta-Trinity National Forest, Weaverville |
www.fs.usda.gov/stnf

This is one of my favorite places on the planet. Lewiston Lake is a narrow lake about 9 miles long with 15 miles of shoreline located directly below Trinity Dam at an elevation of 1,900 feet. It is a great destination for camping, glamping, fishing, kayaking, low-speed powerboating, and bird-watching.

Lewiston serves as the afterbay for Trinity Lake, so it is always kept full to the brim with cool water. The central base of operations is at Pine Cove Marina, which has a launch point and boat rentals. The area is home to seven bald eagles and nine ospreys and sighting them is a daily affair (I've seen bald eagles circle right over the top of my boat).

Though the trip to Lewiston Lake requires a long drive, this is a plus. It's far enough away to provide separation from work and everyday life, a separation that can free you from your problems. Your first sight of the day could be a lake full of water, circles on the surface caused by rising trout, and a boat nestled on the shore nearby. This is as close as it gets to fulfilling the fantasy of having your own On Golden Pond in California.

The best time to visit is in the fall (mid-Sept.-Oct.), when the school season has started and most people have finished their vacations. You can often have your choice of campsites or lodging then. This is also when the fishing is best, when cool nights can set off trout feeding frenzies. The trout seem to know that winter is not far off, and with it, less terrestrial activity and food available.

▽ Lewiston Lake

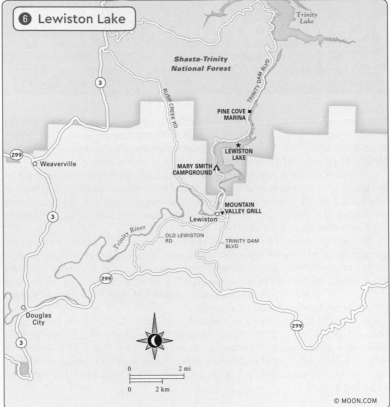

BEST ACTIVITY: FISHING

Fly fishers come from miles around to fish at Lewiston Lake, a cold-water lake that supports trout. Louise Bigham, the owner of the Pine Cove Marina, has developed a trout pen program here. Each year, she releases about 1,000 rainbow trout that range up to 10 pounds. Regulations do not require that anglers use flies, but it is the best way to catch trout.

First-time visitors can rent a boat from Pine Cove Marina, troll flies, and often do great. Shoreliners (often dads with their youngsters) will pick a spot near Pine Cove Marina and use Power Nuggets for bait. They often do just as well. Both are good options for newcomers.

Sometimes the best fishing is at the headwaters of Lewiston, in the 0.5-mile stretch of water below Trinity Dam where the water temperature is in the low 40s. (The best fishing is often in a zone of 45–50°F.) In summer, when water is released out of Trinity Dam, the trout swim up, stage in the headwaters, and wait for food to drift by. When the water releases stop, there is no longer a reason for the fish to hang around. They leave and the bite is over. Access here is by boat.

Another good spot is an area known as the "Terrace." It's located in the center of the lake (roughly offshore from Lakeview Terrace Resort); more specifically, it's downstream from where the peninsula gives way to a terraced lake bottom. The fish often feed here on the edge of the old Trinity

INSIDER'S TIP

Local expert Stanley Mentik experimented for years to develop what we call a "Stanley Special." It's a No. 8 streamer (burgundy head, peacock and rooster hackle) somewhat similar to a leech, Woolly Bugger, or Seal Bugger, which you retrieve just above the moss-covered bottom. One of the best tricks here is to rig a Stanley Special with about 40 inches of fluorocarbon leader behind a Sep's rainbow trout-colored Side Kick Dodger. You then slow troll from the Pine Cove Marina down past what we call "Stupid Corner" (where the lake bends to the right) and catch fish all day long.

You can sometimes get Stanley Specials at **Pine Cove Marina** (9435 Trinity Dam Blvd., Lewiston, 530/778–3878, www.pine-cove-marina.com, 7am-3pm Wed.-Mon.)

River's channel. The crystal-clear water is shallow (3–6 feet deep) and is the site of insect hatches (caddis, midge, callibaetis), a thriving aquatic food chain. I once counted 50 trout here in 45 minutes, almost 1 per minute.

BOATING

Lewiston Lake is calm and quiet, with a 10-mph speed limit that makes it a great place for kayaking and low-speed boating. In June, the water temperature reaches the high 60s offshore at the lower end of the lake, a great spot for paddling and swimming. In a kayak, you can paddle out and watch for bald eagles and ospreys as they hunt the lake for trout.

Pine Cove Marina (9435 Trinity Dam Blvd., Lewiston, 530/778–3878, www.pine-cove-marina.com, 7am-3pm Wed.-Mon.) rents boats including canoes, kayaks, patio boats, and aluminum boats with motors (fuel included). A launch ramp with a large parking lot is a short distance south of the marina.

BEST OVERNIGHT: MARY SMITH CAMPGROUND

Mary Smith Campground (530/275-8113, http://shastatrinitycamping.com) is nestled on the south shore of Lewiston Lake. There are six deluxe tent cabins with log furniture, redwood decks, and lake frontage with views across the quiet, pristine lake. Three cabins have spectacular lake views; two cabins are more secluded and private, located in the pines. Cabin 5A is the closest to the water (about 30 feet). Cabin 3 is close to shore and is the quietest with a great water view. Cabin 9 is ADA-compliant.

There are also 11 sites for tents only; some sites require a short walk, or you can launch your boat and arrive by water. (Avoid site 8 as the tent pad is not level, a nearby trail leads to the restroom, and it is located close to parking). Drinking water and a restroom with flush and vault toilets are available nearby.

Reservations (877/444–6777, www.recreation.gov, fee) are accepted. Open early May-mid-September.

WHERE TO EAT

The **Mountain Valley Grill** (4811 Trinity Dam Blvd., Lewiston, 530/778–3177, 7am-8pm Mon. and Wed.-Thurs., 8am-8pm Fri.-Sun.) is the only game in town unless you're willing to drive into Weaverville. Turns out, there is no reason to make the long drive. Inside the wood-paneled exterior is a down-home café with blue counter seats and a tasty breakfast and lunch

CAMPFIRE STORIES

*A*t Lewiston, we always say there's a big trout out there named Walter, just like the elusive trout in the movie *On Golden Pond*. It turns out that anglers aren't the only ones looking for Walter. During one trip, we had bald eagles and ospreys cruise overhead every 20 minutes or so. At one point, I was able to point my camera straight up and snap the classic soaring shot of the bald eagle's black wings and white head glistening in the sun. Shortly after that encounter, another bald eagle showed up and circled as well.

Birds never lie: A circling eagle means it is looking for food; a hovering eagle means it has sighted food; and a diving eagle means . . . well, you can figure it out. As we watched, the two bald eagles circled and then dove into the water, over and over in a 10-minute span, in a competition to snatch a trout. They both won, flying off with small trout in their talons, then perching on a nearby pine to eat their dinners.

Neither the bald eagles nor our group caught Walter that day, but the eagles did provide a show that offered a special glimpse into nature's ways.

△ *Lewiston Lake camping cabins*

menu. The breakfast burritos are a go-to for locals (order one "grilled"). Mountain Valley Grill will put food on your plate that will make you look forward to your next visit, and they'll remember you with a smile the next time you sit down.

DRIVING DIRECTIONS

From Redding, take Highway 299 west and drive 27 miles over Buckhorn Summit to Trinity Dam Boulevard. Turn right on Trinity Dam Boulevard and drive 10.4 miles, passing turnoffs for Mary Smith Campground, Lakeview Terrace Resort, and a boat ramp. Turn right to enter Pine Cove Marina.

In McCloud, the license plate frames read "Step Back In Time." At this small town east of Mount Shasta, the slow pace of life is like a step back in time. About 1,100 residents live within a five-mile radius of each other and friendships and roots run deep. People know each other from chance meetings at the post office or at the McCloud Market. Mount Shasta looms above the town, a crown jewel with great frontage of its southeast flank and a clear view of the pinnacle summit.

But the top attraction here is the Upper McCloud River with its three water-falls connected by the McCloud River Trail, plus swimming holes, trout fishing, and campgrounds. Fly-fishing the lower McCloud River is something of a cult sport. The miles operated by The Nature Conservancy can provide results for skilled fly fishers on a pristine freestone river.

Camping in the area is excellent. The best site is at Fowlers along the McCloud River Trail, but other U.S. Forest Service camps are nearby, and there are also RV parks in beautiful settings.

What you will remember most, however, are the nice folks you met when you stopped at the McCloud Market or enjoyed a luscious rib eye at Shasta View Lodge. It's a secret, you see—how to slow down. The way to extend your life isn't by trying to pack everything onto a bucket list into a short time frame. Rather, it's to slow down and extend your life to the pace of a walk.

So when you come to enjoy the waterfalls, the McCloud River, and the view of Mount Shasta, wave at the locals. Slow down.

▽ *Middle Falls along the McCloud River Trail*

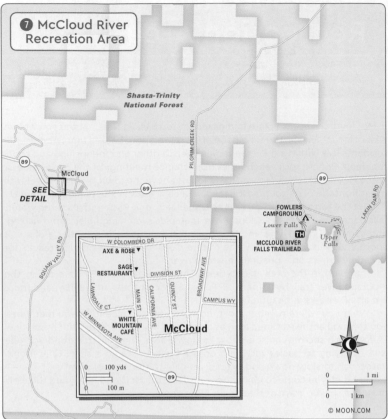

BEST ACTIVITY: MCCLOUD RIVER TRAIL

The **McCloud River Trail** (5 miles, 2.5 hours) is one of the prettiest and easiest walks with the most rewards. The trail is routed along the river and passes all the waterfalls from bottom to top.

From the trailhead at Lower Falls, which has parking and a restroom, it's a one-minute walk to an overlook with an iron railing on the ledge. **Lower Falls** is a 15-foot chute-type waterfall that flows through a gap in the rock. There's a jump-off spot for youngsters to make the leap into the basin below. The trailhead for the McCloud River Trail is on the left.

Walk down a staircase to the first stretch of the trail, which is paved. It is 1.3 miles, past Fowlers Campground on the left (where the trail turns to dirt), to **Middle Falls,** a 60-foot-high, 100-foot-wide silver curtain of water—the kind of place where you can fall in love. From here it's a short but steep climb to a cliffside overlook (also available via a short walk from a parking area).

Continue another 0.5 mile on the trail upstream to **Upper Falls,** a stepped staircase fall in a gorge. As you approach, a short spur to the right leads to the best frontal view of the final chute. Stop here and return to Lower Falls for a round-trip hike of 4 miles, or continue on another 0.5 mile to Lakim Dam. Though the trail is difficult to discern in spots, and Lakim Dam can be reached by car, the reward is well worth it. The small, historic dam

△ *Lower Falls*

creates a pretty, short cascade waterfall and backs up a gorgeous, gin-clear pool with a lookout platform.

For the mobility impaired, you can also drive to staging areas where short spurs (40–50 yards) lead to viewpoints of each of the falls.

FLY-FISHING IN THE NATURE CONSERVANCY

The **Kerry Landreth Preserve at McCloud River** (415/777-0487, www.nature.org) is a 2.5-mile section of river managed by The Nature Conservancy that is world-renowned among fly fishers. It is so pretty that even if the fish don't bite, you can just watch the water pour by and feel like it is cleansing your soul. The wading is slippery and difficult, and the bite can be challenging, but every once in a while the planets align to transport you into fishing heaven.

The tourmaline-colored water is tinted by glacial melt off Mount Shasta and fed by 44°F artesian springs and summer snowmelt. The river's limestone base, outcrops, and gorges give way to long slicks and tailouts.

McCloud's wild, native rainbow trout are blazed with brilliant crimson stripes down each side. (They were used as seed stock to establish trout fisheries in New Zealand, South America, and Europe, making them "the trout of the world.") The McCloud's wild brown trout can reach up to 25 inches and are spectacularly speckled with black, red, and orange spots. These fish can be difficult to catch, which adds to the challenge and intrigue. It's pure magic to cast, hook, and fight these gorgeous trout, then to release them and watch them swim off to fight another day.

Avoid the river section below Ash Camp; it's crowded and you practically have to bring your own rock to stand on. Instead, head downcanyon to the McCloud River Preserve and camp nearby at Fowlers or Ah-Di-Nah Campgrounds. The Nature Conservancy limits fishing access to no more than 10 rods at a time (reserve a spot at mccloudreservations@tnc.org, 415/777-0487, free) and requires the use of flies or lures with single barbless hooks for catch-and-release.

CAMPFIRE STORIES

*Y*ou never see them coming, the most profound days of your life. So it was that dawn morning in early May. Legendary fly fisher Ted Fay had agreed to join me on the McCloud River. We woke up early and drove in darkness into the canyon to the 2.5-mile section operated by The Nature Conservancy. Ted and I did our thing that day, and when we drove out, we were euphoric over the fishing, and we had even sighted some baby bobcats playing in the dirt along the road. We emerged from the national forest and drove up Squaw Valley Road, when suddenly the view appeared. Squaw Valley Meadow, in luxuriant shades of greens, extended for miles toward the foothills, backed by giant Mount Shasta, its white flank glistening against the sky. It was one of the prettiest sights I've ever seen, right up there with the summit of Mount Whitney, the Sierra Crest, and Yosemite Valley from Dewey Point.

△ *McCloud River Preserve in the Nature Conservancy*

For gear I use a Sage 5-weight, 9-foot XP 590-4, with Galvan reel, floating line, 9- to 12-foot 5X (sometimes lighter) fluorocarbon leader, strike indicator for nymphing pocket water; best with two-fly rig with dropper. Flies include Prince Nymph, Copper John, Hare's Ear, caddis for rainbow trout, plus sculpin or Seal Bugger (for browns). All barbs on hooks must be pinched down or removed. The game warden test is to pass the hook through your shirt; if it gets stuck on the way out, you get a ticket.

BEST OVERNIGHT: FOWLERS CAMPGROUND

Fowlers Campground sits beside the beautiful Upper McCloud River at 3,400 feet elevation. Nearby are three waterfalls, including Middle Falls, the centerpiece. The McCloud River Trail is routed along the edge of camp. Upstream through the forest is a near-level walk to Middle Falls, the river's spectacular cascade. There are 39 campsites and one double site for tents or RVs. Picnic tables and fire grills are provided, and drinking water and vault toilets are available. Some facilities are wheelchair-accessible. Leashed pets are permitted.

Reservations (877/444-6777, www.recreation.gov, fee) are accepted. Open year-round, weather permitting.

WHERE TO EAT

For such a small town, McCloud has some of the best restaurants run by the nicest people with the biggest smiles. For breakfast, folks line up for a seat at the **White Mountain Café** (241 Main St., McCloud, 530/964-2330).

The gorgeous **Axe & Rose** (424 Main St., McCloud, 530/408-8322, https://mccloudhotel.com, 11:30am-9pm daily) offers pretty outside dining, a woodsy interior with a vintage bar, and pub-style food. It's linked to the adjacent McCloud Hotel, whose **Sage Restaurant** (Main St. at Division, McCloud, 530/964-2822, 5:30pm-8pm Wed.-Sun.) is the choice for high-end gourmet, from its coconut shrimp appetizers to its filet mignon, paired with a bottle of cabernet.

DRIVING DIRECTIONS

From Redding, take I-5 north for 58 miles to exit 736 and Highway 89. Bear right and merge onto Highway 89. Drive 9.4 miles east to McCloud; the Shasta View Lodge is on the right and the McCloud Market is on the left.

To reach Fowlers Campground: Continue 5.6 miles east on Highway 89 to the signed turnoff (on the right) for Fowlers Campground and the McCloud River Trail. Turn right and drive 1 mile past the access road (on the left) to a fork. Turn left for the campground or right to reach Lower Falls.

At 14,179 feet, Mount Shasta rises like a diamond above a sea of green forest backed by a cerulean sky. Its sphere of influence spans a radius of 125 miles, and its shadow is felt everywhere in the region. This is a mountain of fire and ice, born of volcanoes and gouged by glaciers, coated most of the year in snow-hardened ice. The mountain asks a challenging question that demands an answer: Can you climb it? For the fit and prepared, the answer is: Yes.

There are many great day trips on the mountain, but these are all warm-ups. Once you spend time on Mount Shasta, the mountain will start to call to you, a magnetic pull of attraction. You will feel an unstoppable need to climb to the summit, a pinnacle created by a lava plug dome. I've felt that attraction seven times and, except for one wind-stopper on Misery Hill, I've made it every time. It's likely that, with the right preparation, you can too.

The best first trip is to drive Everitt Memorial Highway and hike from Bunny Flat to Horse Camp. If you want more, you can then launch from Horse Camp and trek to Hidden Valley, Casaval Ridge, Lake Helen, or Green Butte—or all the way to the summit.

The best time to climb Mount Shasta is in June and early July during big snow years. The snow settles and freezes at night, which allows hikers with crampons to walk on the firm surface. Day hiking is best mid-July–September, when the trails from the trailhead to the tree line at 8,000 feet are clear of snow.

▽ *climbing Green Butte ridge*

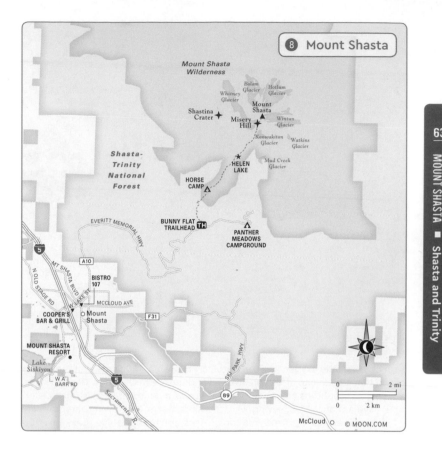

BEST DAY HIKE: BUNNY FLAT TO HORSE CAMP

The day hike from Bunny Flat to Horse Camp (3.6 miles round-trip, 2.5 hours) provides a taste of adventure on the old volcano and leads to the mountain's best launch point for more ambitious treks.

From the parking area at the Bunny Flat Trailhead (6,950 feet), the trail to Horse Camp leads up through a forest of Shasta red firs and climbs to an intersection with the route out of the Sand Flat Trailhead. A sign at the junction points to Horse Camp. Turn right and the follow the trail along a sub-ridge to Horse Camp at an elevation of 7,800 feet. The hike is 1.8 miles one-way with a 900-foot climb.

Upon arrival at tree line, look for the **Sierra Club Hut,** a hiker cabin. Look right and you'll find a spring that provides the sweetest-tasting water on Earth. From Horse Camp, enjoy the view of Helen Lake (a terrace) and Red Banks towering above. Beyond is a choice of destinations: Hidden Valley, Casaval Ridge, Lake Helen, or Green Butte.

Note that the Bunny Flat Trailhead and parking area receives high use from visitors.

BEST BACKPACKING: SHASTA SUMMIT TRAIL

The hike to the top of 14,179-foot Mount Shasta is an epic trek. The challenge is to climb 7,229 feet over ice, snow, and rock in a span of six miles while trying

△ *descending the summit*

to suck what little oxygen you can out of the thin air. It's one of the greatest adventures that hikers (in good condition) have a chance of achieving.

Timing is everything: Time your trip for a day in June or early July when the wind is down on the top, the summit is clear with no thunderstorms, and the route has plenty of snow, which provides an excellent climbing surface for crampons. (The snow acts as mortar for holding boulders in place.)

Most backpackers camp at Horse Camp (first-come, first-served, $5 cash) or Helen Lake (first-come, first-served, free) to get acclimated to the altitude and to shorten the ascent on the second day. Plan on hiking 1 mph (7 hours) on the way up, spending an hour on top, and hiking 2.5 mph (3 hours) on the way down. If you depart Horse Camp at 3:30am, you could be on top by 10am, before the chance of increased winds or thunderstorms threaten.

From Horse Camp, look for the signed Summit Trail (12 miles round-trip from Horse Camp, 10–11 hours or

2 days) about 40 yards past the spring and the Sierra Club Hut. The trail starts across a series of large stones called Olberman's Causeway, then quickly rises above timberline, gaining 1,000 feet per mile.

Head over the first ridge to make the standard first-timer's route up Avalanche Gulch. The hike gets steep, with a 35-degree slope to reach Red Banks, a huge, red volcanic outcrop at about 12,500 feet. When you emerge atop Red Banks, you are nearly 13,000 feet high. Look up to see a false summit ridge, hence the name Misery Hill.

It's a slow 1,000-foot climb up Misery Hill through snow in spring or scree in summer. Once atop Misery Hill, you can look down inside the Shastina Crater to the left, where there are two small turquoise glacier ponds: Clarence King Lake and the smaller Sisson Lake. Look across the sun-cupped glacier field to see Shasta Summit's massive pinnacle of lava jutting straight into the air, emerging into view for the

◉ INSIDER'S TIP

If you have your sights set on summiting Mount Shasta, here's what you need to know:

A wilderness permit and a summit permit (for climbs above 10,000 feet, $25) are required to summit Mount Shasta, available at the Mount Shasta Ranger Station (204 W. Alma St., Mt. Shasta, 530/926-4511, www.fs.usda. gov/stnf, 8am-4:30pm Mon.-Fri.).

For a climber's report, call **Fifth Season's Climbing Report** (530/925-5555).

Gear rentals are available from **Fifth Season** (300 N. Mount Shasta Blvd., Mt. Shasta, 530/926-3606, http://thefifthseason.com, 9am-6pm Mon.-Fri., 8am-6pm Sat., 10am-5pm Sun.).

To hike with a guide, contact **Shasta Mountain Guides** (530/926-3117, http://shastaguides.com).

Hikers should dress in layers and bring a wind shell, a skullcap, climbing boots with crampons, gloves, an ice axe, and glacier glasses. Carry two liters of water and plenty of food and snacks. Plan an early start (2am or 3am) to avoid afternoon wind, clouds, and the chance of thunderstorms. All hikers must pack out waste; special waste pack-out bags are available (free) at the trailhead and at the Mount Shasta Ranger Station.

Side note: Is it possible to hike from the Bunny Flat Trailhead to the Shasta summit and back in one day? Yes, but I don't advise it. The extra 900-foot climb over 1.8 miles with no time to acclimate to altitude makes it a grueling endurance test. A one-day trek from Bunny Flat means 12 hours-(plus) round-trip on the mountain, plus your time on the summit. Add to that the drive time from the town of Mt. Shasta to the trailhead and back, and you face absolute exhaustion. If you need time to organize your gear, food, and water, or if you encounter any gear issues or any slowdowns, that "one-day trip" from the town of Mt. Shasta can end up taking 13-15 hours start to finish.

first time. That is all that is left of the hike to gain the summit.

At the foot of the summit, you will see the route to the top. For the final push (about 10 minutes), grab the rocks and pull yourself up as you suck in the thin air at the tip top of the pinnacle. It is an unforgettable moment. You did it! Sign your name in the logbook housed inside an old rusted metal box, then take in the grand wonders surrounding you. On clear days you can see hundreds of miles in all directions, and the sky is a deeper blue than you ever imagined.

BEST OVERNIGHT: PANTHER MEADOWS CAMPGROUND

The best campsites on Mount Shasta are at **Panther Meadows Campground** (Everitt Memorial Hwy., www.fs.usda. gov, free), located at 7,500 feet above Bunny Flat near the Old Ski Bowl. There are 15 primitive hike-in tent sites available via a short walk from the parking lot. Plan to bring everything you need and to pack out all garbage. Picnic tables, fire rings, and vault toilets are available, and there is a seasonal spring for water (bring

△ *Panther Meadows*

more anyway). Reservations are not accepted; all sites are first-come, first-served. A three-night maximum stay is enforced to minimize long-term impacts. Open July-November.

If you prefer low-cost luxury instead, the best cabin rentals are the cedar chalets at **Mount Shasta Resort** (1000 Siskiyou Lake Blvd., Mt. Shasta, 800/958–3363, www.mountshastaresort.com).

WHERE TO EAT

After a day on the mountain, your reward is the best "Burger, Beer & Fries" combo ($13.50) in the state at **Cooper's Bar & Grill** (111 Morgan Way, Mt. Shasta, 530/926–3101, www.treehouserestaurantmtshasta.com, 10:30am-10pm Sun.-Thurs., 10:30am-11pm Fri.-Sat.), an outpost at the Tree House Restaurant at the Best Western. A full menu is avail-

able, but that three-for-one combo is the best deal around and the quality is top-shelf.

DRIVING DIRECTIONS

From Redding, take I-5 north for 60 miles to exit 738 for Central Mount Shasta. Take that exit and drive 0.3 mile to Lake Street. Turn right and drive 0.4 mile to a stoplight. Fifth Season is on the left and Shasta Mountain Guides is on the right. Continue 0.4 mile; the road curves left and becomes Everitt Memorial Highway for 11.1 miles to the Bunny Flat Trailhead on the left.

In winter, Everitt Memorial Highway is plowed clear of snow from the city of Mt. Shasta to the parking area at Bunny Flat. The road is gated beyond Bunny Flat and there is no access from Bunny Flat to Panther Meadows, South Gate Trailhead, or the Old Ski Bowl.

CAMPFIRE STORIES

A species of mysterious beings, known as Lemurians, are said to inhabit the inner world of Mount Shasta, living in underground caves lined with gold. The legend describes the Lemurians as tiny and states that ancient tribes called them "The Little People." Phylos is the most famous Lemurian. He wears a flowing white robe and can materialize at will. A climbing party once claimed they were invited into his golden temple to listen to soft music.

The Lemurians share the mountain with the Yaktavians of the Secret Commonwealth, said to have built the greatest bells in the universe (tuned so precisely that they can set off avalanches and rock slides). Then, when massive oval lenticulars envelop giant Shasta, inhabitants of another dimension are said to pass into our world at The Gate, a portal located out of South Gate near Gray Butte.

Yet in all my trips, I have never seen a Lemurian, Phylos, or Yaktavian. What about you?

△ *view of Mount Shasta*

When you gaze across Shasta Lake and imagine the fun that awaits, it's kind of like looking into a clear night sky: It seems to go on forever. Shasta Lake is really five lakes in one, with each arm forming a separate lake: Sacramento River Arm, McCloud River Arm, Pit River Arm, Squaw Creek Arm, and the central lake body (Sacramento) near the dam. Add in thousands of little coves and secret inlets and your boat can feel like a spaceship, venturing into the unknown.

Shasta Lake is filled with opportunities for all kinds of boating, water sports, fishing, swimming, and camping and enough space to handle everyone who shows up to have the time of their lives. The lake has 370 miles of shoreline and 1,200 campsites, 11 marinas, 21 boat ramps, 35 resorts, and 400 houseboat rentals. The Department of Fish and Wildlife states that 22 species of fish live in the lake.

Plan your visit for the right time of year, as weather will be key. March-early June and October-early December, the weather is temperate and ideal. Lake levels usually peak around Memorial Day weekend, with the lake high and in good shape March-mid-July. Mid-June-early September, the weather turns hot, with temperatures in the 100s not uncommon. The lake level is also subject to drawdowns in late summer and fall. December-February, expect lots of rain. In some years, the watershed can be among the wettest spots in the state.

▽ *houseboat on Shasta Lake*

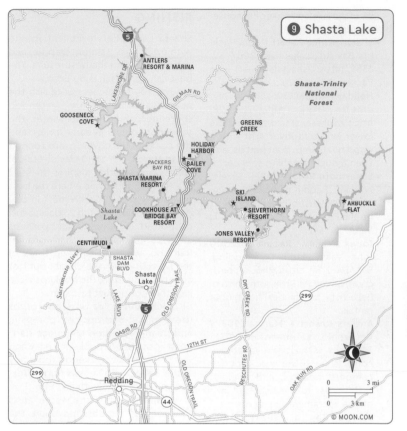

© MOON.COM

BEST ACTIVITY: BOATING

No matter the season, Shasta Lake has room for everybody—water-skiers, wakeboarders, personal watercraft riders, houseboaters, anglers, swimmers, windsurfers—you name it and Shasta can accommodate them all.

In the summer there are hundreds of houseboats out on the lake each day, plus quite a few water-skiers and wakeboarders. In a houseboat, it takes about five or six days to tour the whole lake. With all the houseboaters, it can seem like one giant party, everybody happy with lots of sun, skin, and liquids. If you prefer to escape the fes-tivities, head instead into one of the quiet coves. Most people develop an affinity for one section of the lake and return to it year after year, just like a second home.

The surface temperature of the water at Shasta Lake ranges from the 70s to the low 80s in summer, making the lake feel like a giant bathtub, ideal for water sports. Swimmers should be aware that most of the shoreline areas have steep drop-offs; a better bet is to venture inside the leeward points of the coves, which helps you get away from the summer boat traffic as well. No matter where you take the plunge, children should always be supervised in the water.

Six of the lake's marinas offer houseboat rentals:

- **Shasta Marina Resort** (16814 Packers Bay Rd., Lakehead, 800/959-3359, https://shastalake.net) is at Packers Bay.
- **Holiday Harbor** (20061 Shasta Caverns Rd., O'Brien, 800/776-2628, https://lakeshasta.com) is off the lower McCloud River Arm with a good boat ramp, boat rentals, and even a boat-launching service.
- **Silverthorn Resort** (16250 Silverthorn Rd., Redding, 800/332-3044, https://silverthornresort.com) is on the Pit River Arm north of Bella Vista.
- **Jones Valley Resort** (22300 Jones Valley Marina Dr., Redding, 833/474-2782, https://houseboats.com), on the Pit River Arm north of Bella Vista, has the best houseboat rentals.
- **Antlers Resort & Marina** (20679 Antlers Rd., Lakehead, 800/238-3924, www.shastalakevacations.com) is a full-service spot for campers, boaters, and anglers, with access to the beautiful lake on the Sacramento River Arm.
- **Bridge Bay at Shasta Lake** (10300 Bridge Bay Rd., Redding, 800/752-9669, https://bridgebayhouseboats.com) is west of I-5 near the Pit River Bridge.

For public boat launch ramps, try one of the following:

- **Jones Valley** (north of Bella Vista) is best for access to the Pit River Arm and bass fishing.
- **Bailey Cove** (near I-5) is best for access to the McCloud River Arm.
- **Antlers** (out of Lakehead) provides the best access to the upper Sacramento River Arm of the lake.
- **Centimudi** (near Shasta Dam, in the town of Shasta Lake) provides access to the main lake body. It's often the best access late in the season or when water levels are low.

FISHING

Shasta Lake offers excellent fishing with trout, bass, salmon, crappie, and catfish providing the best results. The best fishing, by far, is by boat.

The key to success is to fish the open water points (i.e., extended shoreline points) in late winter, the secondary points in early spring, and the backs of the coves in late spring.

In **March,** a 7- to 10-day stretch of clear, warm weather inspires the start of a three-month cycle where the bass practically shout "Catch me!" In one day, it's typical to catch 25 bass, a mix of spotted, largemouth, and perhaps a Florida. On one trip with my brother Rambob, we tried to keep track of the number of fish we caught but lost count at around 73; the hookups were just coming too fast to count.

Techniques: For bass, use grubs (best in salt-and-pepper, pumpkin, and pearl) rigged on 1/4-ounce darthead jigs with 3/0 hooks; it's easy and works great. I always keep a rod ready that is set up with Senkos rigged Texas-style or Wacky (with an O-ring).

In **spring,** when the water starts to warm and the bass move into the rocky shallows to get warm, I'll throw hard baits like mini-bass or bluegill.

In summer, there can be a surface bite at first light; that's when Zara Spooks can incite some outrageous action in the early mornings. The bass scatter vertically, with the best success on live minnows at dusk and into the darkness.

Techniques: Troll your lure at the exact right depth. I often use downriggers to get it right, staggering depths and lures so it looks like a big fish is chasing a smaller bait (what I call the cat-and-mouse technique). Troll so that you follow the shoreline contours of the lake.

Winter-spring, it seems that 15–35 feet deep is right; in summer, it's 60–90 feet; and then in fall, surface-35 feet.

Techniques: On the bottom line, I'll set up a big lure (like a five-inch Cop Car Needlefish, Speedy Shiner, Rapala, or similar). On the next line, I'll run a Humdinger, Sparklefish, or smaller Needlefish about 10 feet higher. If nothing happens, I'll change the depths and the lures until I get it right.

On my top day with Gary Miralles, we caught and released 58 trout. On another trip, my pals Clancy Enlow, Ross Sanders, and I got skunked bass fishing. Then Ross caught a trout by accident on a bass lure. We switched over too and caught 27 trout in two hours.

BEST OVERNIGHT: BOAT-IN CAMPS

Late spring-early summer, some of the best camping is at Shasta's boat-in campsites. When the lake is full, you can often create your own boat-in sites on flat spots in the backs of coves. If you rent a houseboat, you can make your own boat-in camp virtually anywhere. Most boaters try to park in as a secluded a cove as possible.

There are four designated boat-in campgrounds:

- **Gooseneck Cove** is on the Sacramento River Arm with 12 boat-in sites for tents. From the boat launch at Antlers (out of Lakehead), cruise seven miles south to the boat-in campground.
- **Greens Creek** is on the McCloud River Arm with seven boat-in sites for tents. The nearest boat launch is at Bailey Cove. Launch your boat and cruise four miles northeast up the McCloud River Arm.
- **Ski Island** is on the Pit River Arm with 29 boat-in sites for tents. The closest boat ramp is at Jones Valley. From Jones Valley, launch your boat and head west (left) for four miles to Ski Island.

- **Arbuckle Flat** is on the Pit River Arm with 11 boat-in sites for tents. It is five miles east of the Jones Valley boat ramp. The last major arm off to your right hides the campground at the back of the cove in the oaks above the shore.

Picnic tables and fire grills are provided at all boat-in campsites, and vault toilets are available. There is no drinking water, and garbage must be packed out. Reservations are not accepted; all sites are first-come, first-served. There is no fee for camping; boat launch fees vary. Open year-round.

WHERE TO EAT

One of the best views of Shasta Lake is from the dining room at the **Cook-House at Bridge Bay Resort** (10300 Bridge Bay Rd., 530/275–3021, https://bridgebayhouseboats.com, 8am-9pm Thurs.-Sun. winter). The view faces north across the lake, with the I-5/Pit River Bridge to the right and the shoreline of Beaver Island to the left. The fish-and-chips are the go-to item on the menu. The rest of the menu can be uneven, not quite measuring up to the view, but, like many patrons, I keep going back.

DRIVING DIRECTIONS

Getting here is easy, a straight shot off I-5. From Redding, take I-5 north for 8.5 miles to exit 687 for Mountain Gate/Wonderland Boulevard. Take that exit and drive 0.2 mile to Old Oregon Trail. Turn right and drive a short distance to Holiday Road. Turn right and drive 0.3 mile to the Shasta Lake Ranger Station and Visitor Center. Pick up a map to determine your next stop.

CAMPFIRE STORIES

*D*uring one fishing trip, my brother Rambob had hooked a bass and was tussling with it. As the fish neared the boat, an osprey plummeted out of the sky, talons forward, and sailed past Rambob's shoulder into the water. It grabbed his bass and then tried to fly off with it. There was Rambob, the bass still hooked but now in the talons of the osprey, 15 feet in the air above the boat. Rambob's rod was bent, and there in midair he continued the tussle, fighting the osprey as if it was the fish. "That's my fish," shouted Rambob. The osprey took the line out into the sky, then Rambob reeled a portion of it back in. Suddenly the fish popped out of the osprey's talons and into the water. As we brought it in the boat, it was barely wiggling.

Well, we did the only thing that seemed right. We released the fish back into the lake, like we always do. It labored away near the surface. And just like that, Mr. Osprey returned in a flash, swung down, grabbed it, and flew off to a perch on a pine tree to dine on lunch.

△ *my son Jeremy fishing Shasta Lake headwaters*

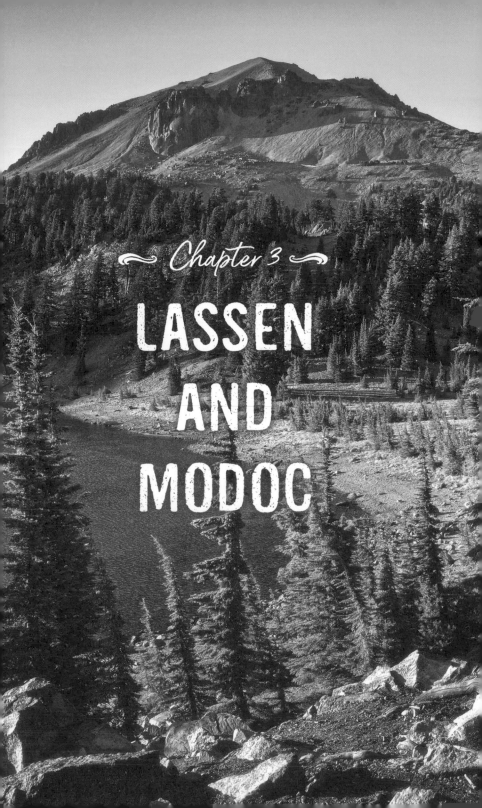

~ Chapter 3 ~

LASSEN
AND
MODOC

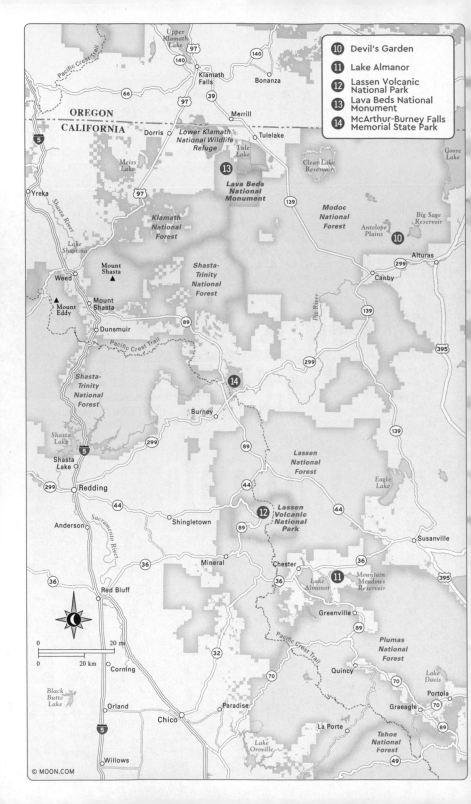

10 Devil's Garden

11 Lake Almanor

12 Lassen Volcanic National Park

13 Lava Beds National Monument

14 McArthur-Burney Falls Memorial State Park

OREGON

CALIFORNIA

Upper Klamath Lake

Klamath Falls

Bonanza

Merrill

Dorris

Tulelake

Lower Klamath National Wildlife Refuge

Tule Lake

Clear Lake Reservoir

Goose Lake

Meiss Lake

13 Lava Beds National Monument

Modoc National Forest

Big Sage Reservoir

Yreka

Klamath National Forest

Antelope Plains

10

Alturas

Lake Shastina

Shasta-Trinity National Forest

Canby

Weed

Mount Shasta ▲

Mount Shasta

▲ Mount Eddy

Dunsmuir

Pacific Crest Trail

Pit River

Shasta-Trinity National Forest

Burney

14

Shasta Lake

Shasta Lake

Redding

Lassen National Forest

Eagle Lake

Anderson

Sacramento River

Shingletown

12 Lassen Volcanic National Park

Susanville

Mineral

Chester

11 Lake Almanor

Mountain Meadows Reservoir

Red Bluff

Greenville

Pacific Crest Trail

Plumas National Forest

0   20 mi
0   20 km

Corning

Quincy

Lake Davis

Portola

Black Butte Lake

Paradise

Graeagle

Orland

Chico

La Porte

Lake Oroville

Tahoe National Forest

Willows

© MOON.COM

⑩ Devil's Garden

530/233-5811 | Modoc National Forest, Alturas | www.fs.usda.gov/modoc

Nearly 40 years ago, I was in a record store when I first saw Bob Seger's hit album "Against the Wind." The album cover had a painting of five wild stallions thundering across the high plains. Wild horses look different, you know. The big stallions seem primordial, wild and free, thick through the neck and shoulders, much larger and stronger than expected. In the fall, their radiant winter coats glow in the late afternoon sun.

The best opportunity to see wild horses in California is across some of the state's most remote landscape. In Devil's Garden, on the Modoc Plateau in the northeastern corner, an estimated 3,000 horses run wild and have done so for the past 140 years. At 5,000–6,000 feet in elevation, their habitat spans 500,000 acres in a place dotted with small lakes and volcanic rocks and peppered with sage, junipers, and wild grass. In spring, the volcanic pockets fill with rainwater and the region turns into a paradise for waterfowl on the Pacific Flyway. Across the plains, wildflower blooms are spectacular.

In Devil's Garden, there is no crowd. In fact, you may not see another person. (In eight hours afield on a Saturday during the peak fall season, I saw one other person, about a half mile away at Big Sage Reservoir.) Amid the solitude, it's the chance to see wild horses that sets an experience here apart. The first time I came here, that song "Against the Wind" echoed through my head as the album cover came to life right in front of me. This is why you go.

▽ *wild horse in Modoc National Forest*

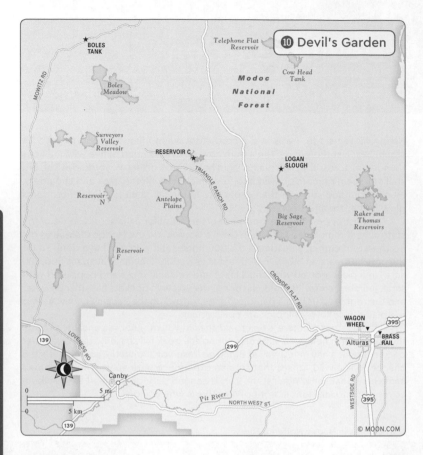

BEST ACTIVITY: WILDLIFE WATCHING

Devil's Garden, in the heart of the Modoc Plateau, is so vast and has so few people that it can be overwhelming to drive in and see nothing but junipers, grass, and volcanic rocks for miles around. You need a strategy, and this is it. In Modoc National Forest, these are the best places to see **wild horses:**

- **Big Sage Reservoir:** On the far southeast shore beyond the campground and dam. Access is via Crowder Flat Road (Forest Road 73). As you drive in on Forest Road 73, you will see a junction on the right for Forest Road 180. Turn right and drive to Big Sage Campground at the foot of Big Sage Reservoir. Cross the dam and look for a rocky Jeep road on the left. Hike along the northeastern side of the lake and scan the surrounding country from the ridge-top viewpoints.

- **Logan Slough:** This feeder creek pours into Big Sage Reservoir. Access is via Forest Road 45N06 from Crowder Flat Road. Drive past the head of the lake and turn right for Logan Slough. This leads to a chasm-like inlet to the lake. With four-wheel drive, you can cross the chasm and hike one of two routes on a rocky Jeep road.

- **Boles Tank:** A lookout in the vicinity of Blue Mountain and Boles Creek. Access is via Forest Road 46N10.

△ *wild horses in Modoc National Forest*

Other good spots include Reservoir M, Crowder Flat, and Emigrant Spring near Pencil Road. Farther away, you can try Drift Fence Tank near Davis Lake and Quaking Aspen near Clear Lake.

When you spot movement, park your vehicle and turn off the engine, being careful not to make any noise (like talking or slamming your car door). Hike upwind to conceal yourself behind a sub-ridge, using ridges, gullies, rocks, and junipers. With a long camera lens, you can eventually get close enough for a photo—an electric experience you will never forget.

FISHING

Reservoir C (Forest Road 44N32, north of Big Sage Reservoir) has the best fishing in Devil's Garden. This pretty lake has a campground and a boat ramp ideal for small boats (kayaks, canoes, and prams). The lake often provides good trout fishing in early summer, then as the water warms, the lake's bass spark to life.

Big Sage Reservoir (Forest Road 180) is a shallow lake four miles long that spans 77,000 acres, with a boat ramp near the campground. Though the lake has bass and catfish, it can sometimes be too muddy to fish.

BEST OVERNIGHT: RESERVOIR C

Reservoir C has a dispersed camping area for tents or RVs. The open sites have lake views, and a boat ramp is adjacent to the campground. The elevation is 4,900 feet, and the stargazing is spectacular. Picnic tables and fire grills are provided, and a vault toilet is available. There's no drinking water (bring your own), and garbage must be packed out. Leashed pets are permitted.

Big Sage Reservoir also has a campground with 11 sites for tents or RVs with similar amenities.

Reservations are not accepted for either campground. All sites are first-come, first-served; there is no fee for camping. Open May-September.

WHERE TO EAT

The most popular spot in the region is the **Wagon Wheel Restaurant** (308 W. 12th, Alturas, 530/233–5166), known for big, hearty breakfasts like chicken-fried

△ *Logan Slough, wild horse habitat*

steak smothered in gravy. It's located right along Highway 299 and is easy to reach.

For dinner, hit the **Brass Rail** (395 Lake View Dr., Alturas, 530/233–2906) and order the rib eye, the best bet on the menu.

DRIVING DIRECTIONS

Big Sage Reservoir: From I-5 in Redding, take Highway 299 east for 136 miles to Crowder Flat Road/Forest Road 73 (3 miles west of Alturas). Turn left on Crowder Flat Road and drive 6.1 miles to Big Sage Road/Forest Road 180. At the boundary for Modoc National Forest, the road turns from asphalt to hard-packed gravel. Turn right on Forest Road 180 and drive 3.3 miles to a fork near the dam. Turn left and drive 0.3 mile to the campground.

Reservoir C: From Highway 299, turn north on Crowder Flat Road/Forest Road 73 and drive 9.5 miles to Triangle Ranch Road/Forest Road 43N18. Turn left on Triangle Ranch Road and drive 7 miles to Forest Road 44N32. Turn right on Forest Road 44N32 and drive 0.5 mile. Turn right on the access road for the campground and drive 0.5 mile to the end of the road.

CAMPFIRE STORIES

I had just finished a great trip to Yellowstone and Grand Teton National Parks. In the Snake River Valley, east of the Tetons, I saw a grizzly bear, an antelope, and a herd of bison—all within a span of 45 minutes. I figured, it doesn't get any better than this.

Then I got the idea to venture to Devil's Garden to find wild horses. After a few hours without sighting any wild horses, I assumed that was it. Then, while driving toward Logan Slough, I caught a glimpse of movement far to the right and stopped. A wild stallion, about a 0.25 mile off, had emerged from behind a juniper. I hiked north behind a ridge, then edged right and used the ridge to conceal my presence. Hiding behind boulders and junipers, I slowly crept ahead for a view. Finally, when I felt I was close, I peered over a rock and 60 yards straight ahead was the alpha stallion of the pack: squared up, nostrils flaring, the dark fur of his massive neck and shoulders glistening in the sun. Content I would come no closer, the stallion turned to his herd of seven and led the way across the Modoc Plateau.

My heart was beating like a bass drum. This encounter truly affected me, and was better than anything I've ever experienced in Yellowstone.

△ *wild stallion in Logan Slough*

⑪ Lake Almanor

530/258-2141 | Lassen National Forest | www.fs.usda.gov/lassen

Big and beautiful Lake Almanor is filled with sapphire-blue water and back-dropped by snowcapped Lassen Peak. Located east of Redding and south of the border to Lassen National Park, this is one of the best recreation lakes in California—an excellent destination for fishing, boating, camping, and exploring the surrounding area.

The reservoir is about 13 miles long with 28,000 surface acres set at an elevation of 4,500 feet. Ringed by conifers, the lake is gorgeous when full. The clear water is ideal for boating, fishing, and water sports, with waterskiing, wakeboarding, and personal watercraft use excellent in July and August.

Lake Almanor works as a destination for a fishing weekend trip and for families who like to use a lakeside campground or cabin to explore the surrounding area. Nearby day trips reach the eastern portions of Lassen Volcanic National Park, including Drakesbad and Warner Valley.

On the warm, calm days of summer, when the lake is full and the sun is hot, Lake Almanor seems like a boater's paradise. Late September-November, the lake is often flat. Winter here starts early and ends late, with cold temperatures in October and lasting well into May. The best time to come is in spring and fall, when the weather warms to the mid-70s by the afternoon.

▽ *view of Lassen Peak from Lake Almanor*

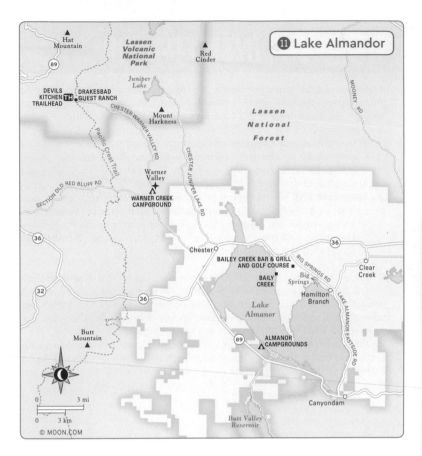

BEST ACTIVITY: FISHING

Lake Almanor is one of best lakes for fishing. Large rainbow trout and brown trout lure anglers in spring, early summer, and fall, while summer sees tons of smallmouth bass ply the waters here. The lake is loaded with pond smelt, which means the fish have plenty to eat and grow big fast. I've hooked many a rainbow trout over 5 pounds and even brown trout over 10 pounds. One summer day, I saw so many smallmouth bass that I gave up counting after 50.

Here are some of the best fishing spots:

- The edge of the **historic river channel** (the route of the Feather River before it was dammed). You'll need a depthfinder on your boat that can track the contours of the lake bottom. Look for an underwater terrace that suddenly drops off to deeper water—that's the historic river channel. Use a downrigger to place your lures at the exact correct depths, then troll your lures along the top edge of the channel.
- **Big Springs,** north of the Hamilton Branch, tucked along the shore inside the bay and the Almanor Peninsula
- **Hamilton Branch** (on the east side)
- The edge of **weed beds** at the north end of the lake. A weed bed extends west of the channel out of Bailey Creek (offshore of the Bailey

It takes some expertise to fool these big trout. First-timers will need to learn the nuances of this lake, which means days with little success until you break through. Here are some of the best methods:

1) Trawl using downriggers to reach precise depths on the edge of underwater ledges and channels, near submerged boulder fields, springs, or weed beds.
2) Jig straight up and down at ledges or springs.
3) Fly cast with sink-tip line; use Midnight Cowboy, black leech, Seal Bugger, and Wooly worm with copper head at edges of weed beds.
4) Baitfish with night crawler under slip bobber at springs.
5) For smallmouth bass, use a live cricket for bait on a No. 8 hook, with a split shot 18 inches above it for weight.

I also use a technique I call the "cat-and-mouse": Off a downrigger on a deep line, I run a jointed Rebel or Rapala. On shallow line above it, I run a Needlefish. (It will look like a small trout is chasing a pond smelt.) With two downriggers and three lines, plus another line on the surface, anglers can make it look like there are four fish in a line.

I troll a 2¼ or 2½-inch Needlefish rainbow-colored lure and add a red-eye sticker to the head of the lure; a 2½-inch Z-Ray, yellow with red spots; a 2¾-inch jointed Rapala (floating), gold/black; marabou trolling flies (no snap swivel); or a 4½-inch rat lure with double treble hooks.

Creek Golf Course) and across to the historic river channel. Large trout often hide under this weed bed and emerge along its edges to feed on hatching insects.

- An offshore spot called the **A-Frame** (named for an onshore A-frame cabin with a green roof) near the outlet area (right along the buoy line) and offshore of the A-Frame.

- The **buoy line** at the outlet between Prattville and the Plumas Pines Resort. There is an outlet tower in a cove where water from Lake Almanor is delivered in a tunnel down to Butt Valley Lake. A buoy line guards this cove and keeps boats out. In summer, this is often the best spot on the lake for smallmouth bass. Use live crickets for bait on a No. 8 hook with a single split shot for weight.

- The best area for smallmouth bass is on the west side of the lake

The best fishing is by boat, but there are exceptions. Hamilton Branch, on the eastern shore of the lake (County Road A13 crosses the upper end of Hamilton Branch), is an extended stream outlet that enters Almanor in a large bay and is protected by the Almanor Peninsula. It often provides exceptional shore fishing for trout. Anglers can cast from shore with Power Nuggets for trout in the 12- to 14-inch class. Another spot popular for shore-liners is the leeward side of the point at Rocky Point Campground.

The drawback here is the weather. The wind comes up out of the north-west something fierce in the early afternoon. In spring and summer, it pays to

△ Lake Almanor scenic view from Rocky Point Campground

be on the water at dawn when the lake is pristine and calm. If a breeze starts to blow by 11am, expect more wind by 2pm and perhaps a gale by 4pm.

Trout fishing is best in spring, early summer, and fall, when it is very cold and windy. Be out before daybreak, before the wind comes up (by 10am), which forces everyone off the lake. In fall, the mornings are frigid, and in winter, the place is covered in 10 feet of snow and abandoned. That leaves a narrow window of good weather in July and August, which is when most people visit and when fishing is the worst. If you come in those warm months, try fishing for smallmouth bass. Use live crickets for bait, a split shot for weight, and cast along the shoreline drop-offs. Let the cricket sink to about 30 feet deep, then twitch it and reel in a few feet—that is when you will get a bite.

Lake Almanor has many boat ramps, but most are at private resorts. The biggest and most popular public ramp is the Canyon Dam boat ramp on the southern end of the lake. A personal favorite is the West Shore ramp, located near the Almanor Campground south of Chester off Highway 89.

VISIT NEARBY WARNER VALLEY

You can use your Lake Almanor campsite or cabin as a launching pad for trips into Warner Valley, the undiscovered southeast corner of Lassen Volcanic National Park—beautiful, wild, and remote. North of Chester, Lassen's Warner Valley offers camping, the gorgeous outpost of Drakesbad, and an easy hike to Devils Kitchen, a unique geothermal area.

The **Devils Kitchen Trail** (4.4 miles, 2.5 hours) heads west above Hot Springs Creek, with a gradual climb of 300 feet. After two miles, you'll immediately understand why it was tagged Devils Kitchen: It's a barren pocket of steaming vents, boiling mud pots, and fumaroles.

At popular **Drakesbad Guest Ranch** (866/999-0914, http://lassenlodging.com), securing reservations is about as difficult as finding Bigfoot. Fortunately, the **Warner Valley Campground** (http://lassenlodging.com/warner-campground, June-mid-Oct., $16) has 17 tent sites along Hot Springs Creek at 5,650 feet elevation. Picnic tables, food lockers, and fire

△ *Devils Kitchen Trail*

rings are provided. Drinking water (until mid-September) and pit toilets are available. About half the sites are reservable and the rest are first-come, first-served. There is a park entrance fee per vehicle.

Access is obscure and circuitous. In Chester, hop onto Feather River Drive and drive 0.75 mile. Bear left for Drakesbad and Warner Valley, and drive 6 miles to Warner Valley Road. Turn right and drive 11 miles to Warner Valley Campground. For the Devils Kitchen Trail, continue 0.5 mile to the trailhead on the left. The last 3.5 miles of road are unpaved, with one steep hill that can be difficult for trailers or RVs.

BEST OVERNIGHT: ALMANOR CAMPGROUND

Almanor (www.fs.usda.gov/lassen) is one of the area's best-known and most popular campgrounds. The U.S. Forest Service campground is set along the western shore of Lake Almanor, across from the Almanor Peninsula. There are two linked campgrounds, North and South, and another campground at Legacy. There are 104 sites at Almanor North and South for tents or RVs. Legacy has 13 sites for tents or RVs. Picnic tables and fire grills are provided, and drinking water and vault toilets are available. A dump station, boat ramp, and beach area are nearby. Some facilities are wheelchair-accessible. Leashed pets are permitted.

Sites at Almanor North and Legacy are first-come, first-served (no reservations). Reservations (877/444-6777, www.recreation.gov, fee) are accepted for the South Campground. Open May-September.

Don't care to rough it? Opt for the cottages at **Bailey Creek Golf Course** (433 Durkin Dr., Lake Almanor, 530/259-4653) on the Almanor Peninsula. The luxury units come with fireplaces, jetted tubs, garages, private decks, and kitchenettes.

WHERE TO EAT

Spend enough time at Lake Almanor and sooner or later you will end up at the **Bailey Creek Bar & Grill** (433 Durkin Dr., Lake Almanor, 530/259-3463, https://baileycreek.com/bargrill, 5pm-8pm Thurs.-Sun.). During the day, the high-class bar offers a good selection of spirits and plenty of salads, appetizers, and sandwiches. The big and hearty dinners include roast turkey, prime rib, and New York steak with all the goodies.

DRIVING DIRECTIONS

From I-5 in Red Bluff, take Highway 36 East and merge with Highway 36. Continue east on Highway 36 for 66 miles to Highway 89. Turn right onto Highway 89 and drive 5.5 miles to Almanor Drive. Turn left and drive 0.7 mile to the Almanor Campground.

CAMPFIRE STORIES

*M*y brother Rambob and I once had a three-hour stretch in which we caught five trout (all over 5 pounds), and then I hooked—and lost—a lake-record, 24-pound brown trout. I know it was the lake record because my field scout and pal, Hal Janssen (the Hall of Fame fly fisher), caught, weighed, and released the same fish about 20 feet from where it got away from me. When I hooked it, the fish was so big that it simply swam away and took out my line until I could see the metal spool on my reel. We panicked, and my brother motored the boat slowly toward the fish until I was able to retrieve line. We should have stopped at 40 yards and then resumed the fight. Instead, without thinking, we motored right up to the fish to get a look and, at 10 feet with no leverage against it, the giant brown trout simply swam around a stump, got an angle, and dislodged the hook. I sat there in the boat for nearly an hour, stunned at the loss and unable to talk, move, or utter a sound.

Even today, when I'm on the lake and the day gets quiet, I look across the water and think about that fish.

△ *my brother Rambob with rainbow trout on Lake Almanor*

Lassen Volcanic National Park has a world-class array of peaks and lakes, geo-thermal basins and backcountry trails, and campgrounds and cabins. Located east of Red Bluff, the park spans 106,000 acres with easy access from Highways 44 and 89. Lassen Volcanic National Park Highway (Highway 89) runs north-south through the park, passing trailheads for Manzanita Lake, Lassen Peak, Summit Lake, Bumpass Hell, and Brokeoff Mountain. At the pinnacle of the park is 10,457-foot Lassen Peak, the southernmost volcano of the Cascade Range.

What awaits you here is a series of stellar recreation destinations with 90 percent less people than you'll find at Yosemite (Lassen only receives about 500,000 visitors per year, 10 percent of Yosemite's almost 5 million). With the exception of holiday weekends, you can usually find a campsite. You'll have most trails to yourself and can rent a kayak and paddle around Manzanita Lake with few others on the water.

In summer, that solitude can disappear in places. The camping cabins at Manzanita Lake are always in demand, and there will be plenty of company on the first mile of the Lassen Peak Trail.

Explore instead some of the park's more remote areas. Out of Butte Lake are the trailheads for the Cinder Cone, Prospect Peak, Painted Dunes, and the Fantastic Lava Beds. In the Warner Valley and Drakesbad area, trailheads lead to the Devil's Kitchen geothermal area, Drakes Lake, and even the Pacific Crest Trail.

▽ *Lassen Peak Trail*

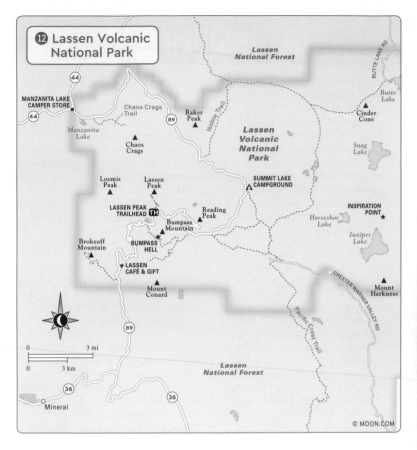

The map shows Lassen Volcanic National Park (12), including:

- Lassen National Forest
- BUTTE LAKE RD
- MANZANITA LAKE CAMPER STORE
- 44
- Chaos Crags Trail
- Raker Peak
- Butte Lake
- 89
- Noble Trail
- Cinder Cone
- Manzanita Lake
- Chaos Crags
- Lassen Volcanic National Park
- Snag Lake
- Loomis Peak
- Lassen Peak
- SUMMIT LAKE CAMPGROUND
- INSPIRATION POINT
- LASSEN PEAK TRAILHEAD
- Reading Peak
- Horseshoe Lake
- Bumpass Mountain
- Juniper Lake
- Brokeoff Mountain
- BUMPASS HELL
- LASSEN CAFÉ & GIFT
- Mount Conard
- CHESTER WARNER VALLEY RD
- Mount Harkness
- 89
- Pacific Crest Trail
- 0 3 mi
- 0 3 km
- 36
- 36
- Mineral
- Lassen National Forest
- © MOON.COM

BEST ACTIVITY: LASSEN PEAK TRAIL

Lassen Peak is a huge volcanic flume with hardened lava flows, craters, outcrops, and extraordinary views in all directions.

The **Lassen Peak Trail** (5 miles round-trip, 3–5 hours) is located at 8,500 feet in elevation on the park road, with a huge parking area at the trailhead. You'll have a good view of much of the trail as it rises up the volcano's flank in a series of switchbacks. The route to the top is a 2,000-foot climb over the span of 2.5 miles (one-way). The first 1.3 miles are routed up the backside of a sub-ridge to Grandview, where you can see Lake Helen below to the south and Lake Almanor across to the southeast. The next mile traverses a series of switchbacks, which helps turn the grade into a more rhythmic aerobic hike. With each step you climb, the views get better: You get a lookout for nearby 9,239-foot Mount Brokeoff, a panorama of the scope of the caldera of the giant 500,000-year-old Tehama Volcano, and to the north, a view of the 32,000-acre burn zone of the Eiler Fire. And that is all before you even make the rim of the caldera.

Within the caldera of Lassen Peak, the jumbled volcanic landscape spans 500 yards. At the top of the rim, the lava plug dome summit emerges into view. This is your destination on the Lassen Peak Trail. From the rim, you sail across the caldera to the foot of

If the trail up Lassen Peak is too crowded, there are plenty of other great hikes in the park:

Bumpass Hell: This is the most popular trail in the park and is great for youngsters. A mostly boardwalk trail (3 miles round-trip) leads to a huge geothermal basin. The trailhead is on Lassen Park Highway.

Cinder Cone: The trail to the Cinder Cone (4 miles round-trip) is a slog through volcanic rubble. From the rim, a trail circles the cone and offers a peek inside the collapsed center of a caldera, plus long-distance views to Lassen Peak. The trailhead is at Butte Lake.

Inspiration Point: This 1.4-mile round-trip hike includes a 400-foot climb to a volcanic crag with panoramic views across the park. The trailhead is at Juniper Lake.

the plug dome, where the trail forks. The left fork routes around the backside of the summit, which you climb to gain a perch on top of the summit.

The air is cool and clean up here, and the sky a deep blue. It feels like you are on the roof of the world. The views are highlighted by Mount Shasta, about 100 miles to the north, while far below to the southeast, giant Lake Almanor looks like a sapphire nestled in a sea of conifers.

The best time to hike the Lassen Peak Trail is when the snow has melted off the route: mid-July-October in most years. In heavy snow years, there can be snow into August. In light snow years, the trail to the top can by clear by June.

MANZANITA LAKE

Manzanita Lake is nestled at 5,890 feet in the northwest corner of the park, near the Highway 44/89 entrance. Kayaking is a hit at this gorgeous lake at the foot of Lassen Peak. The **Manzanita Lake Camper Store** (9am-close daily, first-come, first-served) rents sit-on-top kayaks. Most kayakers cruise the shoreline, paddling around for a while to take in the view of the flank of Lassen Peak towering above.

Manzanita is also the site of a unique wild fishery. Anglers float in tubes or small boats for catch-and-release fly-fishing. Rules mandate using lures or flies with single, barbless hooks (use a leech or Seal Bugger, sink-tip line, strip retrieve). All fish must be released; none may be kept. So if you envision a trout barbecue at your campsite to crown the day, this is not your lake.

The 20 wood **camping cabins** (866/999-0914, http://lassenlodging.com, May-Oct., fee) at Manzanita Lake are cute and popular, nestled in a thinned forest within walking distance of the lake. Cabins come with one or two rooms and include heat, a battery-powered lantern, and platform beds. Camping amenity packages are available. Reservations are accepted up to six months in advance.

BEST OVERNIGHT: SUMMIT LAKE

The most popular campsites in the park are at the **Summit Lake Campground** at 6,695 feet elevation. This is a beautiful spot where deer often visit in the evening in the adjacent meadow just east of the campground. There are two sections: North and South. North Summit Lake has 46 sites for tents or RVs. South Summit Lake has 48 sites for tents or RVs (Loop E is tent-only). Picnic

△ *paddling Manzanita Lake*

tables, fire rings, and bear-proof food lockers are provided. Drinking water is available. Flush toilets are in North Summit Lake; pit toilets are in South Summit Lake. Some facilities are wheelchair-accessible. Leashed pets are permitted at campsites only. **Reservations** (www.recreation.gov) are accepted for Loops B, C, and D; Loops A and E (tent-only) are first-come, first-served. Open late June-October.

WHERE TO EAT

The only meal in the park is at the **Lassen Café & Gift** (21820 Lassen Peak Hwy., Mineral, 530/595-3555, 9am-5pm daily May-Sept.) inside the Kohm Yah-mah-nee Visitor Center, one mile from the southwest entrance. The slim pickings include sandwiches and snacks, ice cream, and drinks.

On the north end of the park, the **Manzanita Lake Camper Store** (39489 Hwy. 44E, 530/767-0077, http://lassenlodging.com, 9am-5pm daily late May-mid-June, 8am-8pm daily mid-June-mid-Oct.) sells sandwiches, ice cream, drinks, and camping supplies.

DRIVING DIRECTIONS

South Entrance: From I-5 in Red Bluff, take the exit for Central Red Bluff-Highway 36/Antelope Boulevard. At the stop sign at Antelope Boulevard, turn right and drive 2.3 miles into a left turn lane for Highway 36. Turn left onto Highway 36 and drive 43 miles to Highway 89. Turn left onto Highway 89 and drive 5.3 miles to the south entrance station.

North Entrance: From I-5 in Red Bluff, drive 15 miles north to Anderson. Take the exit for Anderson/Deschutes Road-Factory Outlets and continue 0.8 mile, merging onto Highway 273 North. Drive 0.2 mile to Factory Outlets Drive. Turn right onto Factory Outlets Drive and continue 0.2 mile to Deschutes Road. Continue on Deschutes Road for 4.2 miles. Turn right onto Dersch Road and drive 12.5 miles to Highway 44. Turn right on Highway 44 East and drive 26 miles to Highway 89/Lassen Park Highway. Turn right onto Highway 89 and drive 1.2 miles to the north entrance station.

CAMPFIRE STORIES

*O*n the morning of a TV shoot for CBS, I looked up from the parking lot at the trailhead for Lassen Peak and saw a small puff of a cloud, the start of a cumulonimbus forming at the summit. "You know what that means," I said to our producer, Jim Schlosser. "We need to get up there in two hours and get the pay-off shots before that cloud buries the summit." And that's what we did. My guests, trail specialists Erica and Sondra Blockman, and our crew hoofed it straight to the summit where we filmed the end of the show, with views of the caldera, the lava plug dome, and panoramas in every direction. On the way down, we stopped every quarter mile or so and turned around to simulate hiking up the trail.

In post-production, we had to cut and move the clips to put them in the right order. A year later the show, called "Land of Fire and Smoke," aired on CBS and won first place Best Outdoors Recreation Show from the Outdoor Writers Association of America. The judges said that "the story had a natural flow and pace, as we joined them on the climb, just like being there heading up the trail, with the anticipation of reaching the summit." Heh, heh, heh . . . little did they know.

△ *heading up Lassen*

Located in remote Modoc County near the Oregon border, Lava Beds National Monument is a one-in-a-million spot with more than 700 lava tube caves, the Schonchin Butte cinder cone, the Mammoth Crater, Native American petroglyphs and pictographs, and battlefields and sites from the Modoc War. There are two worlds here: one aboveground, the other below.

Start your visit with a drive on the Volcanic Legacy Scenic Byway, which runs north-south through the park. Along the way, you'll get a feel for the landscape, with opportunities to explore lava craters, view pinnacles, and visit historic sites. Cruising south through the Devils Homestead Lava Flow, stop at the picnic area near the Fleener Chimneys, where you can admire the 50-foot cones (the holes in their center give them a chimney-like appearance). At the southern border of the park is the Mammoth Crater, where lava gushed in molten streams 30,000 years ago. This was the source of most of the volcanic flows, lava tubes, and caves for the entire region.

More than 700 lava tube caves have been discovered here; 20 caves are available for public access. The longest cave is the 7,000-foot Catacomb Cave, with rooms, gateways, and passageways that vary in size. It's great for youngsters; when the cave ceilings begin to drop, they just slither on through. Adults, on the other hand, must bob, dip, and scramble to squeeze through.

The best time to visit is in summer, when temperatures peak in the mid-80s, because you can always cool off in the caves. Most folks hike in the morning when temperatures are cooler and then, as temperatures warm in the afternoon,

▽ Schonchin Butte cinder cone

⑬ Lava Beds National Monument

venture underground. This is a popular destination for families. Once school starts in late August, visitor traffic diminishes. You might have the place to yourself in late November, when the first snow flies. In December, mule deer bucks with huge antlers migrate into the area and provide the chance for spectacular wildlife photography.

BEST ACTIVITY: CAVING

Lava Beds has the best do-it-your-self caving for youngsters. Some of the caves have been developed for fairly easy access; they are outfitted with ladders, walkways, and lighting. Others caves remain in their original condition.

Well-lit **Mushpot Cave** (770 feet) is the best introductory cave with easy access, but **Catacombs Cave** (6,903 feet) is the feature destination for most. Located along the Cave Loop Road, access is a descent into the cave vertically on a ladder; within 25 feet, on go the headlamps. After a slight turn in the cave, a single shaft of sunlight from the cave opening is left behind. The cave continues 2,000 feet through a series of large rooms connected by small openings under four-foot lava bridges to small chambers. There are a number of dead ends and surprise con-nected tubes. The ceiling is covered with lavacicles and shark-tooth stalac-tites. In the Catacombs, you can see how the floor of the tube is filled with flows of what are called "cauliflower

Volcanic-connected **Medicine Lake** is located just 15 miles south of Lava Beds National Monument and provides lakeshore camping, fishing, and low-speed boating. Combined with the national monument, that's a recreation complex covering 500 square miles with countless lava flows, craters, cinder cones, ice caves, and lava tubes, with Medicine Lake set in the former caldera of a volcano. It is the ultimate playground, especially for youngsters.

Medicine Lake was a caldera (the mouth of a volcano), which then sealed and was filled with water. Fishing here is often good for small trout, with the best bite early in the season when the snow melts and anglers have their first access in six months. Then, when the cold weather arrives in the fall, the fish often bite like dogs, knowing that winter is ahead. Most anglers slow-troll Needlefish along the ledge between the boat ramp and the campgrounds, or fly-fish with black leeches along the tules on the far side of the lake.

Medicine Lake has four campgrounds:

★ **Medicine Campground** has 22 sites for tents or RVs.
Each summer, during the third weekend of July, there is a one-week tribal gathering at the Medicine Campground. The campground is closed to reservations and walk-ins during this time (stay at A. H. Hogue instead).
★ **A. H. Hogue** has 24 sites for tents or RVs.
Reservations (877/444–6777, www.recreation.gov, fee) are accepted for some sites at Medicine and A. H. Hogue Campgrounds. Remaining sites are first-come, first-served.
★ **Hemlock** has 22 sites for tents or RVs.
★ **Headquarters** has 16 sites for tents or RVs, but no lake access. There is no drinking water.
Sites at Hemlock and Headquarters are all first-come, first-served.
Amenities include picnic tables, fire grills, and vault toilets. Three campgrounds have drinking water. A boat ramp is nearby. Some facilities are wheelchair-accessible. Leashed pets are permitted. Open late May-early October.

Directions: From Dunsmuir take I-5 north to exit 736 for Highway 89/ McCloud. Turn right on Highway 89 and drive 26.3 miles to Bartle. Continue 0.6 mile to Harris Spring Road. Turn left onto Harris Spring Road and drive 4.4 miles to Medicine Lake Road. Turn right and drive 26.5 miles to the signed turnoff for Medicine Lake. Turn left and drive 0.3 mile to a T junction. Turn left for the boat ramp and beach day-use area; turn right for the campgrounds.

tongues," streams of lava that resemble a tongue, filled with joined lava boulders that look like cauliflowers.

Plan to bring a bike helmet for low ceilings, kneepads for crawling, boots or athletic shoes for scrambling on the jagged lava boulders, a fleece jacket (temperatures dip to 50°F), and a headlamp plus two flashlights per person with fresh batteries (these are do-it-yourself trips through unlit caves). The visitors center (530/667–8113, 9am-5:30pm June.-Aug., 9am-4:30pm daily Mar.-May and Sept.-Nov., 10am-4pm daily Dec.-Feb.) rents wide-beam flashlights and sells cheap plastic hard hats. Pick up a cave map here as well.

Note: The Cave Loop Drive closes to vehicles 5pm-8am.

HIKE CAPTAIN JACK'S STRONGHOLD

There's a saying: "If only these rocks could talk." At **Captain Jack's Stronghold** (1.7 miles, 1.5 hours), I'd never stop listening to the tales. Captain Jack was a Modoc warrior who used this lava fortress as a hideout. When U.S. troops attempted to move Native Americans off their lands and onto a reservation, this is where Captain Jack made his last stand. In 1873, Captain Jack was betrayed by his own troops, captured, and then hanged. This site was later named for him.

There are two short but rocky trails. The trail to the inner Stronghold is one mile round-trip (30 minutes). The other trail is three miles round-trip (1 hour) around the outer Stronghold. Start on the inner Stronghold Trail. It's a short walk with a few trenches, dips, and a short climb to the lava formation that both looks and feels like a fortress. If only these rocks could talk.

Captain Jack's Stronghold is in the northern region of the park. On the Volcanic Legacy Scenic Byway/Hill Road, look for a signed turnoff at a T intersection to Road 10. Turn east and drive 3.2 miles to the parking area.

BEST OVERNIGHT: INDIAN WELL CAMPGROUND

Indian Well Campground has 43 sites for tents and small trailers in two loops, plus one group site. Picnic tables, fire rings, and cooking grills are provided. Drinking water and restrooms with flush toilets are available. The visitors center is nearby. Some facilities are wheelchair-accessible. Leashed pets are permitted in the campground and on roads only.

Reservations are not accepted; all sites are first-come, first-served. Open year-round.

WHERE TO EAT

When you roll up to Señor Tequila (337 Main St., Tulelake, 530/667–4201), the first thing you will notice is the mural across the top of the entrance—a painting of a worker tending a blue agave (known as tequila agave). This place has the flavor of Mexico. Inside the small restaurant has a friendly feel, with good prices and an authentic menu that keeps the locals coming back. Order your salsa mild or spicy (like my fuego-breathing wife).

DRIVING DIRECTIONS

From Redding, take I-5 north for 68 miles to exit 747 (Central Weed/U.S. 97). At the stop sign, turn right and continue one mile to U.S. 97. Bear right on U.S. 97 and drive 54 miles to Highway 161. Turn east onto Highway 161 and drive 17 miles to Hill Road. Turn right (south) onto Hill Road and drive 12.8 miles to the park boundary of Lava Beds National Monument. Turn right onto the Volcanic Legacy Scenic Byway and drive 9.5 miles to the visitors center. The campground is adjacent to the visitors center.

It's a long drive (about two hours) to get here, so plan to fill the gas tank in Weed or Tulelake (on Hwy. 139) before entering the park.

CAMPFIRE STORIES

*A*t the Catacomb Cave, my guides were my son Kris (age 10 at the time) and his pal Zack, who was all of 65 pounds. They loved the narrow cave openings and crawling segments, where they slithered through like snakes. Both 10-year-olds pressed on, scouting each opening. They discovered plugged branches and hidden chambers, at times crawling through passageways when the ceiling lowered to just a few feet. "The stalactites look almost like cave coral, but not quite," Kris said. Zack, meanwhile, was looking for bats.

Bats are common late in the year, when they take refuge from the cold cave ceilings. During the summer months, bats are only occasionally seen in the caves, usually as folded-up sleeping forms. "The best time to come here would be in winter," Kris said. "That is when you could go into the ice caves and see the ice and crystal formations, and maybe see the bats, too."

"Out of the mouth of babes," goes the saying. They often know best.

△ *Catacomb Cave*

The feeling you get when you first see Burney Falls can imprint on your senses: You will always want to return. Start your trip with the short walk to the overlook, where Burney Falls first comes into view. The waterfall is drop-dead gorgeous, a wide, curtain-like cascade that's 129 feet high and split at the top. Below the brink, lava tubes produce a subliminal flow that emerges from the moss-covered wall, creating a series of trickles, streams, and mini-curtains. It looks as if the canyon wall is alive—there's nothing like it anywhere.

Burney Falls is the gateway to the park. Once you've arrived, you will find a great easy hike, campgrounds (include camping cabins) set in a forest, and a lake in the park's interior with a boat ramp, a small marina with rentals, and an adjacent swimming beach. A section of the Pacific Crest Trail even runs through the park.

The lake has fishing for trout late winter-late spring, smallmouth bass in the early summer, and crappie on warm summer evenings. With a hike, fly fishers can get shoreline access to Burney Creek, which feeds into the park, and a stellar section of the Pit River, which flows out of the dam.

▽ *view of Burney Falls from the Falls Loop trailhead*

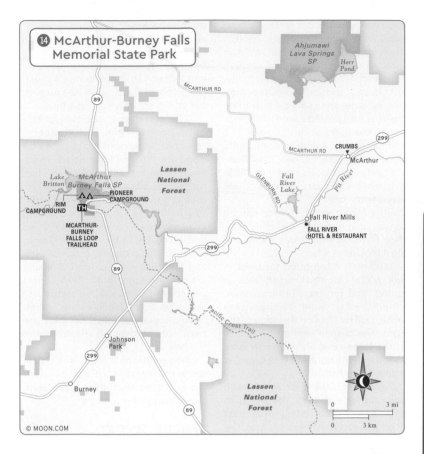

BEST ACTIVITY: FALLS LOOP TRAIL

From the visitors center parking lot, it's only a 100-foot walk to the Falls Overlook and the start of the Falls Loop Trail (1.2 miles, 0.5 hour). The wheelchair-accessible overlook offers a gorgeous view of Burney Falls, with two connected levels for viewing that are edged in by rock walls.

From the Falls Overlook, the paved Falls Loop Trail starts north along Burney Creek. The surrounding forest, canyon, and stream still manage to provide a pristine feel. The trail descends 200 feet into the canyon then skirts the plunge pool of the falls. Two spur trails lead to the water's edge, where you can feel the cold spray on your face.

Follow the trail downstream along Burney Creek to pretty Rainbow Bridge. Turn left and cross the bridge, where the path turns to dirt. Hike upstream along a few switchbacks. At one spot, you are directly adjacent to the subliminal curtain flows emerging from the lava tubes.

The trail rises past the brink of the falls along Burney Creek. At Fisherman's Bridge, stop for pretty photos of the creek. After crossing the bridge, you'll start hiking north back to the Falls Overlook. But before you do, look up and to your left here. Above the far side of the creek, atop a broken-off pine, a mated pair of bald eagles often tend a nest.

LAKE BRITTON

Inside the state park, drive north on Lake Road to Lake Britton, which has a small marina with boat rentals, a boat ramp, and a swimming beach. Though the swimming beach is small, it's a hit with youngsters in July and August. The beach is protected by a buoy line just offshore, and you'll see lots of families. All water sports are permitted on the lake, with posted speed limits near shore, the narrows, and coves. The marina (https://camprrm.com) rents sit-on-top kayaks, canoes, small fishing boats with motors, and those little two-seat pedal boats. All are popular May-September.

The fishing at Lake Britton can be sensation in late April and early May, then turns off with warm water and algal blooms in July.

Fishing is often good for trout in late winter, for smallmouth bass in spring, and for crappie in summer. When the first warm temperatures arrive, troll for trout on the edge of the main river channel and at the mouth of the large cove on the north side. (Get the depth right and troll Cop-Car colored Needlefish.)

April-May, fishing for smallmouth bass can be excellent. The key is to find inshore rock piles, then cast diving shad-type lures, such as the Shad Rap, Bagley mini bass, or lead jigs with a Keitech or Rage Swimmer grub. (Some do well with Ned Rigs.) The best bet on a hot summer evening is for crappie. Use a light to attract gnats and then fish just off the cement block structures in the Narrows. Use small crappie jigs, where you cast and jig (slowly, not fast) right along the cement block supports. When it's right, you have a chance at a bucketful of crappie.

BEST OVERNIGHT: MCARTHUR-BURNEY FALLS MEMORIAL STATE PARK

McArthur-Burney Falls Memorial State Park has good availability for cabins and campsites in summer, especially during the week. On holiday weekends, the parking lots can fill, which causes the park to close until spaces open up. This is a popular destination for families late June-mid-August. Once school starts up in late August, campsites are easy to come by.

The state park has two pretty campgrounds—**Rim** and **Pioneer**—set amid large ponderosa pines on opposite sides of Lake Road. There are 121 sites for tents or RVs, six environmental sites, and one hike-in/bike-in site near the Pioneer Cemetery Trail. There are 24 wood camping cabins (no water or electricity) in two sizes available in the Pioneer Campground. Picnic tables, food lockers, and fire grills are provided. Drinking water, restrooms with flush toilets and showers, and a dump station are available. Some facilities are wheelchair-accessible. Leashed pets are permitted, except on the trails and the beach.

Reservations (800/444-7275, www.reservecalifornia.com, fee) are accepted seasonally. Open sunrise-sunset year-round.

WHERE TO EAT

In the town of Fall River Mills, the **Fall River Hotel & Restaurant** (24860 Main St., Fall River Mills, 530/336-5550, www.fallriverhotel.com, 7am-9pm Sun.-Mon. and Thurs., 7am-10pm Fri.-Sat.) serves the best country-style dinner around. A small bar at the entrance serves locally brewed elixirs from the Fall River Brewing Company.

A few miles north, in the town of McArthur, is the cottage-like front of a restaurant called **Crumbs** (44226 Hwy. 299, 530/336-5451, call for hours), which serves some of the best food in the northern part of the state. Believe it or not, the sushi here is world class, as good as the mega-buck sushi outfits in San Francisco. Turns out the chef is a big-city transplant who landed here in remote Shasta County.

CAMPFIRE STORIES

*W*hen it comes to landmark moments in the outdoors, sometimes you never see them coming. So it was on a visit to McArthur-Burney Falls Memorial State Park. We showed up to see the waterfall at peak flow, and it was sensational, as expected. We hiked the loop—great, expected that, too. Then we launched my boat and caught smallmouth bass in exciting little tussles. We watched a few bald eagles sail overhead then turn north into a cove to land on some pines. Birds never lie, you know. So I cranked up my Honda 115 and motored slowly ahead, then turned north to follow them into the cove. For a few minutes, we floated quietly with the motor off and watched the eagles with binoculars. Suddenly, one flew overhead, hovering in an arc and looking down. We looked into the lake and, right next to us, sighted this huge school of trout near the surface. It looked like a thousand fish or more. But instead of pulling out our rods and casting, we watched the bald eagle above us as it folded its wings and plummeted to the surface. In a flash, it had plucked out a trout. A moment later, another bald eagle joined the easy pickings. And just like that, they were gone and the school of trout dispersed into the depths. It was like peering into a supernatural world.

△ *A bald eagle snatches a trout.*

DRIVING DIRECTIONS

From I-5 in Redding, take Highway 299 east for 50 miles to the town of Burney. Continue 5 miles to the junction with Highway 89. Turn left (north) and drive 5.4 miles to the state park entrance (24898 Hwy. 89) on the left.

The park has a great visitors center, a well-stocked camper store, and friendly rangers.

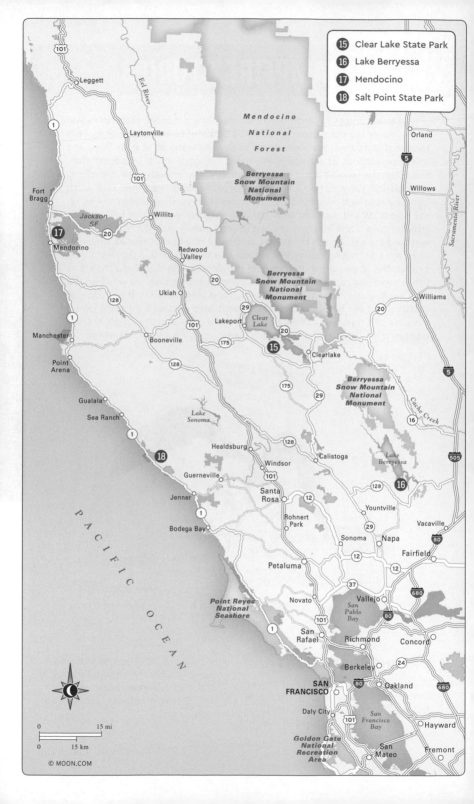

~ *Chapter 4* ~

MENDOCINO AND WINE COUNTRY

Set amid the foothills of Lake County, Clear Lake is the largest natural freshwater lake in California, with 44,000 surface acres and 150 miles of shoreline. The first sight of the lake offers a vision of what lies ahead: boating, fishing, water sports, lakeside lodging, and hiking Mount Konocti for a panorama across the region. The lake is so big it often seems full right to the brim. With Mount Konocti looming above and the surrounding hills bright green in spring, everything feels fresh and clean. It's one of the prettiest sights in California.

Nestled on the lake's peninsula, Clear Lake State Park has good shoreline fishing, a boat ramp with easy access to nearby waters, a great campground (plus those cute park model cabins), and an excellent trail to Wrights Peak.

Dozens of mom-and-pop resorts and private campgrounds are sprinkled along the shoreline of the lake, which means that even on peak weekends, the lake can accommodate large numbers of visitors without feeling crowded.

Clear Lake has almost 100 boat ramps; many resorts have their own boat ramps, in addition to city and county ramps. In many cases, launching a boat is free (or just a few bucks). Every imaginable water sport—even parasailing—can is enjoyed here, and just about every kind of watercraft is available for rent.

The lake is shaped somewhat like an hourglass, with the northern section of the lake much larger and rounder than its southern counterpart. The two sections are somewhat divided by the Buckingham Park peninsula and a few small islands. Anglers, kayakers, and swimmers tend to stick to the shoreline and coves.

▽ *Mount Konocti overlooking Clear Lake*

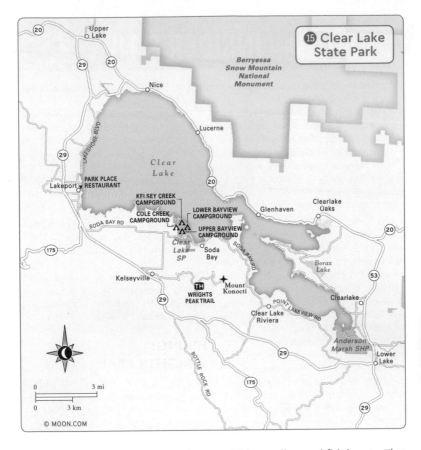

The best time to come is in late spring and early summer, when the sun is warm and the water is cool and clear. (In late summer, the water can become soupy with algae and water grass in some areas.)

BEST ACTIVITY: FISHING

Most folks head to Clear Lake for one reason: It's the best place in California to catch the bass of a lifetime, a five-pounder or better. (According to pro bass angler Scott Green, the average odds here are about 80 percent.) This place is a fish factory for giant bass, catfish, and crappie, with good populations of bluegill as well. The lake is lined with tules, docks, and pilings (many of which are 3–10 feet deep),

which are all natural fish haunts. That kind of structure makes it easier to fish.

The best fishing is in late spring and early summer for bass at the docks in the marinas. Boat activity is light during the week, especially late winter through spring and into early summer. The bass will often stage under the docks and moored boats at marinas around the lake. They also hide in the shade and along the tule-lined shore in the state park and in Kelsey and Cole Creek Sloughs. The best prospects are by boat, and you can fish a dozen or more spots in an extended morning.

Most anglers will rig several rods and rotate casts until hitting on what works best: drop-shot Robo worms; a Senko rigged Texas-style, weight-less, with a wide-gap 4/0 Kamakatsu

Some anglers like to hire a guide for their first time out on a lake. Following are some of the best:

* ★ Bob Myskey of **Bassin' with Bob** (707/274-0373, www.fishclearlake.com)
* ★ Richard Pounds of **Bass Fishin' with Richard Pounds** (707/279-4739, www.bassfishinclearlake.com)
* ★ **Ed Legan Guide Service** (702/497-8938, www.clearlakefamilyguide service.com) specializes in crappie.

worm hook; jig & pig with a Terminator with a pork-rind trailer; hard baits such as a Bagley baby bluegill, Husky Jerk Rapala, Shad Rap, and Ratteltrap. A handful of pros stick to giant swimbaits, such as the Huddleston, or the Weapon jig, 10-inch plastic worms, and flukes, and then fish exclusively for bass in the 10-pound class.

In summer, anglers switch to floating (weedless) frogs. The "frog bite" can be incredible in summer, with casters getting a lot of action from big bass. I've caught bass and bluegill in the sloughs with a fly rod and small poppers, best at dusk when the wind dies down and the surface settles. You can sail out gentle casts atop quiet emerald water and get the fish to grab on the surface with a swirl the size of a washtub, right in front of you.

Some of the best bluegill fishing can be had along the shoreline tules in the state park; just dunk a worm and let the biting begin. The lake also has great crappie fishing, which is best in winter from docks at night—use live minnows for bait. For catfish, the best fishing is outside Rodman Slough at the north end of the lake, in Jago Bay, and in Cache Slough to the south.

In addition to the boat launch and marina at Clear Lake State Park, on the west bank of Cole Creek, the following marinas have public boat launches:

* Lakeside County Park, Finley
* Library Point, Lakeport
* Clearlake Oaks
* Redbud Park and Thompson Harbor Marina, Clearlake
* Lucerne Harbor, Lucerne

Note: Clear Lake now requires mandatory boat inspection for quagga mussels, with inspection stations available seven days a week.

HIKING: WRIGHTS PEAK

Wrights Peaks (4,229 feet) is one of five peaks on Mount Konocti, Clear Lake's ancient volcano, and the mountain's best lookout. The **Wrights Peak Trail** (7.5 miles, 2.5-3.5 hours) is a Jeep-style service road that leads to a fire lookout at the summit. The hike is a near-continuous climb as the route rises 1,650 feet over 3.5 miles. Along the way, you'll pass through an orchard and oak woodlands, with sightings of deer and red-tailed hawks. At the top of the peak are sensational views in every direction. Towering over Clear Lake, the vista stretches for more than 100 miles. Of all the surrounding peaks, Mount St. Helena (to the south) is the most prominent. The best view, of course, is from the fire lookout (open to the public during docent tours). Spur trails lead to Howards Peak and Buckingham Peak.

It takes folks about 1.5 hours to hike to the top and then about an hour to come down.

BEST OVERNIGHT: CLEAR LAKE STATE PARK

If you have fallen in love with Clear Lake and its surrounding oak woodlands, then you won't find a better camp spot than at **Clear Lake State Park.** Located on the western shore of the lake, campsites here may feel close together, but the proximity to the lake's boating and fishing makes the lack of privacy worth it. There are four campground loops with 147 sites for tents and RVs:

- **Kelsey Creek Campground** is on a peninsula between Kelsey Slough and the Clear Lake shoreline, with 65 lakeside campsites and two group sites. This is also where you'll find the park's best best: eight park model cabins (pets not permitted) that come with electricity, heaters and air-conditioning, lights, and fans.
- **Cole Creek Campground** is just past the park entrance, with 26 campsites and two hike-in/bike-in sites.
- **Lower Bayview Campground** has 22 campsites with nice views; sites are within walking distance to the park's swim beach.
- **Upper Bayview Campground** is located on a hill, with 33 campsites.

Picnic tables and fire rings are provided at all sites. Drinking water, restrooms with coin showers and flush toilets, and a dump station are available. A boat ramp, dock, boat battery charging station, visitors center, and swimming beach are located within the park. Some facilities, including the cabins, are wheelchair-accessible. Leashed pets are permitted in the campgrounds.

Reservations (800/444-7275, www.reservecalifornia.com, fee) are accepted and advised late spring-early summer. Open year-round.

WHERE TO EAT

A lakeside setting is a must, right? For a dynamic menu and consistent quality, head to **Park Place Restaurant** (50 3rd St., Lakeport, 707/263-0444, www.parkplacelakeport.com, 11am-8:30pm Sun.-Thurs., 11am-9pm Fri.-Sat.), the best place in Lakeport. Crown the day with an order of the bay shrimp salad or indulge in an array of pasta-based dishes (with garlic bread, of course).

DRIVING DIRECTIONS

From Vallejo, take I-80 to exit 33 for Highway 37/Napa. Take that exit and drive 0.8 mile onto Highway 37, then continue 1.4 miles to exit 19 for Highway 29. Take that exit onto Highway 29 and drive 36.5 miles to Dunaweal Lane. Turn right and drive 1.6 miles to Silverado Trail. Turn left and drive 1.6 miles to Highway 29. Turn right and drive 31 miles (becomes curvy) to Lower Lake and a stoplighted intersection (signed left for Highway 29). Turn left and drive 14.2 miles to Kelseyville and the exit for Main Street. Turn right and drive 0.5 mile to State Street. Turn right and drive 0.4 mile to Gaddy Lane. Turn right and drive 2.1 miles to Soda Bay Road, and then continue ahead 1 mile to the entrance for Clear Lake State Park.

To reach the Wrights Peak Trailhead: From Clear Lake State Park, take Soda Bay Road for 1 mile, then turn left onto Gaddy Lane. Continue straight on Gaddy Land for 2.1 miles to State Street. Turn left on State Street and drive 0.4 mile to Kelseyville and Main Street. Turn left on Main Street and drive 0.2 mile to Konocti Road. Turn left and drive 3.2 miles to Mount Konocti County Park, then continue 3 miles past two parking lots (a restroom is available at the second one). A short distance beyond is a locked gate. Park and walk on a flat dirt road to the signed trailhead on the right.

CAMPFIRE STORIES

Y ou always remember the landmark moments in your life. My family had arrived at Clear Lake around midnight on a warm summer night. After we found a campsite, everyone crawled into their sleeping bags to go to sleep. But I was a little kid who wanted to have fun—not sleep. I'd read a magazine story about how you could go out to the docks at Clear Lake at night and fish under the bright lights with a crappie jig. So off I went to the nearest dock with my rod and reel. At 2:30am, I staggered back to our campsite with a stringer of about 20 crappie. I woke up my mom and dad to show off my catch, and my dad mumbled something like "Am I gonna have to clean all of those?" My mom touched my arm and said, "I'm proud of you." I glowed, and at that moment, a crazy little 11-year-old started to grow up.

△ *fishing Clear Lake State Park*

Located within a short range of Sacramento and the San Francisco Bay Area, Lake Berryessa is one of the best lakes for boating, fishing, and water sports. The lake is 23 miles long and 3 miles wide with roughly 165 miles of shoreline plus five major coves and five recreation areas with boat ramps.

One of the best-known spots is the "Glory Hole." When Lake Berryessa fills, the water spills over into the Morning Glory Spillway, which looks like a giant funnel near Monticello Dam. On summer weekends, the miles of warm, clear water can inspire a wild scene: lots of fast boats, water-skiers, sunbathers, and flowing liquid refreshment of various origins. Midweek, the place is far more peaceful and the natural beauty really shines.

In spring and fall, the water is too cold for most water sports, but it is perfect for fishing, with excellent prospects for bass and trout.

The lake has many secluded coves and islands. Above the western shore, Berryessa-Knoxville Road runs for 12 miles with cutoff roads for Steele Canyon and Capell Cove recreation areas, the visitors center, and the Oak Shores and Smittle Creek Day Use Areas. On the eastern side is an expanse of untouched shore.

Over the years, I've ventured to all of these places, but the strongest image for me is of the lake seen from my plane overhead. As I peer down across the expanse of water, it seems like anything is possible. And in a boat on the water, it is.

▽ *the Morning Glory Spillway a.k.a. the "Glory Hole"*

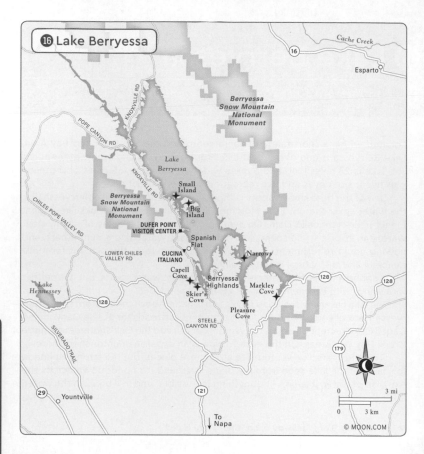

⑯ Lake Berryessa

BEST ACTIVITY: BOATING

The miles of cool, clean water make Lake Berryessa a great destination for boating. In summer, the water temperature climbs into the mid-70s, which makes it perfect for waterskiing, boarding, and personal watercraft. The 5-mph zones welcome kayakers, canoeists, and swimmers.

The lake's shoreline topography divides the lake into natural regions for each activity. The northern section of the lake is a wide expanse of water where jet boats and personal watercraft can go crazy, with all the space anybody could dream of. The northern area feeds south into a spot called the Narrows, which divides and connects the spacious northern waters to the

southern arm of the lake. As you continue south, the lake extends to Monticello Dam and Markley Cove.

The best spots for kayaks, canoes, and nonmotorized boating are deep in the major coves of the lake. At the far north end of the lake (up the Putah Creek Arm), a buoy line marks the 10-mph speed limit where canoeists and kayakers can paddle into this lesser-traveled section. This is bordered on the west by a dramatic granite wall and on the east by a meadow where deer often graze. I've paddled in here, casting for bass along the way, and watched wildlife near the shore that never knew I was there.

Berryessa does not provide free public boat ramps. There are five major recreation sites with boat ramps ($20 launch fee), marinas and boat rentals, and campgrounds. All the best fishing spots are within range of kayaks, as long as you launch at the nearest available boat ramp. However, they are far enough apart that those in kayaks and other hand-powered boats are committing to a single area per launch.

South-north, the five major coves with recreation areas and boat ramps are:

- **Markley Cove** (Markley Cove Resort, 707/966-2134, www.markleycove resort.com)
- **Pleasure Cove** (Pleasure Cove Marina, 707/966-9600, www.go berryessa.com)
- **Capell Cove** (Steele Canyon Recreation Area, 707/968-9179, www.goberryessa.com; Spanish Flat Recreation Area, 707/966-0200, www.spanishflatcamping.com)
- **Oak Shores Day Use Area** (west shore of Lake Berryessa, near the islands, 707/966-2111, www.recreation.gov)
- **Putah Creek** (Putah Canyon Recreation Area, 707/966-9051, www.royalelkparkmanagement.com)

Berryessa Point and Monticello Shores Recreation Area, once popular spots for access, picnics and camping, remain closed to camping by the Bureau of Reclamation. These areas are still open for day-use.

FISHING

At times, Lake Berryessa can be the No. 1 fishing lake in California. At other times, well, not so much. At dawn on a warm day in late spring (April-mid-May), you can have many of the best spots to yourself, where the fish practically shout "please catch me!"

Here is where to go:

- **Skier's Cove** is a long, deep cove located on the southern peninsula of Capell Cove. It is within short range of Spanish Flat and Steele Canyon Recreation Areas and the Capell Cove boat launch.
- The **Narrows** are the two narrow passages that link the main lake body of Lake Berryessa to Pleasure Cove and, farther south, to Markley Cove. On the north side of the Narrows, look for a rocky area that

△ *fishing for largemouth bass at Lake Berryessa*

falls into the lake, called the **Rock Slide.** It's a natural habitat for fish.

- The **Big Island** is on the west side of the main body of the lake and adjoins a smaller island to the northwest.

Bass fishing is best late winter-early summer, with counts of 30–40 catch-and-release common for those who know how. The spots are the Putah Creek Arm (at the headwaters of the lake), the Vineyard (off the northeastern shore of the lake), in the coves on the east side of the central lake body, and Portuguese Cove (out of Markley Cove).

Techniques for Bass: Use a green Senko rigged wacky style, green or salt-and-pepper Zoom twist-tail grubs and white flukes for depths 10–25 feet deep; Rebel Pop-R or Zara Spook during surface bites; chartreuse spinnerbaits (with silver blades) when windy.

In the fall, when the lake turns over, the trout come up to the top 10 feet of water and fishing can be spectacular (the best fishing is often with minnows). When the lake establishes a thermocline in summer, it's like the trout are locked in a jail 25–40 feet deep. You can find the key to that jail.

Techniques for Trout: Use downriggers to test depths until you get it just right. Troll Needlefish, Humdinger, Triple Teaser, R-Lure, or Sparklefish, or drift along the shoreline with a live minnow under a bobber.

BEST OVERNIGHT: PLEASURE COVE MARINA

One of the best camping ideas ever is the park model cabin. The cabins are built off-site on a trailer platform and then towed into the park. Tack some lattice around the base of the cabin, add a deck, and just like that, you've got a lakefront cabin at a campsite. That's how **Pleasure Cove Marina** (6100 Hwy. 128, 707/966-9600, www.goberryessa.com) created the Lake Berryessa Cabin Rentals. These little wood-sided cabins are real pretty, with decks overlooking the lake, and they come with a small refrigerator, a microwave, and an indoor bathroom; there's a charcoal barbecue grill outside. Choose from two sizes: one that sleeps up to four people or another that sleeps up to eight. Note that dogs are not allowed in the cabins.

Reservations are accepted online, and there's a two-night minimum. Open year-round.

Pleasure Cove Marina also rents houseboat, with three models that range 59, 60, and 70 feet.

WHERE TO EAT

The thing I've learned about Italian restaurants is that before you can form an opinion, you have to learn something about the owner. This will tell you what you need to know about the food. So it is at Cucina Italiana (4310 Knoxville Rd., 707/966-2433) at Spanish Flat. Here it all starts here with the owner, Stefano, and it just gets better from there. Say hello, and then take a look at the plates on the tables for what's good (personally, I'm a fan of the seafood). Whatever you order, you really can't miss.

DRIVING DIRECTIONS

From Vallejo, take Highway 29 north to merge with Highway 221 North. Drive 2.6 miles (the road becomes Soscol Avenue), then continue 0.5 mile to Highway 121/Silverado Trail. Turn right on Silverado Trail and drive 2.7 miles to signed turnoff for Highway 121. Turn right on Highway 121 and drive 12.3 miles to Highway 128/Capell Valley Road. Turn left and drive 4.8 miles to Berryessa-Knoxville Road. Turn right and drive 6.6 miles along Lake Berryessa to the turnoff (on the right) for the Dufer Point Visitor Center (5520 Knoxville Rd., 707/966-2111, noon-3pm Mon.-Fri., 10am-5pm Sat.-Sun. late May-early Sept., noon-3pm Sat.-Sun. early Sept.-late May). Berryessa-Knoxville Road passes the Spanish Flat area en route to the visitors center.

CAMPFIRE STORIES

There's been so many magic days out on Lake Berryessa. With angling wizard Jim Munk, I've had 60-fish days for bass. One time at the Vineyard, I caught an 11-pound catfish by accident. With novelist John Lescroart, I caught trout and salmon one after another. When then–book dealer Tom Hedtke cast a lure off the side of a boat at Markley Cove, I watched him nail a stunning 5-pound smallmouth bass. Dusty Baker, Elvin Bishop, and I once floated into Skier's Cove, casting ahead of the boat for bass, trailing live minnows under bobbers for trout, and having the time of our lives.

Back when my brother Rambob returned home from the front lines of Vietnam, we went straight to Berryessa. For the first time in my life, I was so grateful just to be in a boat with him, alive and well, that it didn't matter if the fish were biting or not.

But the most unforgettable day was when I was in my canoe with my friend, publisher Ed Ow, who was running a houseboat, recognized me from about 100 yards off. He steered toward me to say "hi" and, as he neared, he discovered that houseboats don't have brakes. That houseboat ran right over the top of my canoe and dumped us both in the warm water. "Sorry about that, Tom," he said, and then we went aboard and let the hot sun dry us out, laughing like hell.

△ Lake Berryessa

⑰ Mendocino

707/937-5804 | Mendocino County | www.parks.ca.gov

This is a classic spot on the Pacific coast where you'll fall in love with hidden coastal coves, redwood forests, and classic waterfalls. Within the village of Mendocino, quaint shops are loaded with treasures, but the real treasures are the inshore coastal waters and nearby redwood forests.

The town of Mendocino is surrounded by eight state parks with plentiful access to coastal beaches, historic sites, and scenic hiking trails. You'll find campgrounds at Russian Gulch and Van Damme State Parks, as well as hiking trails to the headlands and beach access into Mendocino Bay. Opportunities abound for kayaking in wind-sheltered lagoons and bays or just watching the sun set beyond the surf and sea. Kayaking is sensational in Mendocino Bay and Big River Lagoon, and the views from the water are just as good.

At the tip of town is Mendocino Headlands State Park (end of Main Street). From the parking lot, it's a short walk to Point Mendocino, where the ocean views seem to extend across what feels like forever. A stepped trail curves down to Portuguese Beach, backed by high cliffs and fronted by Mendocino Bay.

Mendocino used to receive heavy fog in summer, but climate change has given rise to more clear days on the coast. For the best weather and the prettiest days, plan your visit mid-March-April or mid-September-November.

▽ *Mendocino*

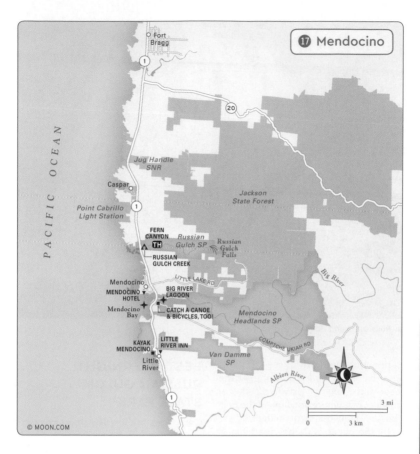

© MOON.COM

BEST ACTIVITY: RUSSIAN GULCH FALLS

The hike to **Russian Gulch Falls** (5.1 miles round-trip, 2.5 hours) is an easy walk along pretty Russian Gulch Creek to an overlook of Russian Gulch Falls. The first 2 miles along the Fern Canyon Trail are nearly flat as the pocked trail passes bracken and sword ferns before entering the redwoods with an understory of ferns, wild blackberries, and sorrel. At 2.3 miles, you'll reach the junction for the Falls Loop Trail. Turn left and, after a short climb, hike the final 0.7 mile to the waterfall. You get a full frontal of the 36-foot cascade as it pours into Russian Gulch. After you've had your fill, turn right and descend a short distance to the foot of the plunge pool. Continue across

a bridge over the creek for another angle of the falls, then return the way you came.

The trailhead is located inside Russian Gulch State Park, two miles north of Mendocino on Highway 1. The trailhead is at the end of the campground.

KAYAKING

Kayaking trips are a popular summer activity on the Mendocino coast. North of Mendocino is Big River Beach, the launching point for premium kayaking trips into Mendocino Bay (west) and Big River Lagoon (east).

Pick a calm morning with a light surf and venture west under the Highway 1 Bridge, then paddle across **Mendocino Bay** to Point Mendocino and the headlands. The views are sen-

△ *Russian Gulch Falls*

sational to the north of the cliff walls and the arcing beach frontage. At the headlands, you can play in a series of small coves, where you float in the currents and feel the surge in the eddies.

If the ocean is rough, head inland instead to kayak the **Big River Lagoon.** (The official name is Big River Estuary State Marine Reserve.) The lagoon is well shielded from coastal winds and provides gorgeous flatwater paddling. There are often good numbers of migratory shorebirds here.

To explore the Big River Estuary, rent a canoe from **Catch a Canoe & Bicycles Too** (1 S. Big River Rd., Mendocino, 707/937–0273, www.catchacanoe.com, 9am-5pm daily). For other guided trips, **Kayak Mendocino** (707/813–7117, www.kayakmendocino.com) launches Sea Cave Nature Tours from the beach at Van Damme State Park (Highway 1, 3 miles south of Mendocino).

From Highway 1, take the Big River Road exit. The beach is located on the north side of the Big River, just below the Highway 1 Bridge.

BEST OVERNIGHT: RUSSIAN GULCH STATE PARK

Campsites are nestled deep in a redwood canyon along Russian Gulch Creek. These are some of the prettiest and most secluded drive-in campsites on the Mendocino coast. There are 26 sites for tents or RVs, four equestrian sites, and one group site. Picnic tables, fire grills, and food lockers are provided. Drinking water, coin showers, and flush toilets are available. A seasonal junior ranger program includes nature walks and campfire programs. A day-use picnic area and beach access are nearby. Some facilities are wheelchair-accessible. Leashed pets are permitted in the campground and on some trails.

Reservations are accepted (800/444–7275, www.reservecalifornia.com, fee) April-October. Sites are first-come, first-served mid-to-late March and mid-September-October. Open mid-March-October.

INSIDER'S TIP

If there's a shopper in your crowd, they'll be in heaven strolling the shops of downtown Mendocino, one after another. **Rainsong Shoes** (10483 Lansing St., 707/937–1710, www.rainsongshoes.com), has the best array of sandals around. **Gallery Bookshop and Bookwinkles Children's Books** (319 Kasten St., 707/937–2665, www.gallerybookshop.com, 9:30am-6pm Sun.-Thurs., 9:30am-9pm Fri.-Sat.) and **Main Street Book Shop** (990 Main St., 707/937-1537) can fulfill all your reading needs, while **Out of This World** (45100 Main St., 707/937–3335, www.outofthisworldshop.com) is a fun-filled toy store worthy of both kids and adults.

If you don't like to shop but your partner does, the solution is to hike or kayak in the morning to get your ya-yas out. Then, your partner can shop while you take a seat at the bar in the Mendocino Hotel, where you can post your trip photos online.

WHERE TO EAT

For lunch I like to take a seat in the woodsy bar at the **Mendocino Hotel** (45080 Main St., 707/937-0511, www.mendocinohotel.com, 6pm-9pm Sun.-Thurs., 6pm-9:30pm Fri.-Sat.) and order a bowl of the house-made clam chowder, or maybe split a turkey bacon avocado sandwich. But at dinnertime, I always make the short drive south to the **Little River Inn** (7901 Hwy. 1, Little River, 707/937-5942, www.littleriverinn.com, 6pm-close daily), where the petrale sole with gulf shrimp is out of this world.

DRIVING DIRECTIONS

From San Francisco, cross the Golden Gate Bridge and take U.S. 101 north for 83 miles (past Cloverdale). Take exit 522 for Highway 128 and turn left onto Highway 128. Drive 0.8 mile, then turn right (well signed, still on Highway 128) and drive 55 miles north along the Navarro River to Highway 1. At the junction of Highways 128 and 1, turn right onto Highway 1 and drive 10 miles north to the Big River Bridge. Continue 0.3 mile north to Mendocino and take the first exit on the left for Main Street.

Coming from points north and east, take I-5 to Highway 20 and drive west, past Clear Lake, to U.S. 101 North. Drive 12.6 miles on U.S. 101 to the exit for Highway 20 West. Take that exit and drive 0.3 mile to a stop sign. Turn left and drive 2.8 miles to Willits. At a stoplighted intersection for Highway 20, turn left and drive 33 miles to Highway 1. Turn left and drive 8.1 miles to Mendocino and the exit on the right for Main Street.

⑱ Salt Point State Park

707/847-3221 | Jenner | www.parks.ca.gov

The dramatic shoreline of Salt Point State Park is memorable to anyone who visits it. This gorgeous piece of the Sonoma coast is highlighted by ocean breaks that pound against rocky crags; deep, quiet coves and inshore kelp beds; and protected marine reserves. Across the park's 6,000 acres, coastal outcrops and stacks lead to a series of protected coves—Gerstle Cove, Stump Beach Cove, Fisk Mill Cove, and Horseshoe Cove. Beneath Gerstle Cove is a rare underwater park and reserve: Gerstle Cove State Marine Reserve, where no form of marine life may be taken or disturbed within the protected area. Inland are coast redwoods and Bishop pine forests that transition to coastal grasslands. Throughout the park, short, outstanding hikes provide stellar ocean views.

Start your visit at the park's **visitors center** (10am-3pm Sat.-Sun. Apr.-Oct., $8 day use) near Gerstle Cove, where you can pick up a map to the park's sights. Hike to the Pygmy Forest, drive north to the Sentinel Rock Viewing Platform overlooking Fisk Mill Cove, or take a side trip to explore the adjoining Kruse Rhododendron State Natural Reserve. Whatever you do, don't miss the scenic stroll along the bluff.

▽ *rock formations at Salt Point State Park*

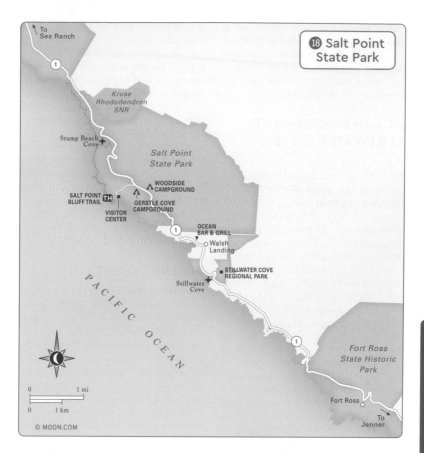

To Sea Ranch

1

Kruse
Rhododendron
SNR

Salt Point
State Park

Stump Beach
Cove

WOODSIDE
CAMPGROUND

SALT POINT
BLUFF TRAIL

GERSTLE COVE
CAMPGROUND

VISITOR
CENTER

OCEAN
BAR & GRILL

Walsh
Landing

STILLWATER COVE
REGIONAL PARK

Stillwater
Cove

PACIFIC OCEAN

1

Fort Ross
State Historic
Park

0   1 mi
0   1 km

© MOON.COM

Fort Ross

To
Jenner

BEST ACTIVITY:
SALT POINT BLUFF TRAIL

The **Salt Point Bluff Trail** (2.4 miles round-trip, 1.5 hours) is routed above ocean cliffs from Salt Point north to Stump Beach Cove. This pretty walk races above the shore with a series of spectacular views of the coves below and across the ocean. From the trailhead (located near the visitors center), walk 1.2 miles north for a series of awesome views of the park's dramatic rocky shoreline. Cross over Warren Creek (a seasonal stream) and continue north across the 100-foot-high ocean bluffs. You can practically feel the crashing of the waves below as the ocean spray rockets skyward. The trail winds around and down to Stump Beach Cove, a pretty, sandy

△ *Salt Point Bluff Trail*

beach where the calm waters are in sharp contrast to the nearby breakers.

From here, it's possible to extend the hike two miles north to the Sentinel Rock Viewing Platform and the overlook of Fisk Mill Cove.

OCEAN KAYAKING AT STILLWATER COVE

There's a launch point at Gerstle Cove for kayaking, but a better choice exists less than four miles south at **Stillwater Cove Regional Park** (22455 Hwy. 1, Jenner, 707/847-3245, www.sonomacounty.ca.gov, $7 parking). Set in a deep cove on the Sonoma coast north of Jenner, Stillwater Cove is home to one of the best sea kayaking destinations on the Pacific Coast. On the west side of Highway 1 is a sheltered beach that expands to a rock-peppered shore along Stillwater Cove. There is a pullout near the foot of the cove where you can park, unload your kayak, and then drop down to the beach. (A tow dolly with beach wheels is advised for heavier kayaks.)

A separate parking area is north of the park's main entrance and provides access to the Stillwater Bluff Trail (0.25 mile), which offers views of the rock-strewn shore and access down to the water's edge.

BEST OVERNIGHT: SALT POINT STATE PARK

Salt Point State Park has two campgrounds:

Gerstle Cove Campground, located on the west side of Highway 1, has 30 sites for tents or RVs. The trailhead to the cove overlook is located between camps 9 and 10, so if you don't want people walking past your camp, pick a different site.

Woodside Campground is located on the east side of Highway 1, where it has 79 sites for tents or RVs contained within two large loops. Two trailheads—one in the lower loop (between camps 33 and 34) and another on the upper loop (between camps 88 and 89) provide access to Gerstle Cove.

Picnic tables and fire rings are provided, and drinking water and flush toilets are available. Firewood is available for purchase. In summer, interpretive programs may be offered at the campground. The picnic area and one hiking trail are wheelchair-accessible. Leashed pets are permitted, except on trails.

Reservations (800/444-7275, www.reservecalifornia.com, fee) are accepted. Open year-round.

WHERE TO EAT

The **Ocean Bar & Grill** (23255 Coast Hwy., Jenner, 707/847-3158, www.oceancovelodge.com, noon-8pm Sun.-Thurs., noon-10pm Fri.-Sat.) sits perched on a hillside on the east side of the Coast Highway. An outdoor courtyard near the entrance promises gorgeous views of Ocean Cove and across the Pacific. Order the fish-and-chips or a bowl of clam chowder from the menu, grab a seat, and enjoy the view. The restaurant is located inside the Ocean Cove Lodge, 0.5 mile south of the boundary to the state park.

DRIVING DIRECTIONS

From U.S. 101 near Petaluma, exit at Railroad Avenue and turn left, driving 0.4 mile to Stony Point Road (the second right). Turn right and drive 1.7 miles to Roblar Road. Turn left and drive 6.5 miles to Valley Ford Road. Turn right and drive 5.5 miles to a junction with Highway 1 (on the left). Continue straight on Highway 1 for 36.5 miles, past Bodega Bay and Jenner, to Salt Point State Park.

Picnic areas are located at South Gerstle Cove, Stump Beach Cove, and Fisk Mill Cove off Highway 1.

CAMPFIRE STORIES

*F*rom a blufftop lookout at Salt Point State Park, a game warden and I, with binoculars in hand, watched a family of poachers dive, collect, and transport illegal abalone to shore. Other family members waited on shore, then stuffed the booty into garbage bags and carried them to their vehicles. Another game warden was alerted by radio and the bust was made in the parking lot. It was yet another in a string of felony cases of abalone poaching from the Sonoma coast.

According to the California Department of Fish and Wildlife, abalone cannot sustain their populations amid illegal commercialized take and sale. Abalone require about 10 years to reach seven inches. State divers measure the distance between abalone on the rocks of the sea bottom. When they are about 10 feet apart (or farther), it becomes difficult for the sea snails to crawl and find each other to mate. At this point, more restrictive rules are set in motion. Sport divers must use no air assist (that is, you hold your breath and free-dive). Yet lawbreakers pay no heed to these rules, and often use scuba gear in order to take every abalone they can get their illegal mitts on to sell as contraband to restaurants. Some of the abalone illegally taken here have been tracked to a black market in Los Angeles.

Poaching has devastated abalone populations to the point that legal sport diving, though not the cause of the decline, was banned for three years, into 2021. There is no guarantee the populations will rebound to the point that a sport season will be allowed again. We've already seen this movie in San Mateo County, where abalone diving is still banned after poachers wiped them out.

For that one day with the game wardens, catching a ring of poachers at Salt Point State Park, it felt like the good guys had won.

△ *Salt Point State Park*

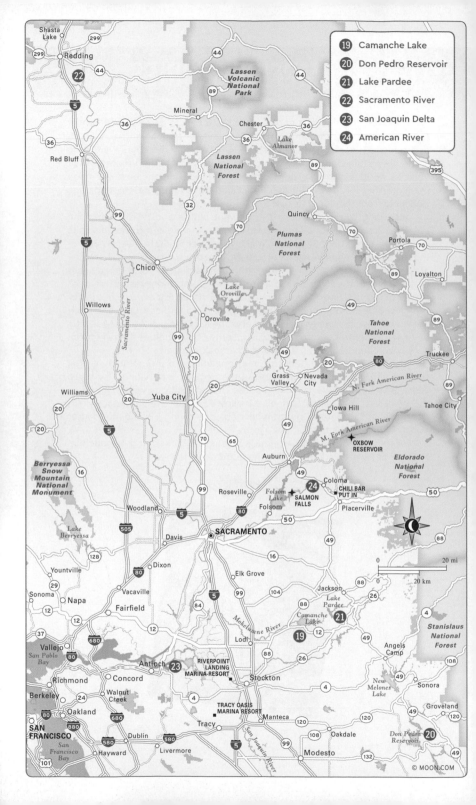

19 Camanche Lake
20 Don Pedro Reservoir
21 Lake Pardee
22 Sacramento River
23 San Joaquin Delta
24 American River

Shasta Lake
Redding
299
299
44
22
5
Lassen Volcanic National Park
44
44
89
Mineral
36
Red Bluff
36
Chester
36
Lake Almanor
395
Lassen National Forest
89
99
5
32
70
Quincy
89
70
Plumas National Forest
Portola
70
Chico
Lake Oroville
Loyalton
89
Willows
Oroville
Tahoe National Forest
89
99
70
Truckee
80
5
Williams
20
Yuba City
20
Grass Valley
Nevada City
N. Fork American River
Tahoe City
89
20
65
70
49
Iowa Hill
M. Fork American River
Berryessa Snow Mountain National Monument
16
99
Roseville
Auburn
49
OXBOW RESERVOIR
Eldorado National Forest
50
Woodland
505
80
Folsom Lake
49
24
SALMON FALLS
Coloma
CHILI BAR PUT IN
Placerville
Lake Berryessa
Davis
SACRAMENTO
Folsom
50
88
128
16
49
Dixon
Yountville
80
Elk Grove
88
Jackson
88
26
Sonoma
29
Napa
Fairfield
84
99
104
Lake Pardee
21
4
Vacaville
5
Mokelumne River
Camanche Lake
19
12
Angels Camp
Stanislaus National Forest
12
12
Lodi
49
108
37
680
88
26
49
Sonora
Vallejo
80
San Pablo Bay
Antioch
23
RIVERPOINT LANDING MARINA-RESORT
Stockton
New Melones Lake
49
Richmond
Concord
Walnut Creek
4
Groveland
Berkeley
24
TRACY OASIS MARINA RESORT
Manteca
120
120
80
Oakland
680
Tracy
4
Oakdale
49
SAN FRANCISCO
580
Dublin
580
120
108
99
Don Pedro Reservoir
20
San Francisco Bay
Hayward
Livermore
5
San Joaquin River
Modesto
132
49
101

© MOON.COM

0   20 mi
0   20 km

Chapter 5

SACRAMENTO AND GOLD COUNTRY

⑲ Camanche Lake

866/763-5121 | Sierra foothills | www.lakecamancheresort.com

Set in the Sierra foothills east of Lodi at 325 feet in elevation, Camanche Lake is the best lake in the region for boating, water sports, fishing, and camping. The big lake spans 7,700 acres with 55 miles of shoreline and has full marinas and recreation facilities. There are two major recreation areas—North Shore and South Shore—and though you must pay entrance fees for both, your reward is that everything is top-shelf across the board. The water is clear and warm, and visitor turnout is high, especially during the peak months in late spring and early summer.

This lake has a rich history from the gold-mining era, with remnants and artifacts from the 1850s submerged in the waters at the head of the lake. In drought years, when the lake just about hits rock bottom, the foundations and structures from a former gold rush town are uncovered from the lake bottom.

I try to venture here every spring with Bob Simms, the KFBK-1530 radio host. For a few days at least, it feels like anything is possible. And often, it is.

▽ *Camanche Lake*

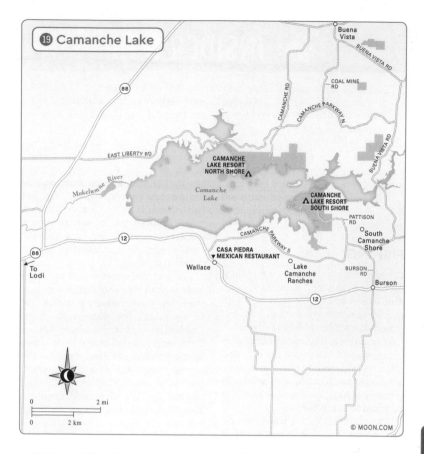

BEST ACTIVITY: BOATING

Camanche Lake has the best of everything when you're in a boat. Just find something that floats and you're in business. The lake has large boat ramps at both the North and South Shores, as well as full-service marinas, boat rentals, tackle and bait, and food services. There are three demarcations for boating and water sports, with enough space for everyone:

- The first is the **central body** of the lake between the dam (on the west shore) and the North Shore islands. This is the best spot for water sports such as waterskiing, tubing, and wakeboarding.
- The **Upper Lake** area and the section above the **Narrows** is popular for low-speed activities, such as fishing and kayaking. There's a 20-mph speed limit with no waterskiing, tubing, boarding, or personal watercraft allowed.
- The **South Shore Cove,** adjacent to the South Shore recreation area, is within 200 feet of the shore. The 5-mph speed limit is ideal to protect those who are fishing, kayaking, or swimming.

A wide variety of boats, kayaks, and paddleboards are available to rent. Kayak rentals can be reserved in advance online (http://kayakcamanche.com). Marinas (7am-4:30pm daily) are on the North and South Shores; each rents boats and sells last-minute supplies and gear. The North Shore

Anglers searching for trout know that the R-Lure is unique to this area. Pick one up on the way to Camanche Lake at **Fisherman's Friend** (440 E. Kettleman Ln. #A, 209/369–0204, 9am-6pm Mon.-Sat.) in Lodi, about 30 miles west off Highway 99.

marina offers boat storage.

Note: If you're bringing your own boat, all boats must be certified mussel-free before launching.

FISHING

On the first warm days of spring, Camanche Lake turns into fishing gold. This is a premier lake for bass, with extensive submerged structures and mine tailings (piles of rocks and ditches left by 19th-century miners) that provide excellent habitat for the fish. And there is a wide variety of fish here: bass, trout, crappie, bluegill, and catfish. On a spring or early summer weekend, it's possible to catch them all.

The best spots for **trout** include the stretch between Big Hat Island and Little Hat Island, in the central body of the lake. You can also try the rock wall off the mouth of China Gulch (near the Narrows), and the area near the Lancha Palana Bridge at the head of the lake. For the best techniques, troll a Rainbow Runner rigged with a single hook, then add half a nightcrawler on the hook. Or try a J-7 or J-9 Rapala, colored in fire tiger or clown, and an R-Lure.

Camanche can produce small **bass,** but if you hit it right in late winter or early spring, the bass are often an average of two pounds or better. To hunt for bass, use a depth finder to search for piles of rocks, ditches, and submerged extended points, and plan to be on the water at dawn and dusk. You'll want to use live minnows for bait, hooked vertically through the lip on a

No. 8 hook with a single split shot. Or try deep-diving crankbaits (Bagley Balsa Diving B, Strike King) in shad patterns, spinnerbaits, or finesse worms rigged Texas-style. The bass here are color-conscious and light-shy, so test different colors.

Do not use heavy line. (I never go heavier than 8-pound in marine-green, Vanish or fluorocarbon, and often go to 6-pound.) The water that enters Camanche Lake comes from Pardee Dam, set upstream on the Mokelumne River. Pardee catches most of the winter storm runoff and snowmelt, and as a result, Camanche doesn't muddy up. It's clear and green, a beautiful sight, but it can make the fish line-shy.

BEST OVERNIGHT: CAMANCHE LAKE RESORT

Camanche Lake Resort (209/763–5121) has every lodging choice to fit your trip, with more than 550 campsites, as well as cottages, mobile homes, and vacation rentals. Most campsites and rental units are in recreation areas on the North Shore and the South Shore of the lake.

Primitive campsites on the **North Shore** feature grassy spots with picnic tables set above the lake. There are few trees and the sites feel largely exposed, but the view of the lake is pretty. There are four campgrounds with 219 sites for tents or self-contained RVs (no hookups). Blue Oaks is the largest campground, while Rabbit Creek and Peninsula Campgrounds

△ *Camanche Lake*

WHERE TO EAT

The North Shore's **Northern Bites Café** (2000 Camanche Rd., Ione, 209/763-5924, www.northernbitescafe.com, 9am-4:30pm Thurs.-Mon.) will do in a pinch, but if you hang out at Camanche Lake, sooner or later you're going to end up at **Casa Piedra Mexican Restaurant** (7998 CA 12, Wallace, 209/763–1046). There's nothing else in the vicinity. The Mexican food is good across the board—start with the fish tacos. The menu includes American food, with decent pizzas. It's family-owned, and I've always liked the prices and the service.

DRIVING DIRECTIONS

Sacramento offers the easiest starting point for this trip. Directions are based on whether you're heading to the North or South Shores, which have different addresses.

To reach the North Shore: From Sacramento, take Highway 99 south for 25 miles. Take exit 273 for Liberty Road. Turn left onto Liberty Road and drive 15.4 miles to Camanche Parkway North. Continue onto Camanche Parkway and drive 4.5 miles to Camanche Road. Turn right and drive 0.9 mile. Turn left (still on Camanche Road) and continue 0.1 mile to the North Shore entrance (2000 Camanche Rd., Ione).

To reach the South Shore: From Sacramento, take Highway 99 south for 27 miles. Take exit 271 (toward Jahant Road) for Highway 99/Frontage Road. Turn left and drive 200 yards to East Jahant Road/East Woodson Road. Turn left and drive 9.3 miles to Mackville Road. Turn right and drive 1.2 miles to Highway 12/88E. Turn left and drive 1.1 miles. Continue straight onto Highway 12 and drive 5.1 miles to Camanche Parkway South. Turn left and drive 5.1 miles to Pattison Road. Continue straight onto Pattison Road and drive 2.2 miles to Bret Harte Drive. Turn right onto Bret Harte Drive and continue a short distance to the South Shore entrance (11700 Wade Ln., Valley Springs).

accommodate RVs. All sites come with picnic tables, barbecues, drinking water, restrooms with hot showers, and laundry facilities. Campers here enjoy access to a café (open year-round) and an ice cream parlor (late May-early Sept.).

There are seven campgrounds in **the South Shore** area, which is better for RVs (with hookups). There are 330 sites for tents or RVs in a large, exposed overflow area; it's a way to keep from getting stuck for a spot on popular weekends. Coyote Flat Campground is popular; it's close to the lake and there's a chance to view wildlife. There are also two alcohol-free campgrounds (Riverview and Oaks). The South Shore campgrounds share the same amenities as the North Shore, but the facilities are more developed and include a trout pond (stocked), a snack shop (late May-early Sept.), and an amphitheater for movies in summer. Some of the facilities at each shore are wheelchair-accessible. Leashed pets are permitted.

All reservations are accepted online (www.lakecamancheresort.com, fee). The resort is open year-round.

CAMPFIRE STORIES

*D*uring one trip to Camanche Lake, my pal Bob Simms, the KFBK-1530 radio host and something of a Sacramento Valley legend, got this wild look in his eye and said, "Let me show you something you've never seen." Off we went in our boat, heading to the headwaters of the Mokelumne Arm. As we neared the head of the lake, a series of old, rusted-out pieces of metal, machinery, and footings appeared along the shore. "These are all remnants from the gold-rush days," Simms said. "If only these rocks could talk, eh?" Each unknown piece of partially buried rusted metal holds the story of someone's hopes and dreams from the 1850s.

Every time we see an artifact or mining tailings, Bob always gets this funny little grin and says, laughing, "If only these rocks could talk."

△ *the great Bob Simms at Camanche Lake*

⓴ Don Pedro Reservoir

800/708-7814 | Lake Don Pedro | www.donpedrolake.com

My pal Dan Bacher, who's in the California Outdoors Hall of Fame, is one the few guys with more miles on his truck than mine (570,000 vs. 425,000 miles). He often rates Lake Don Pedro as the No. 1 lake in California. And when it's full, it is one of the best lakes around for boating, water sports, and fishing. There are thousands of hidden coves and little spots where you can park your boat, make camp, and then play in the water during the day and fish the evening bite.

This giant lake covers nearly 13,000 surface acres with 160 miles of shoreline and many extended lake arms. The primary headquarters is the Don Pedro Marina, on the south end of the lake. Near the northern head of the lake, Moccasin Point provides a quieter campground and boat ramp.

The elevation is just 800 feet, so water temperatures can climb to 70°-80°F in the summer. This is when boating and water sports, houseboats, and camping take over the lake.

Don Pedro offers an ideal destination for a do-it-yourself trip for campers with boats and anyone who likes to fish, boat around, or ply the waters.

▽ *Don Pedro Reservoir*

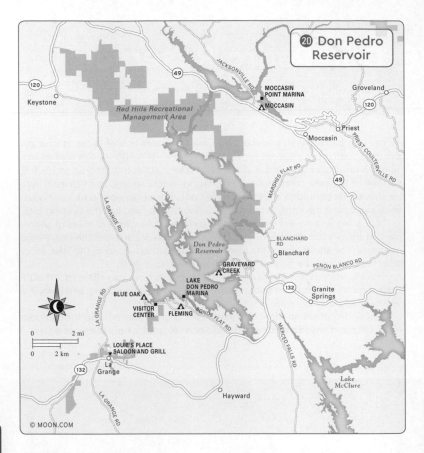

Groveland

Keystone

Red Hills Recreational Management Area

MOCCASIN POINT MARINA
MOCCASIN

Moccasin

Priest

Blanchard RD
Blanchard

PENON BLANCO RD

GRAVEYARD CREEK

LAKE DON PEDRO MARINA

Granite Springs

BLUE OAK

VISITOR CENTER
FLEMING

0   2 mi
0   2 km

LOUIE'S PLACE SALOON AND GRILL

La Grange

Lake McClure

Hayward

© MOON.COM

BEST ACTIVITY: BOATING AND WATER SPORTS

On summer days, the surface temperature at Don Pedro can climb into the high 70s and even 80s, while just a few feet down, everything feels cool and clean. This makes the lake perfect for boating, swimming, and water sports. You can put on a life jacket and just float around with your favorite elixir in hand (some even bring floating coolers). Just wear plenty of sunscreen (including on your shoulders and the tops of your ears) and a hat.

Two full-service marinas are available with boat rentals, mooring, and boat storage. Bait and tackle are also available.

At the south end of the lake, **Lake Don Pedro Marina** (11500 Bonds Flat Rd., La Grange, 209/852-2369, https://lakedonpedromarina.com) acts as the primary headquarters for the lake, with boat ramps at Blue Oaks and Fleming Meadows Campgrounds. Most of the fast boating, waterskiing, wakeboarding, and ripping around in a personal watercraft is done on the main lake here. The lake's open southern end receives sufficient wind in the afternoon to make sailing and windsurfing popular in early summer. The marina rents small boats as well as houseboats (houseboats have a separate dedicated marina). When the lake level is high, houseboat rentals become popular and guarantee a quiet floating site in a hidden cove out of the traffic. There's a designated

swimming area on the south shore at Fleming Meadows, as well as a swimming lagoon and a nearby concession stand. A **visitors center** (Bonds Flat Rd., 8am-4:30pm daily May 15-Sept. 15, 8am-4:30pm Mon.-Fri. Sept. 16-May 14) is near Don Pedro Dam.

At the north end of the lake, **Moccasin Point Marina** (11405 Jacksonville Rd., Jamestown, 209/989-2206, https://moccasinpointmarina.com) offers a quiet alternative to Lake Don Pedro Marina, with a boat ramp located next to the campground. The lake's northern end sits in a deep, narrow canyon that's ideal for fishing, canoeing, kayaking, or floating in a raft.

There are no beach areas, but people swim anyway, either accessing the lake from the shoreline or jumping off their boats. (Shoreline areas often have steep drop-offs, so children should always be supervised and wear life jackets.)

FISHING

Don Pedro is one of the fishiest lakes around. Trout, bass, panfish—it's all good, and in some years the kokanee salmon can be top-shelf. Most of the time, it's the bass fishing that will float your boat. In some years, Don Pedro's gets a bonus plant of fingerling largemouth bass on top of the lake's natural production. Due to the large amount

of aquatic food in the lake, survival rates of those baby bass are high and the fish grow quickly. The result is a lake full of bass.

The fish move according to season and water temperature.

Bass fishing is best in late winter and spring, when water temperatures range 50–65°F and lake levels are highest. In late winter, the bass are often 30–40 feet deep off the main lake points. As winter ends and the first days of spring arrive, the bass rise to 20 feet deep at secondary points. As the water warms, the bass move into the backs of coves and often surface to 15 feet deep. In summer, they slide back down to 20 feet. By mid- to

△ *fishing on Lake Don Pedro*

late summer, the bass can scatter vertically down to 100 feet deep.

During the first cool nights of fall, the trout fire back into life and fishing can be excellent. It is often best in mid- to late October, when the lake turns over and the warm surface layer sinks and is replaced by cool, oxygenated water full of food and fish.

For the best techniques, use plastics (Keitech, Rage) and grubs, often rigged Texas-style, worked slowly along the bottom. The fish often take it on the drop, so you need a rod; the best are medium-heavy, where you can develop a touch not to miss the bites. The lake is best fished vertically; horizontal retrieves get zilch.

With both trout and kokanee, you can always switch over. The best trolling takes place from the Rodgers Creek Arm (south end near Highway 132) north to the Jenkins Hill peninsula and from Middle Bay north to the Highway 49 bridge. The key is always depth. I test different depths with a downrigger, trailing the lures off the clips attached to the downrigger wire line.

Don Pedro can produce large kokanee, at times averaging 1.5–2.5 pounds by mid-August. The best areas include Middle Bay and Jenkins Hill. The fishing generally picks up by mid-May and lasts into early September.

BEST OVERNIGHT: MOCCASIN POINT CAMPGROUND

There are three developed campgrounds (Fleming Meadows, Blue Oaks, Moccasin Point) at Lake Don Pedro and two boat-in campsites (Graveyard Creek, Wreck Bay). The best of all these are the quieter sites at Moccasin Point. Moccasin Point juts into the water directly across from the Tuolumne River Arm at the northeastern end of the lake. The campground sits adjacent to a boat ramp near a full-service marina and is easily accessible off Highway 120. There are 78 sites for tents and 18 sites for RVs with full

hookups (some sites are pull-through). Picnic tables, fire rings, food lockers, and barbecue units are provided at all sites. Drinking water, restrooms with showers, dump station, group picnic area, Wi-Fi, fish-cleaning station, propane gas, ice, small store, boat ramp, motorboat and fuel, moorings, and bait and tackle are available. Some facilities are wheelchair-accessible.

Note that as the lake level recedes in late summer, sites at the head of the lake can become distant from the water.

Reservations (209/852–2396, www.donpedrolake.com, fee) are accepted. Open year-round.

WHERE TO EAT

Louie's Place Saloon and Grill (30048 Yosemite Blvd., La Grange, 209/853-2050, 11am-9pm Sun.-Mon., 11am-10pm Thurs.-Sat.) doesn't have to be good—after all, there's no place else around—but it is. Set in a historic building out in the country, Louie's Place serves good American food, cold beer, and wine, and does it all with a smile as soon as you walk in the door. There's always a few Harleys parked out front or a truck with a boat on a trailer. This is a place for travelers who care about good food, cold drinks, nice folks, and a fair price.

DRIVING DIRECTIONS

Lake Don Pedro is in the San Joaquin Valley sandwiched between Modesto to the west and Yosemite National Park to the east. The quickest way to get here is from Highway 120 in Manteca.

From Manteca, drive 19 miles east on Highway 120 East to Oakdale. At the stoplighted intersection, turn left (staying on Highway 120) and drive 25 miles east. At the exit for Highway 120/Yosemite, turn right onto Highway 120. Pass a junction at 3.4 miles and continue east on Highway 120/49 for 6.3 miles to Jacksonville Road. Turn left on Jacksonville Road and drive 0.6 mile (requires two jogs to stay on Jacksonville) to the Moccasin Point Marina.

CAMPFIRE STORIES

*A*t Don Pedro, my old friend Clyde "The Wrench" Gibbs (a master mechanic for United Airlines) would have nothing to do with the high-end marinas, developed campgrounds, and great bass fishing. Instead, he'd head out on the lake with his family and friends and create a boat-in campsite in a pretty cove, then give it a try for Don Pedro's big red-ear sunfish. He'd use a worm under a bobber and fish inside the shade lines of coves near any submerged structure. That bobber would start to dance and Clyde would go out of his mind, getting so focused and locked in that I thought beads of blood might start to form on his forehead. Then he'd hook up, and nobody enjoyed a tussle with a sunfish more than Clyde. I enjoyed watching him more than catching one myself. His face would soften, and then he'd smile that special smile as he released the fish back into the lake and it would dart away.

On those summer evenings at Don Pedro, it was the best of times.

△ *Don Pedro Reservoir*

East of Stockton in the Sierra foothills, Lake Pardee spans more than 2,000 acres with 37 miles of shoreline. The Mokelumne River feeds Pardee Reservoir, where water is then released downstream into Camanche Reservoir. Together, these are bookend lakes for anglers and boaters.

What sets Lake Pardee apart is that it is kept full. Of the lakes across the Gold Country, Pardee always has the highest water levels, often 90–100 percent full. Personal watercraft, swimming, and water sports are not allowed, which makes it perfect for trout fishing and low-speed boating.

In early November, Pardee Recreation Area closes for the winter, when it provides habitat for migratory bald eagles, waterfowl, and songbirds. It reopens in mid-February, and if you come then, seeing all the birds, especially the bald eagles, can top your trip. In the early spring, when the lake is full and the surrounding hills are green with blooming wildflowers, the lake is beautiful. The wildflowers usually peak in late March and early April. When summer arrives, it's blistering hot with zero shade.

Time it right, and this can be a great place to camp with an RV, fish for trout, and enjoy the wildflowers in spring.

▽ Lake Pardee

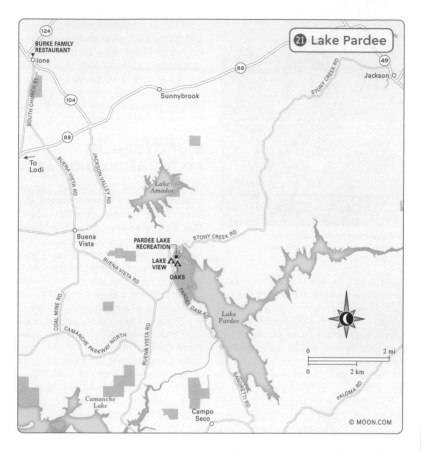

BEST ACTIVITY: FISHING

Lake Pardee is one of the best lakes around for trout and kokanee salmon. It helps that you don't have to worry about a guy ripping around on a WaveRunner, plowing the shoreline and ruining the fishing. We usually venture up the Mokelumne Arm to troll for big trout and bass. For trout, use a depth finder to find the historic Mokelumne River channel and then troll along its edge. The vicinity of the island is also good, as is the south edge of the dam and the nearby shoreline.

In the early season, we troll 10–20 feet deep, and occasionally put something on the near surface, and then again, something deeper, 30–40 feet down, to cover the surface to a 40-foot range. We try different lures until we hit on the magic. Favorites include the blue-silver Sparklefish and R-Lures (local favorites out of Lodi), Cop Car-colored Needlefish, blue-purple Humdinger, and jointed Rapala in gold-black and Fire-Tiger.

While catch numbers are not the highest up the Mokelumne Arm, you always have a chance for a monster-sized rainbow or brown trout. For the highest catch rates, the extended shoreline—roughly within a mile or so of the boat ramp—always seems to produce the best results. Most anglers use boats to get on the water early and troll from the boat launch right down the north arm. Start in the center of the lake, then work along the east side, turning east down the long channel arm of the lake.

△ *fisherman holding a 6-pound largemouth bass caught at Lake Pardee*

Though Pardee is not known as a great lake for bass, the fishing can be good here, with a sprinkling of largemouth bass in the 10-pound range. (Pardee produced the state-record smallmouth bass at 9.82 pounds.) The lake is full of structure, so use a depth finder and fish the shoreline points and coves.

Switch over to bass, usually with grubs on jigheads or rigged Texas-style. In the same area, youngsters can bait-dunk along the shore for bluegill and sunfish; panfish tend to bite as summer arrives and the water warms.

BOATING

If you love to kayak, canoe, or cruise around in one of those pedal boats, then you came to the right place. Pardee Lake is quiet and tranquil for those kayaking, canoeing, or paddling because no personal watercraft (WaveRunners, Jet Skis), waterskiing, wakeboarding, or other water sports are allowed.

Pardee's boating facilities include a full-service **marina** (6:30am-4pm daily) in the recreation area on the northeastern arm of the lake. The marina has a 10-lane paved boat ramp, boat moorings and storage, and fishing and pontoon boat rentals.

The lake speed limit is 25 mph, with signed 5-mph areas in the Pardee Recreation Area. Most boaters heed a "common courtesy" rule that makes the lake safe and comfortable for those with small, low-speed craft, such as kayaks or small fishing boats. For many, this is a perfect fit.

BEST OVERNIGHT: PARDEE RECREATION AREA

Come 10pm at the Pardee campgrounds, a magic moment arrives: It's quiet. There's no parties and no noise. That's because 10pm to 8am is "quiet time" at the campground and it is seriously enforced. The campground host will kick out quiet-time violators, telling them never to return. This keeps it quiet so you can get your sleep in anticipation of a big day on the lake.

There are two main campgrounds with more than 100 campsites: **Lake View Campground** has RV sites and **Oaks Campground** has sites for tents or self-contained RVs. A café (7am-2pm Fri.-Sun. mid-Feb.-early Sept.) and store, showers, laundry facility, marina with boat launch, boat rentals, boat docks with slips, swimming pool (open seasonally), and Wi-Fi. The Oaks Campground is more secluded. Some sites are wheelchair-accessible. Campfires are only allowed in fire rings, and wood gathering is not permitted. Firewood is available for purchase at the store.

Reservations are accepted by phone (800/416-6992). Open mid-February-early November.

WHERE TO EAT

A sense of history paired with good food and drinks can be a killer combo. At Pardee, I always make the 15-minute drive to the historic Ione Hotel, home of the **Burke Family Restaurant** (25 W. Main St., Ione, 209/274-4161, https://burkefamilyrestaurant.com, 11am-9pm Wed.-Sat., 10am-8pm Sun.). Though the place has seen a number of chefs and owners through the years, the

CAMPFIRE STORIES

*I*n past years, the Pardee concessionaire would play favorites, letting in a few handpicked friends from the radio business and allowing them to fish Pardee prior to opening day. What was funny (at least to Bob Simms and me) is that we'd never get invited. But we'd show up incognito during the legal season and do a lot better than those good 'ol boys who got to pre-fish the opener. Of course, it helps to have a guy with Simms's local knowledge.

A new concessionaire took over in 2019, and those good 'ol boys were out of luck anyway. Heh, heh, heh. We laugh every time we think about it.

△ *Lake Pardee fishing hole*

saloon-style bar and gold rush atmosphere always impresses. On my last visit, I had the rib eye and my pal Bob had the chicken; with a cold elixir and a glass of wine, we felt they hit it out of the park. Your mileage may vary.

DRIVING DIRECTIONS

From I-5 in Stockton, take Highway 4 east for about 3 miles to Highway 99 north. Turn north onto Highway 99 and drive 2 miles. Turn east onto Highway 88/Waterloo Road and drive 23 miles to a junction with Highway 12 (blinking light). Stay left on Highway 88 and drive 11 miles to Jackson Valley Road (past two short bridges). Turn right and drive 3.4 miles to Buena Vista (a four-way stop). Turn right again and drive 3.1 miles to Stony Creek Road. Turn left and drive 1.2 miles to the Lake Pardee **entrance** (4900 Stony Creek Rd., Ione, 209/772–1472 for gate access) on the right.

Gate hours are 5am-11pm daily mid-February-early November. There is an entry fee of $10.50.

530/365-1180 | Redding to Anderson | www.sacramentoriver.org

The Sacramento River is the lifeblood of Northern California. From its source at the base of Mount Shasta, it runs some 500 river miles south to San Francisco Bay. The prize section is the stretch from Redding to Anderson.

The river flow releases from the depths of Shasta and Keswick Dams, which means that the water is cold even when summer temperatures are scorching hot. The first 20 miles of river is ideal for easy floats in rafts and tubes. When I've done this, I've felt like Tom Sawyer on the Mississippi River.

There is plenty of room for everyone on the river and plenty of fish. This section of water is one of the best stretches of river for fly-fishing for trout. In the fall, huge salmon in the 15- to 25-pound class migrate upstream.

One thing that keeps Redding from being a first-class recreation destination is the hot weather in summer. The sun can feel like a branding iron, scorching everything it touches. Temperatures in the 100°F range are typical, and a hot siege can jack them up to 110°F. This is when you want to cool off by rafting or floating the river on inner tubes. In fall and early winter, the temperatures start to cool and the fishing turns excellent.

▽ *The Sundial Bridge streches across the Sacramento River in Redding.*

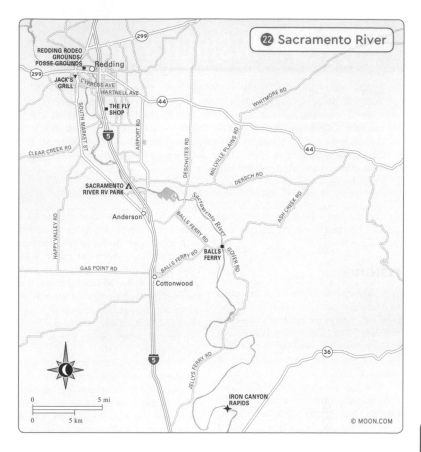

REDDING RODEO GROUNDS/ POSSE GROUNDS
Redding
299
299
JACK'S GRILL
CYPRESS AVE
HARTNELL AVE
44
THE FLY SHOP
SOUTH MARKET ST
5
AIRPORT RD
WHITMORE RD
CLEAR CREEK RD
DESCHUTES RD
MILLVILLE PLAINS RD
44
SACRAMENTO RIVER RV PARK
DERSCH RD
Anderson
Sacramento River
ASH CREEK RD
HAPPY VALLEY RD
BALLS FERRY RD
BALLS FERRY
GOVER RD
GAS POINT RD
BALLS FERRY RD
Cottonwood
5
36
JELLYS FERRY RD
IRON CANYON RAPIDS
0   5 mi
0   5 km
© MOON.COM

BEST ACTIVITY: FLOATING THE SACRAMENTO RIVER

From Redding to Anderson, the Sacramento River runs emerald green, bordered by cottonwoods and alders in a gorgeous upland riparian zone. Wildlife is abundant, especially blue herons and wood ducks. You may see turtles sunning on logs or rocks, while deer and wild turkeys are common along the shore.

For an easy float, the best put-in is the boat ramp next to the Redding Rodeo Grounds (local guides call it the **Posse Grounds**); it's adjacent to the Redding Convention Center, where parking is available. The take-out is at Balls Ferry in Anderson. This scenic, relaxing trip is 20 river miles with no surprises.

If you want more, though, you can find it. About 10 miles south of Balls Ferry awaits the trip's biggest challenge: **Iron Canyon Rapids.** The Class II rapid is located in the canyon below the Jones Ferry Bridge, where the water rumbles through miniature cliffs and lava outcroppings.

Along the way are a few Class I rapids that can be dealt with by taking "an inside line" away from the white water. Some make the 56-mile run all the way down to Red Bluff for a three-day, two-night paddle.

A boat ramp and take-out is available at **Balls Ferry** (Ash Creek and Gover Road, Anderson). Wear a hat for the bright sun, apply a layer of

In operation since 1978, **The Fly Shop** (4140 Churn Creek Rd., Redding, 800/699-3474, www.theflyshop.com, 7:30am-6pm daily, until 9pm Fri.) has risen to legendary status, something akin to the famous fly-fishing shops outside Yellowstone National Park. The Fly Shop runs 15-20 guided trips a day on the river; they have more guides and fish more rivers, streams, and lakes than anyone else. Their up-to-date fish reports alone make this place a must-stop before any fly-fishing trip.

sunscreen, and wear a life jacket that fits (it's needed if you go kerplunk in the cold water).

FISHING

The Sacramento River from Redding to Anderson can provide some of the best catch rates for trout anywhere in the West. The best fishing is mid-October-November, and yet it can also be sensational for shad in spring and salmon in fall.

The big question is this: Can you fish from the shore? The answer may be yes, but is often no. When the river releases out of Keswick and is running below 7,000 cubic feet per second (cfs), there is an opportunity for shoreline prospects (wading out and casting) in the town of Redding. One of the better spots is within 40 yards upstream of the Sundial Bridge.

In the spring, the Tehama Riffle (downstream of the Tehama Bridge) can provide good shore fishing for shad.

When the river is flowing over 9,000 cfs (flows at 9,000-12,500 cfs are common in summer), shore fishing is impossible—you need a boat. From a boat, you can see how the character of the river changes from mile to mile. Guides with drift boats take fly fishers into the prime section (from the Posse Grounds to Anderson) and side drift with nymphs and a strike indicator. The Prince Nymph, Copper John, and Hare's Ear often work great, and most anglers will catch-and-release.

For trout, anglers make shore-side casts with weighted nymphs (often with a dropper) and a strike indicator on the surface, which can catch 5-20 trout per day. The river used to produce trout in the 10-pound class, but these days that trophy catch is rare. Some anglers use Glo Bugs with a split shot (what is called "boon-dogging Glo Bugs"), while others use a single nightcrawler.

In the fall, salmon arrive in large numbers (peaking in September and October) on their migratory journey, often stacking in holes or on ledges (such as the Old Mouth of Battle Creek out of Balls Ferry). The best fishing is mid-August-September, with salmon averaging 15-25 pounds. Guides in sled boats—flat bottoms and jet drives—will back-troll using sardine-wrapped Kwikfish, or back-bounce with roe clusters for bait.

BEST OVERNIGHT: SACRAMENTO RIVER RV PARK

Several full-facility campgrounds and RV parks are available along the Sacramento River and in nearby adjacent towns. But the **Sacramento River RV Park** (Quartz Hill Road, Redding) makes the best headquarters for a boating or fishing adventure on the river. The park has a boat ramp, and fishing guides launch here daily. You also get great long-distance views

△ *fishing on the tranquil Sacramento River near Redding*

of Mounts Shasta and Lassen. There are 140 sites for RVs with full hookups (some pull-throughs) and 10 sites for tents in a shaded grassy area. Picnic tables, restrooms with showers, coin laundry, cable TV, free Wi-Fi, two tennis courts, basketball hoops, horseshoes, a clubhouse, and a large seasonal swimming pool are available. Some facilities are wheelchair-accessible. Leashed pets are permitted.

Reservations (530/365-6402, www.sacramentoriverrvresort.com, fee) are accepted. Open year-round.

WHERE TO EAT

Hang around Redding long enough and sooner or later you'll hear about **Jack's Grill** (1743 California St., Redding, 530/241-9705, https://jacksgrill redding.com, 4pm-10pm Mon.-Sat.). Locally owned and operated since 1938, it's the best off-the-radar steakhouse in Shasta County and is No. 1 for locals.

DRIVING DIRECTIONS

From I-5 in Redding, exit west on Highway 299 West/Central Redding. Drive 1 mile over the Sacramento River to Auditorium Drive. Turn right and drive 0.5 mile (Civic Auditorium on the right) to the Sundial Bridge parking lot.

To reach the Sacramento River RV Park: Drive south on I-5 for 5 miles to the Knighton Road exit. Turn right (west) and drive a short distance to Riverland Drive. Turn left on Riverland Drive and drive 2 miles to the park at the end of the road.

CAMPFIRE STORIES

*W*e popped a champagne cork, toasted the Sacramento River, and took off from the Posse Grounds in our canoe. Seven days and 400 river miles later, we arrived at Fisherman's Wharf in San Francisco and hoisted our glasses once again. In between, we tried to emulate the voyageurs of Hudson's Bay Company, a crew of us paddling in a 37-foot canoe. We paddled by day, under a full moon, and into the night, camping on sandbars inside of river bends. That first day out of Redding was the best: The fish were jumping, wild turkeys and deer watched us from the shore, and ospreys, Canada geese, and bald eagles sailed past.

As the currents and paddle strokes sent us downstream, it felt like we'd found paradise. And for a while there, we had.

△ *That's me, second from the back.*

The San Joaquin Delta provides an escape portal for people from the San Francisco Bay Area and the Sacramento Valley. Fed by the San Joaquin and Sacramento Rivers, this giant spiderweb of more than 1,000 miles of waterways extends from San Pablo Bay west to Stockton in the Central Valley and south nearly to Tracy.

This area was once a vast marshland. According to Delta historian Hal Schell, Chinese laborers worked for 13 cents per cubic yard to build the original levees in the Delta. "That work was eventually converted to clamshell dredges, because it was cheaper," Schell said. By 1930, Delta levees had created 55 islands. Today, the Delta is rimmed by roads perched on the tops of levees and linked by 70 bridges and a few old-time cable ferries.

The Delta levees are lined with tules, cottonwoods, and grass, a habitat that supports one of North America's most diverse and abundant arrays of birdlife. Just get yourself in a boat and out on the water. Your reward will be miles of wide-open space for boating and bird-watching, dawn paddles and mid-morning wakeboarding, and fishing at dusk for bass. In a boat, you can change the course of your life in an instant simply by making a turn and entering the spiderweb of rivers, sloughs, bays, and estuaries.

On summer weekends, it can get wild out here with parties, fast boats, water sports, and a lot of people. The best time to visit is during the week in late summer or weekends in early fall. The people are few, the wind is down, and the temperature feels perfect.

▽ *sunset on the San Joaquin Delta*

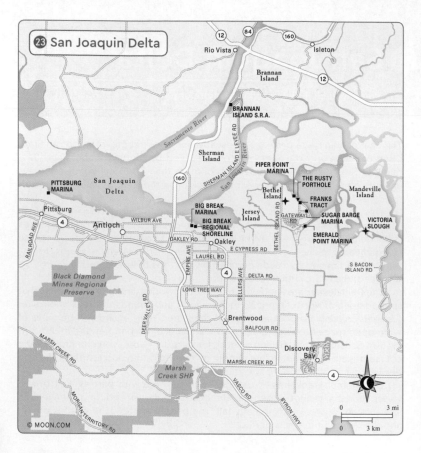

BEST ACTIVITY: BOATING

Just launch your boat and away you go. There are 40 small marinas and more than 100 boat ramps. Good launch points are in Antioch at **Big Break Regional Shoreline** (69 Big Break Rd., Oakley). Some of the best jump-off points for kayaking and boating include:

- **Pittsburg Marina** (51 Marina Blvd., Pittsburgh, 925/439-4958, www. pittsburgmarina.com, 8am-5pm daily, free), west of Brown's Island
- the on-site beach launch at **Big Break Regional Shoreline** (69 Big Break Rd., Oakley, www.ebparks. org, 8am-7pm daily June-Sept., 8am-6pm daily Oct. and Mar.-May,

8am-5pm daily Nov.-Feb., free)
- **Sugar Barge Marina** (1440 Sugar Barge Rd., Bethel Island, 925/684-9075, https://sugarbarge.com, hours vary, fee)
- **Emerald Point Marina** (4234 Stone Rd., Bethel Island, 925/684-2388, www.emeraldpoint-marina.com), a private marina on the Holland Tract
- **Piper Point Marina** (3861 Willow Rd., Bethel Island, 925/684-2174, http://piperpointmarina.com, 8am-5pm Mon. and Wed.-Thurs., 8am-7pm Fri.-Sun. June-Sept., 8am-5pm Wed.-Mon. Oct.-May) and Russo's Marina (3995 Willow Rd., Bethel Island, 925/684-2024, https://russosmarina.com, 8am-5pm Mon.-Fri., 7am-6pm Sat.-Sun.), on the eastern shore of Bethel

Anglers know that the best bites are at the turn of the tides: During high tides, the bass will often move deep into the tule berms; on low tides, they get flushed out of the tules by low water and can be found under the adjoining weed mats.

Here's some of my favorite techniques: I use Senko worms (dark green and maroon sparkle) rigged with offset No. 4/0 Gamakatsu hooks (no weight), white spinnerbaits, Rattletraps, and tons of other stuff. Another winner can be Keitech grubs and Rage worms rigged on jigs, or Texas-style. In summer, when weed mats form in coves along tules, what is called the "frog bite" can take off. This is where you cast plastic frogs on the weed mats and twitch them across the surface. The bass can explode through the mat after that frog like a bomb being detonated.

Striped bass provide good fishing in fall. Use threadfin shad for bait, or troll Bombers on the San Joaquin River. Some of the best spots include west of the Antioch Bridge (with good trolling from Mayberry Slough to the Antioch PG&E power plant), Big Break, Blind Point (at the mouth of Dutch Slough, the connector slough that runs from the south end of Bethel Island west to Big Break), the mouth of False River (near Buoy 25), the Santa Clara and San Andreas shoals (with good trolling in fall and spring), and the lower Mokelumne River.

On the Sacramento River side, the best spots are near the power lines near Decker Island (south of Brannan Island SRA), the Rio Vista Bridge (Hwy. 12), and Isleton. Boat ramps are available at Brannan Island SRA, Rio Vista Launch Ramp and Sandy Beach County Park, all of which are located on the Sacramento River.

Island fronting Franks Tract

Launching here puts Dow Wetlands, Brown's Island, Sherman Lake, Big Break Regional Shoreline, Franks Tract, Old River, and a mosaic of sloughs, cuts, and coves within reach. The Middle River, Grant Line Canal, and Victoria Cut are additional bets. You can also turn into a slough to find quiet water.

What you bring determines where you'll go:

Water-skiers and **wakeboarders:** The three best spots for smooth, warm water are Snodgrass Slough (near Walnut Grove), False River, and Middle River. Don't underestimate the value of these sheltered areas. The sloughs are better protected from winds than wide-open areas like Franks Tract or Sherman Lake (where the San Joaquin and Sacramento Rivers join). At times the wind can be howling on the Sacramento River, while 15 miles away, False River on the San Joaquin is being stroked by a gentle breeze.

Windsurfers: Two popular spots are Ski Beach (on the Middle River) and Swing Beach. Both are located near Franks Tract. The best beach access is at low tides in the sloughs, which are reachable only by boat. I love motoring out the San Joaquin River from Stockton to Mildred Island, a submerged flat with beautiful views of Mount Diablo and (often) spectacular sunsets.

FISHING

With an abundance of food and habi-

△ on the Delta

tat, the San Joaquin Delta has some of the best fishing for big largemouth bass around. There are tremendous numbers of bass here (many big ones). A lot of people think the world-record bass will someday be caught in the Delta.

A typical morning for me is about 25 tugs, a dozen hook-ups, and then landing a half dozen or so. Sometimes better, sometimes worse.

I prefer to launch at **Franks Tract** or Brannan Island State Recreation Area (SRA). I'll run out to the edge of Franks Tract along the tule-lined False River, which is excellent for largemouth bass. There's dozens of good fishing spots in extended walls of tule berms, coves overgrown by weed mats, tule-lined points, and submerged fence lines from fields flooded by levee breaks.

The **Victoria Slough** is another good spot. The waterway connects Old River (near Clifton Court Forebay) to Middle River.

The **Tracy Oasis Marina** Resort (12450 W. Grimes Rd., Tracy, 209/835-3182, www.tracyoasismarina.com)

provides access to the Grant Line, a straight-line slough that is popular with wakeboarders. Just upstream, past the South Tracy Bridge, the river is blocked with boat ramps on each side, and this is often a good spot for bass.

Out of Stockton, the best place to launch is at RiverPoint Landing Marina Resort (4950 Buckley Cove Way, Stockton, 209/951-4144, www.riverpoint landing.com) and its adjacent Buck Cove boat launch. This provides access to the San Joaquin River, where you can cruise past Windmill Cove to Spud Island. The shore is good for bass fishing. This stretch also provides "fast water" that is fun for tubing, wakeboarding, and waterskiing.

BEST OVERNIGHT: BRANNAN ISLAND SRA

Brannan Island State Recreation Area (Hwy. 160, 916/777-6671, www.parks. ca.gov, sunrise-sunset) fronts the Sacramento River Delta and is designed for campers with boats. The proximity of the campgrounds to the 10-lane

△ *kayaking*

boat launch deserves a medal. What many people do is tow a boat here, launch it, keep it docked, and then return to their campsite to set up. This strategy allows campers to come and go as they please, boating, fishing, and exploring the Delta.

A stay here means that you also get access to Three Mile Slough and Seven Mile Slough, both great for kayaks or canoes and accessible for power-boats. You can then connect into the vast matrix of the interior Delta.

There are two campgrounds—**Willow and Cottonwood**—with 102 sites for tents or RVs, 13 walk-in sites, and six group sites. Picnic tables and fire rings are provided. Drinking water, restrooms with coin showers, a dump station, and a boat launch are available. Some facilities are wheel-chair-accessible. Leashed pets are permitted in some areas.

Reservations (800/444-7275, www.reservecalifornia.com, fee) are accepted. Open year-round.

WHERE TO EAT

The **Rusty Porthole Bar & Grill** (3895 Willow Rd., Bethel Island, 925/684-3607, https://rustyporthole.com, 7am-9pm daily) is a little woodsy hole-in-the-wall restaurant and bar on Bethel Island. The docks are so close that you can cruise up Franks Tract in your boat and feast. It's a local gem, with good (not fancy) seafood, steaks, and spirits.

DRIVING DIRECTIONS

From San Francisco, take I-80 east over the Bay Bridge for 6.4 miles (stay in the far right lanes). Over the bridge, the freeways split between I-80 and I-580. Bear right onto I-580 and drive 1.5 miles to the exit for Highway 24. Take Highway 24 east and drive 13.3 miles to Walnut Creek and the exit for I-680 North. Take I-680 North and drive 4.4 miles to the exit for Highway 242 North. Take that exit and drive 3.2 miles on Highway 242 North, merging onto Highway 4 East. Drive 12.4 miles on Highway 4 to Antioch. Take exit 27 for Contra Loma Boulevard for about 0.2 mile. Turn left and drive 200 yards. Continue onto L Street and drive 1.3 miles to a roundabout. Take the second exit of the roundabout and drive 0.1 mile to the **Antioch Marina Harbor** (1 Marina Plaza, Antioch).

To reach Brannan Island SRA: At the merge with Highway 4 East, drive 16.4 miles to Highway 160. Continue onto Highway 160, crossing the Antioch Bridge, and drive 10 miles to the park entrance on the right.

CAMPFIRE STORIES

*O*ne fall day, I was out on the Delta with former 49er coach George Seifert and the great Barry Canevaro of Fish Hookers Sportfishing (http://fishhookers.com). At one point, George looked across the water and said, "You know, the best thing about being out here is you get to feel like a little kid again." We all smiled because we knew just what he was talking about.

As a boy, I grew up going to the Delta with my brother and our dad to fish for striped bass, catfish, and largemouth bass. And when she was a little girl, my wife, Denese, did the same thing with her dad; they would fish for catfish and talk about the future.

It's easy to lose sight of these kinds of moments—to become overwhelmed with traffic, the long hours at work, and people everywhere you look. When you push off onto the water in the San Joaquin Delta, all that goes away. For a little while, you can remember what it feels like to be a kid again.

△Catfish George Powers

This is one of the best rafting rivers in the United States. The heart of the American River is in Coloma, located off Highway 49 between Placerville and Auburn in the gold country of the Sierra Nevada foothills. Each summer, more than 100,000 people float down the river's white water.

There are three branches of the American River, and each provides a great rafting experience. The South Fork American River provides the best introductory rafting trip, an easy 3-mile cruise from Coloma to Lotus, which can be extended 13 miles to Folsom Lake. On the Middle Fork American River, it gets a bit rougher; when you sail down Tunnel Chute, it feels like getting shot out of a cannon. The North Fork American River offers a roller-coaster ride through wilderness.

The town of Coloma is also the site of the Marshall Gold Discovery State Historic Park, where tours, hikes, and gold-panning demonstrations bring a sense of history to visitors of all ages.

The best time to visit is late May-mid-August, when rivers flows are ideal for rafting.

▽ *campground on the South Fork of the American River at Coloma*

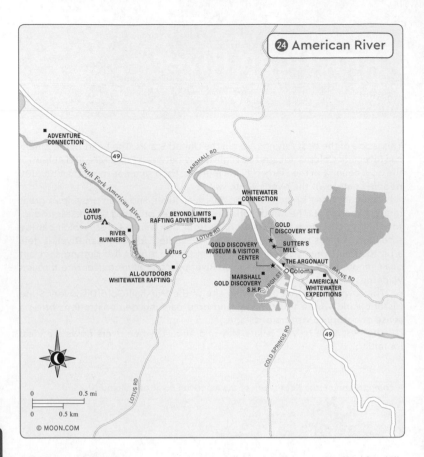

BEST ACTIVITY: RAFTING

South Fork American River

Coloma to Lotus: For a taste of the South Fork, take the three-mile introductory run from Coloma to Lotus. Guided floats start at a noon and take about 90 minutes. This is ideal for first-timers or those who have children and want to experience some time on the water.

Lotus to Folsom: The primary run on the South Fork is 13 miles from the Lotus put-in to the take-out at Folsom Lake. You get all the white-water fun with none of the danger. This section has hot weather, cool water, and rapids rated Class I, II, and III, conditions that makes it great for all ages and skill levels. The surrounding foothills are gorgeous in late spring and early summer when golden poppies and wildflowers brighten the landscape.

Chili Bar: The 20-mile ride from the Chili Bar put-in to the take-out at Salmon Falls Bridge is a step up in challenge. This run is rated Class III+ and includes more than 20 named rapids with monikers like Meatgrinder and Troublemaker. The scenery has an open, rugged feel with lots of historic gold rush sites along the way.

Middle Fork American River

The Middle Fork is the site of the spectacular **Tunnel Chute,** built some 150 years ago by gold miners. The put-in is just below **Oxbow Reservoir.** From here, it is a two-day run, river camp-

△ *rafting the Middle Fork of the American River*

ing along the way. As you approach the Chute, you float through frothing whitewater, then plummet into the tunnel only to be shot out as though being fired out of a cannon. There's nothing else like it.

The Middle Fork is almost inaccessible by road or on foot. If you bring a fishing rod, you can cast for trout that have never seen a fly or a lure.

North Fork American River

When you first lay eyes on the North Fork, you need to ask yourself, "Am I ready for this?" From the put-in at **Iowa Hill** down the nine river miles to the take-out, you face a roller-coaster ride that's rated Class IV-IV+. The stretch takes you through a wilderness canyon with aquamarine water and an awesome boulder-lined shore. It's a bucking bronco of nonstop white water for the first five miles. Most folks stop for a shore lunch to catch their breaths. The last four miles settles down to a series of Class IIs. Enjoy the ride, the beauty, and your experience.

The only vehicle access is six miles downstream at Yankee Jim Road, a four-wheel-drive route. The only people you'll see all day are other rafters.

SIDE TRIP TO MARSHALL GOLD DISCOVERY STATE HISTORIC PARK

One day in 1848, carpenter James W. Marshall was taking a fateful stroll by the sawmill that he was building for John Sutter and saw specks of gold shining in the water. Marshall's discovery sparked the California gold rush and one of the greatest migrations in U.S. history.

That history is now preserved at the **Marshall Gold Discovery State Historic Park** (310 Back St., Coloma, 530/622-3470, www.parks.ca.gov, 8am-6pm daily summer, hours vary fall-spring, $8). When you first arrive, you will see a restored village of wood buildings from the gold rush. Get a park map from the **Gold Discovery Museum** (10am-5pm daily Mar.-Oct., 9am-4pm daily Nov.-Feb.), which details 50 landmarks, including the

△ *rafting the North Fork of the American River*

exact site where gold was first discovered. Follow the Gold Discovery Loop Trail (3.6 miles round-trip) past a full-size replica of **Sutter's Mill** and to the **Gold Discovery Site,** the spot on the South Fork American River where Marshall made his discovery. Other restored buildings include the tiny one-bedroom Mormon cabin, the Chinese-operated Wah Hop and Man Lee stores, the old blacksmith shop, and the Price-Thomas home. If you have children, let them try their hand at gold panning; they will never forget it.

BEST OVERNIGHT: CAMP LOTUS

Camp Lotus (5461 Bassi Rd., Lotus) is set on 23 acres at 700 feet in elevation and features 0.5 mile of frontage on the South Fork American River. The camp is a popular take-out for rafters on the introductory run from Coloma, and it's also the put-in for the trip from Lotus to Folsom Lake. In summer, you'll see plenty of rafters and kayakers. Several swimming holes are in the immediate vicinity. Wineries are nearby, and gold panning, hiking, and fishing are popular activities.

There are 30 grassy tent sites and 10 sites for RVs (partial hookups). Four cabins and a tepee are also available. Picnic tables and fire grills are provided. Drinking water, restrooms with showers, Wi-Fi, dump station, general store with deli, volleyball, horseshoes, and raft and kayak put-in and take-out areas are available. Some facilities are wheelchair-accessible.

Reservations (530/622–8672, www.camplotus.com, fee) are accepted, and are required on weekends. Open February-October.

WHERE TO EAT

The Argonaut (331 Hwy. 49, 530/626-7345, www.argonautcafe.com, 8am-4pm daily, dinner 5:30pm-9pm Fri.-Sat. late May-Aug.) is a tiny place just steps from where James Marshall discovered gold in 1848. Luckily, a meal won't cost you a pile of gold. The food is good and includes sandwiches, soups, chili,

INSIDER'S TIP

An overview of the forks of the American River can be found at The American River (www.theamericanriver.com). Several rafting companies are based near Lotus and offer an array of trips for all levels of experience:

★ **Adventure Connection** (800/556-6060, http://raftcalifornia.com, Lotus)
★ **River Runners** (530/622-5510, www.riverrunnersusa.com, Lotus)
★ **All-Outdoors Whitewater Rafting** (925/932-8993, www.aorafting.com)
★ **Beyond Limits Adventures** (530/622-0553, www.rivertrip.com)
★ **American Whitewater Expeditions** (800/825-3205, www.american whitewater.com)
★ **O.A.R.S.** (800/346-6277, www.oars.com)
★ **Whitewater Connection** (530/622-6446, www.whitewaterconnection. com)

and pie from nearby Apple Hill. Eat at one of the small tables on the café's side patio and you can enjoy a view of the South Fork American River. Picnic tables are also available in back.

DRIVING DIRECTIONS

From Sacramento, take I-80 Business/ US-50 East (signed for I-80 Business/ Sacramento/South Lake Tahoe) and drive 5.3 miles to merge with U.S. 50 East. After merging onto U.S. 50 East, drive 32 miles to Shingle Springs and the exit for Ponderosa Road. Take the exit for Ponderosa Road and drive 0.3 mile to South Shingle Road. Turn left and drive 0.2 mile to North Single Road. Turn right and drive 4 miles, veering right onto Green Valley Road. Continue straight for 0.6 mile as Green Valley Road veers left and becomes Lotus Road. Continue on Lotus Road and drive 6.7 miles to Highway 49/ Coloma Road. Turn left onto Bassi Road to reach Camp Lotus.

To reach Coloma and the Marshall Gold Discovery State Historic Park: Continue X miles on Lotus Road. Turn right onto Highway 49 and drive 0.5 mile to Coloma. The state park will be on the right.

CAMPFIRE STORIES

*I*n summer, the weather here is sunny and warm. Spending day after day in a raft, the cool water of the American River feels ecstatic. The best one-day run is the 20-mile float from Chili Bar to Salmon Falls. The succession of Class III+ rapids provides exhilaration, rather than fear. And once you survive getting through the "Meatgrinder," you'll realize that you had a hell of a time doing so.

One time I tried doing this trip "wildcat-style" (without a guide) in a small, light, self-bailing raft. I hit a break on the tailout of a rapid at the wrong angle and the side current from an eddy flipped me. Just like that, I joined "The South Fork American Swimming Club, Freestyle Event." Heh, heh, heh. No problem. I worked my way over to the calm water of an eddy, made sure everything was still attached, and laughed at my new status as a "Member of the Club."

△ *rafters float down the American River near Coloma*

Chapter 6

LAKE TAHOE AND THE NORTHERN SIERRA

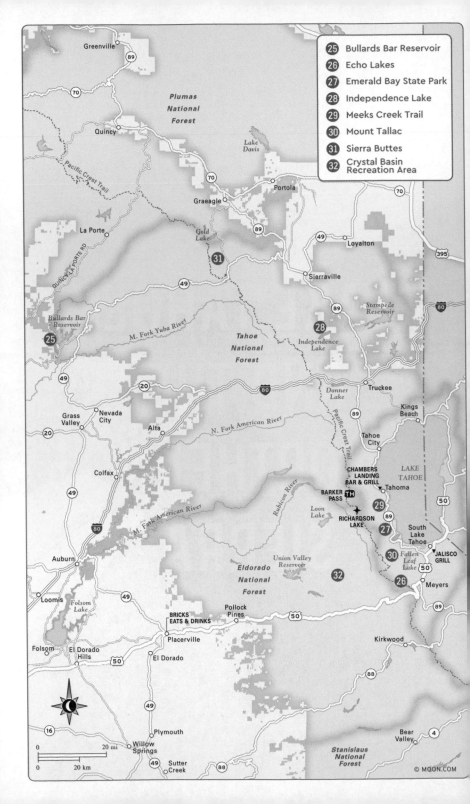

㉕ Bullards Bar Reservoir

877/692–3201 | Dobbins | https://bullardsbar.com

Bullards Bar Reservoir stands out like a silver dollar in a field of pennies. This gorgeous lake is set in the northern Sierra frontcountry at an elevation of 2,300 feet. It has 55 miles of shoreline and spans 4,700 surface acres, much of it nestled deep in the Yuba River Canyon. The reservoir is long and deep, with a gorgeous curving dam across its narrow outlet. The folks who control the plumbing at Bullards Bar somehow manage to keep the reservoir nearly full through most of summer, even in low-rain years when other reservoirs are dust bowls.

The expansive reservoir provides excellent boating and water sports. Venture up the lake and you will find shoreline coves, flats, and submerged terraces and rises, the habitat for giant spotted bass along with lots of smaller bass and kokanee salmon.

One special element at Bullards Bar is boat-in camping. In addition to two boat-in campgrounds, boaters can create their own primitive campsites anywhere along the lakeshore. The coves and flats all provide great campsites, including some of the best boat-in sites in the state.

There are two seasons at Bullards Bar and they rarely intersect. For fishing, come during the cold days of winter for a chance at world-class spotted bass. When summer arrives, boating, water sports, houseboating, and boat-in camping takes over the lake.

▽ *Tom Hedtke casts at Tunnel Cove at Bullards Bar.*

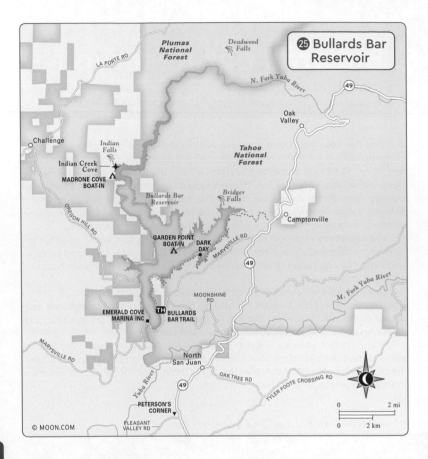

Map labels (left to right, top to bottom):

Plumas National Forest

Deadwood Falls

㉕ Bullards Bar Reservoir

LA PORTE RD

N. Fork Yuba River

49

Challenge

Indian Falls

Oak Valley

Indian Creek Cove
MADRONE COVE BOAT-IN

Tahoe National Forest

Bullards Bar Reservoir

Bridger Falls

Camptonville

OREGON HILL RD

GARDEN POINT BOAT-IN

DARK DAY

MARYSVILLE RD

49

MOONSHINE RD

M. Fork Yuba River

EMERALD COVE MARINA INC

TH BULLARDS BAR TRAIL

MARYSVILLE RD

North San Juan

49

OAK TREE RD

TYLER FOOTE CROSSING RD

Yuba River

PETERSON'S CORNER

PLEASANT VALLEY RD

© MOON.COM

0   2 mi
0   2 km

BEST ACTIVITY: BOATING EMERALD COVE MARINA

is the starting point for recreational boaters. Tucked down at the south end of the reservoir near Bullards Bar Dam, the marina rents boats (including houseboats) and Jet Skis and has a boat ramp at adjacent Cottage Creek.

The water quality of the lake is superb, full of clear, cool water and with an average surface temperature of 78°F in summer. The warm water makes it great for water-skiers, wakeboarders, and tubers. On a hot summer afternoon, it can be a kick just to strap on a life preserver and float around for an hour. However, the steep shoreline makes this a poor place for children to go wading; be sure they wear life jackets at all times.

Explore the lake by boat to discover an array of surprise waterfalls. At the northeast end of the lake, in the cove where Bridger Creek enters the lake, is **Bridger Falls,** where clear streams of water run over the top of granite into a cool swimming spot.

Navigating north up the north Yuba River arm of the lake, look for Indian Creek Cove on the left. Just past this is **Indian Falls,** a gorgeous cascade where silver-tasseled flows run over the top of a crowned rock.

At the northern tip of the main Yuba River arm, near the headwaters, is the lake's hidden gem—**Deadwood Falls.** The flow starts as a silver chute and then feathers out to fall into a

For a panorama of the lower end of Bullards Bar Reservoir, take a walk on the **Bullards Bar Trail** (2 miles, 1 hour) for views up the lake. From the Vista Point Trailhead (on Vista Point Rd., a signed spur off Marysville Rd.), it's a short walk to an overlook where you can gaze across the water to Emerald Cove and the dam. You can then walk as short or as long as you wish (most walk out for a mile and then return). The trail extends seven miles along the eastern shore of the lake and is intersected by a series of trails from other access points along Marysville Road. Vista Point has a picnic area adjacent to the trailhead.

plunge pool. The waterfall is only accessible when the lake is full; in April, May, and June, it can be spectacular. To find it, look for a pumphouse near the head of the lake. An unsigned trail from the pumphouse leads one mile along Deadwood Creek to the waterfall—a gorgeous spot.

FISHING

Bullards Bar is known for world-class spotted bass, with multiple records caught in winter on deep-water swimbaits by patient anglers who fish submerged islands and terraces (40–60 feet deep with swimbaits). In spring, fishing moves to the secondary points in coves, and then, in late spring, to the backs of coves. The average size bass may be small, but you can catch scads of them. In summer, bass are mostly small but eager. Plan to fish 10–20 feet deep along the sloped bottom with your favorite plastic.

In winter and spring, **Dark Day** is the recommended boat ramp for anglers.

Head into the lake and turn left, tracking the contours of the lake bottom and looking for submerged domes (underwater areas that rise up to form sunken mesas and flooded islands). In winter, world-class-size (10-pounders and such) spotted bass will stage here, right on top of the mesas. Cast a swimbait and retrieve

so slowly that it scarcely moves, right on the bottom, right on top of these mesas. The bite is not a grab; it's more of a slow weighting on your rod. You don't strike, but rather reel down to the fish, sense the weight, and let the hook penetrate the mouth without a mighty stroke. What you'll find here is that virtually all of these world-class fish are released. Nobody I know has kept one.

On one trip, my pal Tom Hedtke switched to a crappie jig and caught and released something like 20 bass in less than two hours.

In late spring, the lake starts to stratify in temperature zones, and fishing for kokanee salmon can be a sure thing. Most will troll with a dodger trailing a lure, such as a Kokanee Killer, Mini Kokanee Pro, Double Whammy, or Wedding Ring. The kokanee at Bullards Bar are often small, but their red meat is a delicacy regardless.

BEST OVERNIGHT: BOAT-IN CAMPGROUNDS

Bullards Bar has the best array of boat-in campgrounds in the Sierra Nevada. **Garden Point Boat-In,** on the western shore of the northern Yuba River arm, has 16 tent sites. The accessible **Madrone Cove Boat-In** has 10 tent sites on the main Yuba River arm, along the western shore at an elevation of 2,000 feet. Picnic tables

△ *houseboats on the lake formed by Bullards Bar Dam*

and fire grills are provided at both sites, and vault toilets are available. There is no drinking water, and garbage must be packed out. Leashed pets are permitted.

In addition, boaters can create their own **primitive campsite** anywhere on the shore of Bullards Bar Reservoir (six people maximum per site). Bring a large tarp for sun protection and plenty of water. Garbage must be packed out. A portable chemical toilet and a camping permit are required for all boat-in sites, including Garden Point and Madrone Cove.

Advance reservations and the camping permit are available from **Emerald Cove Marina** (12571 Marysville Rd., Dobbins, 530/692-3201, fee), which also has a general store. Open mid-April-mid-October.

WHERE TO EAT

Location is everything. So when in the vicinity of Bullards Bar, I always end up at **Peterson's Corner** (26310 Hwy. 49, 530/292-3747, 11:30am-2am Mon.-Sat., 9am-2am Sun.). It's a bit of a drive from the lake, at the corner of Pleasant Valley Road along Highway 49. When you walk in, right away you'll see that this is an old-school bar and grill complete with mirrored beer signs behind the bar. Some love the pizza, others the burgers, but the Philly cheesesteak is a must-order. It's all a good fit for the many folks who roll through here.

DRIVING DIRECTIONS

From I-80 in Auburn, take Highway 49 north for 27 miles to Nevada City and the junction with Highway 20. Turn left to stay on Highway 49 and drive 20.4 miles to Camptonville and Marysville Road. Turn left on Marysville Road and drive 2.6 miles to Dark Day Road. Turn right and drive 0.8 mile to the Dark Day boat ramp (straight ahead) and campground (on the left).

To reach Emerald Cove Marina: Continue 3.5 miles south on Marysville Road. Turn right for the Cottage Creek launch ramp and marina.

CAMPFIRE STORIES

*T*o a cult-like following of anglers, Bullards Bar is known as the one of the best lakes to try to catch world-record spotted bass.

My lifetime-best bass was caught here in 45°F water. To be honest, it didn't fight all that hard, and when it appeared at my boat the size of it stunned the heck out of me. In the dead of winter, your next cast at Bullards Bar could bring a world record, too.

The best strategy is to come in winter. With a fishfinder, you can search out underwater ledges and hills. Cast toward the wind-driven side of these ledges, where wind blows food in against the ledges; this is where the aquatic food chain is rich and the fish will hold. Fish 40–60 feet deep with a giant swimbait (like a Huddleston, Keitech Fat, or similar) and barely move the lure in the cold water. The bite from the big ones is less a grab than a nearly indiscernible pull. Most anglers handle the big fish carefully: They weigh them, take a quick photo, and then release them.

△ *Emerald Cove Marina on Bullards Bar Reservoir*

㉖ Echo Lakes

530/543–2600 | Desolation Wilderness, Lake Tahoe Basin Management Unit | www.fs.usda.gov/ltbmu

The Echo Lakes serve as the primary gateway to the Desolation Wilderness. The gorgeous alpine setting is carved in granite and surrounded by forest, nestled at an elevation of 7,414 feet in a deep, glacial-carved canyon with spike-tipped 9,938-foot Pyramid Peak and 9,238-foot Ralston Peak towering overhead.

At one time, this was two separate lakes, but a small dam on Lower Echo Lake raised the water level. A little channel pretzels through a narrow cut to connect Lower and Upper Echo. Afternoon sunlight and a light breeze cover the surface of Echo Lake with refracted silvers. By evening, the lake, often calm at dusk, takes on a different appearance: deep, beautiful, and almost foreboding.

Echo Lake Chalet has historic knotty-pine cabins, a small marina, and the renowned hiker's boat taxi, which can transport hikers to the head of the lake and the trailhead for the Pacific Crest Trail (PCT). For day hikers, the boat taxi eliminates five miles (round-trip) that would otherwise be hiked along the PCT. The taxi also provides a jump start into the Desolation Wilderness, with extended day trips to many destinations.

Every year, it is a watch-and-wait game of suspense to see when Echo Lake Chalet, the boat taxi, and the PCT will become accessible. Your best bet is to aim for July 4th and into summer.

▽ *Echo Lake*

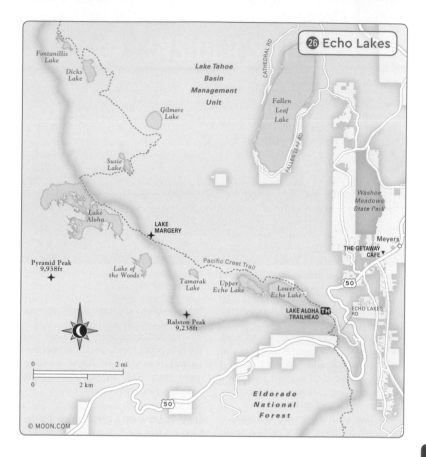

BEST ACTIVITY: HIKE TO LAKE ALOHA

The trail out of Echo Lake provides access to some of the best views and prettiest lakes in Desolation Valley. The feature destination is **Lake Aloha** (6.8 miles round-trip, 4 hours with boat taxi; 12 miles round-trip, 7 hours without), and you can venture to several other gorgeous lakes in the vicinity.

From the parking lot above the lake, walk 0.25 mile downhill to Echo Lake Chalet on the edge of Echo Lake. The **boat taxi** (fee charged each way, hours vary sunrise-sunset, summer only) is located at a dock at the small marina. It leaves whenever more than two people show up. (For those skipping the boat taxi, the PCT trailhead is to the right at water's edge near the outlet.) A day-hike **permit** is required, available (self-serve) from the trailhead at Echo Lake.

It's a pretty 20-minute ride across the lake as the boat sails through a curving channel that connects to Upper Echo Lake. As you emerge on Upper Echo Lake, look for a famous rock cabin used to stage paintings and photographs along the shore to your right. Ralston Peak towers to the left.

Depart the boat taxi at the northern end of Upper Echo Lake and look for a short, 0.1-mile spur to the junction with the PCT. From the PCT junction, it's 3.4 miles (one-way) to the eastern edge of Lake Aloha. Start with a steady climb to a ridge. Just before the ridge, turn around to enjoy

△ Lake Aloha is a glacial basin found in the Desolation Wilderness.

the stunning view of the lakes behind you. Gorgeous!

After topping the ridge, the hike becomes an easy saunter. Stay on the PCT for Lake Aloha. (Along the way, you'll pass several signed junctions with numerous trails leading to various lakes in very short distances.)

When you arrive at Lake Aloha, you'll see a stark, pristine, and sprawling lake that extends for two miles and is circled by landmark peaks. The crest of the Crystal Range is to the left; ahead are Mosquito Pass (8,422 feet), Jacks Peak (9,856 feet), and Dicks Peak (9,974 feet); to the right is the backside of Mount Tallac (9,735 feet).

BACKPACK TO BARKER PASS

(32.8 miles one-way, 3–4 days)

The Desolation Wilderness (and neighboring Granite Chief Wilderness) is filled with sculpted granite domes and hundreds of gemlike lakes. All is pristine, one of the prettiest sections of the 2,650-mile PCT, yet access is easy. The combination makes this one of the most heavily used and most desired wilderness areas. This section hike starts at Echo Lake and exits at Barker Pass, where you'll have a vehicle waiting for you.

Trailhead quotas are enforced for overnight treks, and a **wilderness permit** (Lake Tahoe Basin Management Unit, 530/543-2600, www.fs.usda.gov/ltbmu) is required.

Day 1: Lower Echo Lake to Lake Aloha

(6.8 miles)

The trip starts at Echo Lake Chalet, hops onto the PCT, then climbs through the pines past Upper Echo Lake to continue north toward Triangle Lake (4.2 miles one-way), one of dozens of lakes you pass on your northward route on the PCT. Plan your first night at Lake Aloha.

Day 2: Lake Aloha to Dicks Lake

(10 miles)

Hiking north on the PCT, the lakes come and go in spectacular fashion: Heather, Susie, and Gilmore Lakes, and finally Dicks Lake (at 9,380 feet). There are so many, in fact, that you can plan on a perfect campsite near a lake every night, providing you don't mind

INSIDER'S TIP

From the PCT trailhead near Echo Lake Chalet, you can parlay this trip out to visit a series of small lakes, something I like to call the Desolation Lakes Circuit.

Tamarack Lake (3.8 miles one-way): From the boat taxi on Upper Echo Lake, take the PCT northwest for 1.1 miles, climbing 466 feet to a signed trail junction. Turn left and descend 0.5 mile to gorgeous Tamarack Lake. A short distance beyond is Ralston Lake and little Cagwin Lake (0.4 mile one-way).

Lake of the Woods (4.9–6.4 miles one-way): Take the PCT north for 2.2 miles, climbing 950 feet to a trail junction. Turn left and descend 280 feet over 0.7 mile to gorgeous Lake of the Woods (8,080 feet), backed by a stark, glacial-swept wall and fronted by lakeside campsites amid sparse pines. The lake and campsites are extremely popular for day hikes and picnics, as well as for backpacking.

From Lake of the Woods, the trail continues 1.5 miles along the south shoreline of the lake to reach gorgeous Ropi Lake, which is connected to Toem Lake and Gega Lake.

Lake Margery (4.8 miles one-way): Continue hiking on the PCT, passing the turnoff to Lake of the Woods. In a short distance, look for a signed turnoff on the right for Lake Margery, a speck of a water hole. The 0.4-mile side trip loops down to Lake Margery and back up to the PCT.

△ *Tamarack Lake*

the company of other hikers drawn by classic beauty. The views are dramatic as well, across miles and miles of glacial-carved granite. Plan your second night at Dicks Lake.

Day 3: Dicks Lake to Richardson Lake
(11 miles)

Continuing north, the trail skirts the ridgeline, keeping the higher knobs to the east as it gradually descends toward Richardson Lake, just beyond the Desolation Wilderness boundary, where you then enter the Granite Chief Wilderness to the north. Plan your last night at Richardson Lake.

Day 4: Richardson Lake to exit at Barker Pass
(6 miles)

From Richardson Lake, head north to exit the trail at Barker Pass, elevation 7,650 feet. A trailhead and parking area is available at Barker Pass. This is where you'll want to have a shuttle vehicle (or a prearranged pick-up) waiting. To get there from Highway 89, look for the signed Kaspian Campground on the west side of the highway and Barker Pass Road. The road leads 8.4 miles into Blackwood Campground and beyond to the parking area and trailheads.

BEST OVERNIGHT: ECHO LAKE CHALET

Located on the southeast shore of Lower Echo Lake, **Echo Lake Chalet** (9900 Echo Lakes Rd., Echo Lake, 530/659-7207, www.echochalet. com, summer only) rents nine historic knotty-pine cabins that come with electricity, hot and cold running water, and bathrooms with showers (bedding and linens provided). All but one of the cabins have kitchenettes, cookware,

and utensils. A boat ramp, dock, and marina are nearby, as is a small store. Small, quiet, and clean pets are permitted with prior approval and a deposit, and must be attended at all times.

Reservations are required, and there is a two-night minimum stay. Open late May- mid-September.

WHERE TO EAT

If you're staying in South Lake Tahoe, you'll pass through Meyers en route to Echo Lake. The **Getaway Café** (3140 U.S. 50, Meyers, 530/577-5132, www. tahoegetawaycafe.com, 7am-2:30pm Mon.-Fri., 7am-3pm Sat.-Sun.) serves the best breakfast in Tahoe. Stop here to gorge on breakfast with a Mexican edge and pack in those carbs for your hike.

The **Echo Lake Chalet** (8am-5:30pm daily summer) has a grocery store and soda fountain. Stop here for water, snacks, a trail lunch, or any supplies you might need on the trail.

DRIVING DIRECTIONS

From Placerville, take U.S. 50 east for 45 miles (toward South Lake Tahoe and Echo Summit) and look for Sierra at Tahoe Ski Resort on the right. Continue 1.8 miles to signed Johnson Pass Road (and a brown Sno-Park sign). Turn left and drive 0.6 mile to Echo Lakes Road. Turn left and drive 0.8 mile to the Echo Lakes parking lot. Walk 0.25 mile downhill to the marina and trailhead.

Guests of Echo Lake Chalet can drive down the hill to the small parking area, but day-use parking is restricted to the area at the top of the hill. On peak weekends in summer, the day-use lot (and parking along the shoulder of the road) fills. Get there early. A chemical restroom is available near the parking area.

CAMPFIRE STORIES

*O*n one of my trips here, I thought that the captain of the hiker's boat taxi looked familiar: a young, confident woman with an outdoorsy tan and a look in her eye that hinted of many adventures. Sure enough, she was Sydney Miller, a former classmate of one of my boys. She had become an anthropologist and spent time at destinations around the world. She guided us across Lower Echo Lake, through the channel that pretzels its way to Upper Echo Lake. As we disembarked at the small dock, we asked Sydney what was next for her. "I'm headed this weekend to the Maldives Islands (an atoll in the Indian Ocean)," she beamed.

When it comes to the outdoors, Sydney is living proof that you are limited in this life only by what you can imagine.

△ *Sydney Miller pilots the Echo Lakes boat taxi.*

Emerald Bay is a place of rare and divine beauty—one of the most striking, and popular, state parks in the country. With its deep cobalt-blue waters, surrounding ridgelines, awesome glimpses of Lake Tahoe out the mouth of the bay, and little Fannette Island, there may be no place more perfect to paddle a kayak.

So few places can evoke an emotional response at first glance. Lake Tahoe is one of the rare natural wonders that make you feel something special just by looking at it. To capture this essence of purity, sit on the ridge above Emerald Bay and take it in deep. One of the greatest feelings you can have can upwell from someplace rarely touched.

You can take it a giant step further by hopping in a boat. Boating in Emerald Bay is one of the area's premier outdoor experiences, topped off by an overnight stay at one of the boat-in campsites. The beauty is incomparable. Out in a boat, you are in the middle of clear blue waters, surrounded by a mountain rim often topped with bright white snow. It is always a remarkable, often breathtaking, sight.

To make your visit the best possible, it is critical that you make extensive plans for lodging and recreation; reservations are mandatory on weekends. Or better yet, go during the week. The regional visitor bureau estimates that the Lake Tahoe Basin gets more than three million visitors per year, but many put it closer to five million. The highest use occurs on winter weekends during the ski season, followed by the summer, Fourth of July-early September. There are two periods of relatively light use: after the ski season has ended (April and early May) and then again in the fall after summer (early September-mid-November).

▽ *sunrise on Emerald Bay from the top of Eagle Falls*

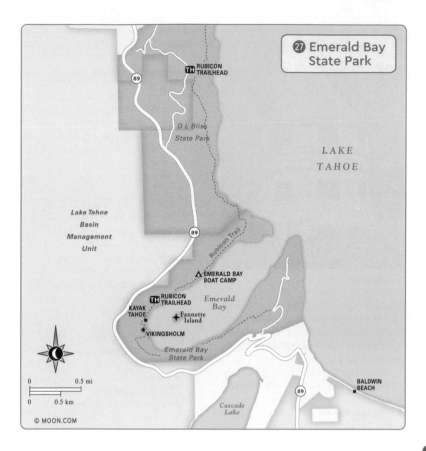

A few weekdays during these shoulder seasons can even make a world-renowned site like Emerald Bay feel like it's your own.

BEST ACTIVITY: FANNETTE ISLAND PADDLE AND PEAK

On a calm, summer morning, it can be ecstasy to sit in the pocket of a kayak and paddle down the center of Emerald Bay. Surrounded by some of the purest and bluest water in the world, you feel enveloped by the mountain rim. From the shore, pine forests rise to a granite ridge high on the northern shoulder of Mount Tallac. Your destination: the remote Tea House built in 1929 on Fannette Island in the middle of Emerald Bay.

To make this trip work, pick a morning when the wind is down. Drive to the Emerald Bay Overlook along Highway 89 and plan to park before 10am in order to grab a spot. From the parking lot, descend almost 500 feet over the course of one mile along the Vikingsholm Trail (a service road). Here's the catch: It's a 500-foot climb back up on the return trip.

Turn right and continue south toward **Vikingsholm** (http://vikingsholm.com). Set at the foot of Emerald Bay, Vikingsholm is considered one of the greatest examples of Scandinavian architecture in North America. It was built in 1929 and is constructed of granite boulders. The castle-like structure features turrets, hand-carved beams, and a sod roof. The **interior** (available via tour, https://sierrastateparks.org,

△ *Vikingsholm*

10:30am-4pm daily late May-Sept., $15) is furnished with authentic artifacts and reproductions. Vikingsholm is listed on the National Register of Historic Places.

From the beach in front of Vikingsholm, hike north along the Rubicon Trail, past the pier, to the rental location for **Kayak Tahoe** (www.kayaktahoe.com, 10am-close daily summer, no reservations, cash only). Hop in a kayak and then enjoy the 10-minute paddle to Fannette Island. After landing, hike the short trek to the summit and the remains of the stone Tea House, which was built by the owner of Vikingsholm.

Enjoy one of the greatest 360-degree views in the state. You are surrounded by the deep blue water of Emerald Bay as it meets the forested slopes that rise to an arcing mountain rim high above. Looking toward the foot of the bay, admire a full frontal of Eagle Falls. Nothing can replicate how it feels to turn and take this all in.

When you put it all together, this is one of the easiest and best paddle-and-peaks anywhere.

HIKE THE RUBICON TRAIL

The **Rubicon Trail** (1–9 miles round-trip, 0.5–5 hours) provides one of the best panoramas across Lake Tahoe. From D. L. Bliss State Park, you can walk an easy 0.5-mile (1 mile out and back) for a sweeping view of Lake Tahoe. The ambitious few can continue hiking south to the foot Emerald Bay and visit Vikingsholm (4.5 miles one-way, 9 miles round-trip).

Note: While you could start the hike in Emerald Bay State Park, it's not advised. Parking availability is poor along the road, plus this gives you a 500-foot ascent on a service road. Avoid both by starting at D. L. Bliss.

The Rubicon Trail starts at Calawee Cove Beach in D. L. Bliss State Park (530/5257277, www.parks.ca.gov). The trailhead is signed Lighthouse/Rubicon Trail and is routed from Rubicon Point to the Old Lighthouse, an easy 2-mile (round-trip) destination for most day hikers. The Rubicon Trail is cut into a slope facing the lake, with 100-foot drop-offs straight down to the waterfront. Cable-type rails are in place in some sections for safety. Many just venture out for the view, enjoy the tons of ground squirrels mooching for some trail mix, then return.

On summer afternoons, the trail is popular and crowded, especially along the first mile. Start instead around dawn, when you will have the trail to yourself and can watch the sunrise cast magical colors across the Tahoe Basin.

BEST OVERNIGHT: EMERALD BAY BOAT CAMP

Emerald Bay State Park has one of the best boat-in camps anywhere. A series of 20 boat-in campsites are available on the northern shore of Emerald Bay, a spectacular trip for those who paddle in via kayak. The sites are set in a pine forest with water views, and a boat dock is nearby. Even when Tahoe is packed, there are times when you can paddle right up and find a site. A reservation makes this a sure thing, of course. Drinking water and vault toilets are available.

If you bring (or rent) your own kayak, you can launch from **Baldwin Beach** (Baldwin Beach Rd., 650/322–1181, late May–mid-Oct., $8–10 parking) outside Emerald Bay for the eight-mile round-trip paddle and make a day of it. It's a great moment when you paddle around Eagle Point and enter Emerald Bay. You see miles of pure water, towering mountain ridges, and, at the foot of the bay, the best view of lower Eagle Falls. (If you paddle outside Emerald Bay, stay close to the shore and be alert for fast boats offshore of Baldwin Beach.) Be sure to check the weather forecast before this trip, as afternoon winds can turn the water rough between Baldwin Beach and Eagle Point.

Kayak Tahoe (530/544–2011, www.kayaktahoe.com) has a rental location on Baldwin Beach. From Highway 89, between the Emerald Bay Overlook and the junction with U.S. 50, turn north on Baldwin Beach Road.

For those who need to car camp, there are two drive-in campgrounds available. The Upper Eagle Point Campground has 33 sites for tents or RVs; it's located near the Rubicon Trailhead. The Lower Eagle Point Campground has 63 sites for tents or RVs; it's located near Eagle Point at the mouth of Emerald Bay. Picnic tables, food lockers, and fire grills are provided. Drinking water and restrooms with flush toilets and coin showers are available. Leashed pets are permitted in the campground.

Reservations (800/444–7275, www.reservecalifornia.com, fee) are accepted. Open early June-mid-September.

WHERE TO EAT

There are a lot of high-end restaurants in South Lake Tahoe, where the chefs worry about how to artfully arrange three spears of asparagus on a plate. And then there's a whole 'nother way to go about it. **Jalisco's Mexican Grill** (Town & Country Shopping Center, 2660 Lake Tahoe Blvd., South Lake Tahoe, 530/600–1775, 11am-8pm Mon.-Sat.) may not look like much, just a neon "Open" sign and Mexican flag-colored drapes in the window, but it's always great. There's nice folks, no crowds, and good, down-home Mexican food. I've been coming here for years, so don't be surprised if you see a guy in a black hat hunkered down in the back corner working on a chicken taco, tostada, and chile relleno with a Bohemia in hand.

DRIVING DIRECTIONS

From South Lake Tahoe, take Highway 89 north for 9 miles to the Emerald Bay Overlook parking lot on the east side of Highway 89. Most park along the shoulder of Highway 89 (on the west side of the road between the visitors center near Eagle Falls), then take a short walk and cross the road to reach the trailhead. Plan to get here by 10am in order to secure a spot.

To reach D. L. Bliss State Park: Continue 2 miles north on Highway 89 to the park entrance on the right.

There is a $10 parking fee for both Emerald Bay and D. L. Bliss State Parks.

CAMPFIRE STORIES

To do Tahoe right, you have to do it by boat. One day, I decided to do *all* the boats. At dawn, we fished out my sport cruiser just offshore of the Stateline casinos. As morning took hold, we rented a kayak and paddled into Emerald Bay. As the sun heated things up, we took a high-speed ride out of Timber Cove on the **Thunder Boat** (530/544-5387, https://action-watersports.com). Then, believe it or not, I took a waterski lesson out of **Camp Richardson** (800/544-1801, www.camprichardson.com). I learned that when you go kerplunk, you find out that water is *cold*. To settle down, we took the giant MS *Dixie II* paddle wheeler out of **Zephyr Cove** (800/238-2463, www.zephyrcove.com) for a dusk cruise.

The only thing I missed that day was paddling a SUP. Well, there's always next time.

△ exploring Emerald Bay State Park by water

The first time I sighted Independence Lake was from the air, off the left wing of my airplane as I was flying from Mount Shasta to Lake Tahoe. Upon approaching Truckee, I looked down and saw an amazing jewel of a lake set in a deep, forested canyon in the High Sierra. The sapphire lake was at 6,949 feet elevation, tucked out of sight from any road. It was one of the prettiest lakes I'd ever seen, and I could hardly wait to venture there.

Flash forward to the present. The Nature Conservacy has since bought the lake and the surrounding property and opened it for public access. On calm mornings, paddling across the clear, mirror-like waters in a kayak is a fantasy come true. Even better is the fact that The Nature Conservacy provides these kayaks for free use. All you have to do is get here.

The old logging road to the preserve can be blocked by snow until late June and sometimes into July. And on afternoons in late spring and early summer, the wind can howl through the canyon, making it dangerous for small craft. But most of the time, these things are not an issue. When I looked down from my plane, I thought I had found paradise. Turns out, I had.

▽ *Independence Lake*

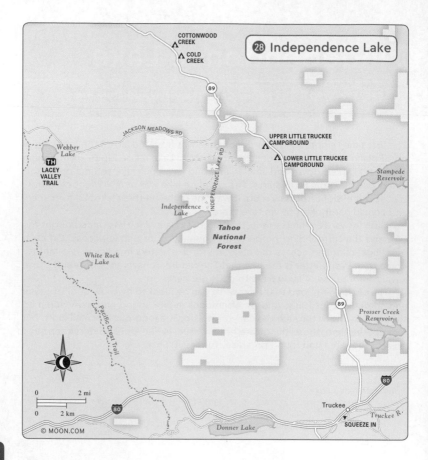

BEST ACTIVITY: KAYAKING

At sunrise, the surface of Independence Lake turns into a perfect mirror. The forested ridges, often crowned with snow on the flanks, are reflected on the lake surface so perfectly, it looks as if you could walk on it. When you sit in the pocket of a kayak and paddle ahead, it's euphoric.

The Nature Conservancy provides free boats for use on the lake June-October. That's right: free. There are eight kayaks (including two tandems), three pontoon float tubes, and three 14-foot aluminum boats with 10-horsepower outboards (motorboats are available every other week). Reservations are not accepted; all craft are first-come, first-served, so plan to arrive early (between 9am and noon), especially on weekends.

There are a few rules: Private craft are not permitted (you can't bring your own boat). Boats, kayaks, and float tubes from outside the preserve are not allowed.

FISHING

Let me tell you a campfire story. In the 1940s, there was no such thing as Independence Lake. There were only two small lakes, called Loon Lakes, separated by a ridge. When a forest fire vanquished the canyon, the salvage logging cut all the trees down right to the water's edge. A lot of the old logging equipment, like booms

△ *kayaking on Independence Lake*

and cables, were left behind. A small dam was built at the outlet, which created a single lake, and Independence Lake was born.

Independence has the largest population of large cutthroat trout in California; however, they are under strict protection (catch-and-release only), and anglers are required to use artificial lures with single barbless hooks.

The best spot to fish is the windward side of the underwater land bridge that used to separate the two lakes. (It's about three-quarters of the way to the far end of the lake. Those with portable, battery-powered depth finders can easily find it.) The best prospects for cutthroat are when there is a breeze on the lake with an overcast sky, or at dawn or dusk. Brown trout are light-shy; they bite at dawn and dusk and hide during the day, often preferring large lures the size of small kokanee.

The water is gin-clear and the fish are line-shy in calm water conditions (boats are not allowed out in windy weather). Anglers must use lightweight, low-visibility fishing line (think near-invisible fluorocarbon leaders and 8-pound ultra-green line) to have a chance. If you use heavy line for the large fish, you'll never get a bite; the fish will wrap the line around the old logging booms and break off. In the Rocky Mountains, where cutthroats are common, anglers use Jake's Spin-o-Lure, gold with red dots, or large, dark

streamers like leeches or Seal Buggers.

Put it all together and you have history, intrigue, and the chance for a spectacular catch like no other.

BEST OVERNIGHT: TAHOE NATIONAL FOREST

There is no camping at Independence Lake. However, there are four small campgrounds in the **Tahoe National Forest** (Sierraville Ranger District, 530/994–3401, www.fs.usda.gov/tahoe), north of Truckee along Highway 89. All are within range of Independence Lake.

- **Cold Creek** is upstream of the confluence of Cottonwood Creek and Cold Creek at 5,800 feet elevation. There are six sites for tents or RVs (no hookups). The campground is 20 miles north of Truckee on the left side of Highway 89.
- **Cottonwood Creek** is at 5,800 feet elevation with 48 sites for tents or RVs (no hookups). The campground is 20 miles north of Truckee on the right side of Highway 89 (0.5 mile past Cold Creek Camp).
- **Lower Little Truckee River** is at 6,200 feet with 12 sites for tents or RVs (no hookups) and two walk-in tent sites. The campground is 12 miles north of Truckee on the left side of Highway 89.
- **Upper Little Truckee River** is at 6,100 feet along a pretty trout stream with 21 sites for tents or

Webber Lake (www.truckeedonnerlandtrust.org) is about 13 miles northwest of Independence Lake and first opened to the public in 2018. Though smaller than Independence Lake, Webber Lake shares its off-the-radar beauty. The lake is kept full year-round and has a campground, good low-speed boating, and some big rainbow trout.

On the southwest shore of the lake, the **Lacey Valley Trail** (1–6.8 miles, 1–3.5 hours) is a pretty walk to the largest mountain meadow in the region. Wildflowers bloom into August and sightings of deer, and even bear, are common. From the trailhead on Webber Lake Road, the route climbs gently south and extends into a series of mountain meadows: Lower and then Upper Lacey Meadow. To the west towers 8,093-foot Webber Peak. The trail is routed 3.4 miles one-way along the Lacey Creek watershed to another trailhead and parking area along Meadow Lake Road. Most just hike into the meadows and then return the same way.

Campground (46 sites) **reservations** (www.truckeedonnerlandtrust.org, $30–39) are accepted online. Open spring-October 15.

Driving Directions: From I-80 in Truckee, drive east and take exit 188A (also signed for Highway 89) for 0.3 mile to Donner Pass Road. Turn left and drive 0.2 mile to a traffic circle. Take the second exit to Donner Pass Road and continue 0.3 mile to another traffic circle. Take the second exit to Highway 89 and drive 14 miles to Bear Valley/Cottonwood Road. Turn left and drive about 80 yards to Jackson Meadows Road. Turn left and drive 8.1 miles to Henness Pass Road (signed for Webber Lake). Turn left onto the dirt road and drive 0.25 mile to a gate (the lake is on your left). Bear right at the fork and drive 0.25 mile to a road signed for Lacey Meadows. Turn left and drive 0.6 mile to the parking area.

RVs (no hookups) and one group site for up to 25 people. The campground is 11 miles north of Truckee on the left side of Highway 89.

Picnic tables and fire rings are provided, and drinking water and vault toilets are available at all campgrounds. Leashed pets are permitted.

Reservations (877/444–6777, www.recreation.gov, fee) are accepted. Open May-October.

WHERE TO EAT

There are tons of places to eat in northern Tahoe, but only one where you can order the omelet of your dreams. At the **Squeeze In** (10060 Donner Pass Rd., Truckee, 530/587-9814, www.squeezein.com, 7am-2pm daily), there are more than 60 spelling-challenged omelets on the menu. Choose from "107 quadrillion different possible 'omelette' combinations, best with 'spudz,'" or invent your own. At this friendly little spot in downtown Truckee, the ability to spell might be lacking, but the ability to cook is out of this world.

DRIVING DIRECTIONS

Independence Lake is 20 miles north of Truckee. You'll need a high-clearance vehicle to access the lake. A Forest Service map may be helpful for navigating roads.

CAMPFIRE STORIES

*I*t was a snowy, windy day in early September and the water at Independence Lake was too rough for my canoe. The land was privately owned at the time, so I ended up hunkering down with the caretakers for a spell. They told me the tale of the ghost of Independence Lake.

Across from the caretaker's lodge was a boarded-up structure, a 150-year-old resort where several people had reported seeing a ghost. The ghost appeared in the window of the long-closed resort, wearing a plaid shirt and blue jeans.

Some say the ghost is the spirit of a person who drowned here in the 1940s, a photographer whose boat capsized on a windy day, or even the pilot of a plane that crashed on a nearby ridge in a snowstorm in 1950.

Whether you believe in ghosts or not doesn't matter. What matters is that the people here do. After all, they've seen one.

From Truckee, take Highway 89 north for 15 miles to a turnoff signed for Independence Lake, Webber Lake, Jackson Meadow Reservoir. Turn left and drive 1.5 miles on a paved road to a junction signed for Independence Lake—5 miles. Turn left and drive 2 miles on the dirt road to a fork signed for Independence Lake—3 miles. Turn right and drive 0.5 mile to another fork. Bear left and drive across a stream; if you do not cross a stream just after this fork, then you have taken the wrong fork. Continue to the signed entrance road for Independence Lake Preserve. Continue to the parking area (well-signed). Preserve staff are on-site daily May-October, and the parking lot can fill on weekends. Plan to pack out all trash.

530/543-2600 | Lake Tahoe Basin Management Unit |
www.fs.usda.gov/ltbmu

When spring arrives in the Sierra, all your senses start firing off. After six months of winter, the warm weather returns, the snow starts to melt, and miles of trails are unveiled week by week. It is a magical time, and the sights, sounds, and smells can imprint you for life.

The Meeks Creek Trail is my favorite way to commemorate the arrival of spring in Tahoe. While you get occasional long-distance views of Lake Tahoe, that is not what drives this trip. Rather, it's the small, pristine lakes: a series of six gorgeous alpine lakes crowned by Rubicon Lake and its world-class beauty. As you hike, you'll hear the rush of Meeks Creek, fed by melting snow, and listen for the mating calls of blue grouse (a deep whoomph, whoomph, whoomph in three or four pulses). The scent of pine duff fills the air, and the alpine zone has a pure freshness that fills each breath.

This trip is popular in summer, with people at every lake, and is a great day hike: Stay the night at nearby Meeks Bay Campground or perhaps at a cabin rental in Tahoma or Homewood and hike the trail during the day. You can extend the trip (and escape the crowds) by turning this into an overnight backpacking trek and spending the night at your choice of lakes or by venturing beyond to connect with the Tahoe Rim Trail.

Before summer arrives and the crowds inundate the Desolation Wilderness, you can often have this trail virtually to yourself.

▽ *Meeks Creek*

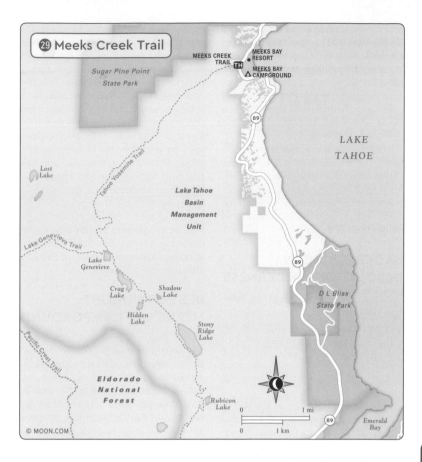

BEST ACTIVITY: MEEKS CREEK TRAIL

The **Meeks Bay Trailhead** is located at an elevation of 6,230 feet along the west side of Highway 89; there is parking adjacent to a gated dirt road and a historic cabin. (If altitude is an issue for you, take an Advil and drink plenty of water before you embark on the trail.) A self-service permit for day hiking (required) is available at the trailhead.

The first 1.4 miles belies what is to follow. The hike starts with a walk on a flat dirt road (Forest Road 14N42) along the valley floor with a long-distance glimpse of Rubicon Peak (9,183 feet). At the end of the valley is the boundary sign for the Desolation Wilderness. At a giant cedar off to the right, the road turns to trail.

From here the trail climbs, a rhythmic stride for most, and then is routed along pretty Meeks Creek with a series of pretty cascades. The trail crosses a creek over a log bridge at 3.3 miles and rises 1,100 feet to **Lake Genevieve** (at 4.6 miles) at about 7,300 feet elevation. It's the first of a half dozen lakes and, like most all lakes in Desolation, it's pristine and pretty. This is a common spot for a lunch break and a swim in summer. For most, the best is yet ahead.

Hike another 0.5 mile upstream to **Crag Lake** (at 5.1 miles). At the foot of the lake, you'll find boulders where can take a seat and absorb the expanse of beauty. The lake is nestled at the foot of a mountain ridge and an unnamed crag, where you can get mirror images off the surface of Crag Lake.

A right fork leads to small **Hidden Lake** (at 5.7 miles), a good side trip. Also beyond the main trail from Crag Lake are Shadow and Stony Ridge Lakes, and then the big payoff, Rubicon Lake (at 8.1 miles).

Campsites are available at all the lakes, but for day hikers, Crag Lake is the most popular turnaround point. It's a short distance past Lake Genevieve and a bigger lake, with a dramatic ridge looming overhead and many good sites for lunch.

BACKPACKING IN DESOLATION WILDERNESS

For a two-day backpacking trek, **Rubicon Lake** (8.1 miles one-way from the trailhead, 6 hours; 16.2 miles round-trip, 1–2 days) is your destination and the best overnight stay. It is also the best stopping point to get acclimated before continuing on to the Tahoe Rim Trail (see Insider's Tip).

From Crag Lake, follow the Meeks Creek Trail to **Shadow Lake** (at 5.9 miles). It is small and, in summer, cov-ered with lilies. From Shadow Lake, it's less than half a mile farther to **Stony Ridge Lake** (at 6.3 miles), the largest of this series of lakes. It's then nearly two miles, with a steep stretch at the end, to gorgeous **Rubicon Lake,** for a total elevation gain of 2,000 feet from the trailhead. Rubicon is edged by forest on one side, with granite slabs feeding into the lake in spots on the other. From above the lake, you get glimpses of the Tahoe Rim. For people who love wilderness, a moment like this is worth more than gold.

Backpackers must purchase a Desolation Wilderness **permit** (www.recreation.gov) in advance and pick it up at one of four ranger stations prior to arrival at the trailhead.

BEST OVERNIGHT: MEEKS BAY CAMPGROUND

Meeks Bay is a beautiful spot along the western shore of Lake Tahoe. Both campgrounds and cabin rentals are available here and in nearby Tahoma and Homewood. The **Meeks Bay Campground** is operated by the Forest Service and has 20 sites for tents or RVs (no hookups) and 16 sites for tents only. Picnic tables, food lockers, and fire grills are provided. Drinking water and flush toilets are available. Some facilities are wheelchair-accessible. Leashed pets are permitted, but not on the beach.

Reservations (877/444-6777, www.recreation.gov, fee) are accepted. Open mid-May-mid-October.

Also nearby is **Meeks Bay Resort** (7941 Emerald Bay Rd., 530/525-6946), which has a popular campground that is often booked well in advance for July and August. There are 23 sites for RVs with full hookups (some pull-through) and 14 tents sites. Lodge rooms, cabins, and a house are also available. Picnic tables, bear lockers, and fire grills are provided. Restrooms with showers and flush toilets, a snack bar, a gift shop, and a camp store are available.

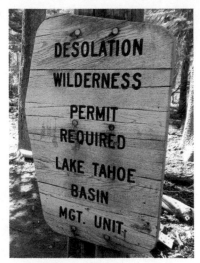

△ *Desolation Wilderness*

From the Meeks Creek Trail, it's possible to connect with the **Pacific Crest Trail/Tahoe Rim Trail** for a backpacking adventure. From the Meeks Creek Trailhead, hike 4.6 miles southwest with a gain of 1,100 feet to Lake Genevieve and a trail junction. Turn right and hike 3.7 steep miles as you climb out of the lake basin to the Pacific Crest Trail/Tahoe Rim Trail (elevation 7,880 feet).

A left turn here leads south into the Desolation Wilderness and 1.5 miles to beautiful Middle Velma Lake. Beyond to the south lies the heart of the Desolation Wilderness and, in summer, some of its most crowded but beautiful lakes and campsites.

A right turn on the Tahoe Rim Trail leads north out of the Desolation Wilderness and into the Granite Chief Wilderness. Turn right and continue 2.7 miles to a spur on the right; this leads 0.3 mile down into the basin for Richardson Lake, where you'll spend the night. For those who pass Richardson Lake, there's a campsite at Bear Lake, available on a spur (that turns into a 4-wheel-drive road) from the PCT. It's the closest lake site to Barker Pass and gets a fair amount of traffic. For overnight use, a wilderness permit (Lake Tahoe Basin Management Unit, 530/543-2600, www.fs.usda.gov/ltbmu) is required.

Reservations (877/326-3357, www.meeksbayresort.com, fee) are accepted. Open mid-May-mid-October.

WHERE TO EAT

Many people go to Tahoe for one reason: to look at the lake. **Chambers Landing Bar & Grill** (6300 W. Lake Blvd., Homewood, 530/525-9190, www.chamberspunch.com, 11:30am-4:30pm Wed., 11:30am-9pm Thurs.-Tues.) has a sensational view with outdoor picnic tables and shade umbrellas. The place is famous for its punch. I'm not a punch guy, but I've seen people get slonkered on the stuff, walking out with dreamy smiles on their faces. The pub-style fare is decent enough to draw crowds in summer. Chambers is located just north of the Meeks Bay Trailhead.

DRIVING DIRECTIONS

From Sacramento, take I-80 east roughly 100 miles to Truckee and Highway 89. Turn right on Highway 89 and drive 13.6 miles to Tahoe City. Bear right (still on Highway 89) and drive south for 10.5 miles to the trailhead on the right.

From South Lake Tahoe, take Highway 89 north and drive 17 miles (past the bridge over Meeks Creek) to the dirt access road and trailhead on the left.

Look for a historic cabin and gate next to a parking area.

Note: The trailhead is located near the entrance of Meeks Bay Resort, on the opposite side of the road. If you drive south over the bridge at Meeks Creek, you have gone too far.

CAMPFIRE STORIES

*A*s with many people who live for the outdoor experience, I value how places make me feel. In spring, when the ice melts off the alpine lakes of the Tahoe basin, I put hiking the Meeks Creek Trail at the top of my list above just about everything.

While parking here for one trip, I set my cell phone on the railing of my pickup truck bed and then booted up, belted my pack, put on my black hat, and ventured off for a solo hike. It was a long one that day, a 16-miler to Rubicon Lake and back. I returned to the truck at dusk and my cell phone was still sitting there, on the railing of my pickup truck, right where I had left it.

The hike had been so beautiful and filled me with so many sensations that I never even realized I had left my phone behind until I saw it sitting there, untouched. Never missed it, not for one second.

△ *Crag Lake on Meeks Creek Trail*

530/543–2600 | Lake Tahoe Basin Management Unit |
www.fs.usda.gov/ltbmu

On top of Mount Tallac, amid a jumble of rocks and boulders that make up the crown of Tahoe's preeminent mountain, there's a single rock perch that tops the 9,735-foot summit. Alongside it are more slabs that seem made for taking a seat and soaking in the views. And the views are why you're here.

Mount Tallac affords views like no other, across a sea of pines and aspens to Cascade Lake, Emerald Bay, and Lake Tahoe. The eastern horizon is topped by Monument and Freel Peaks and Mount Rose in Nevada. A look west into the Desolation Wilderness is equally profound, across distant Aloha Lake to huge snow-packed slopes that reach to Pyramid Peak, Mount Price, and the rim that crests Crystal Basin. And directly beneath your rocky perch, the slope plummets 3,000 feet to Fallen Leaf Lake.

Of course, the view from the top of Mount Tallac is paramount, but the entire experience is unforgettable. On my trips up Mount Tallac, I often run into ranger friends and outdoors writers. Once, on the flank of Mount Tallac, I took a seat on the rocks and then soaked in the view of Gilmore Lake below. On the way down from the summit to Gilmore Lake, I trekked off-trail and flushed a blue grouse. The whole thing was so spectacular that I never wanted to leave.

The best time to hike Mount Tallac is in early-mid-July, when the route is clear of snow. The trail up to Gilmore Lake is usually clear by mid-late June. Or come in early fall (Sept.-early Oct.), when people are few and the cold mornings are crystal clear.

▽ *Lake Tahoe, as seen from Mount Tallac*

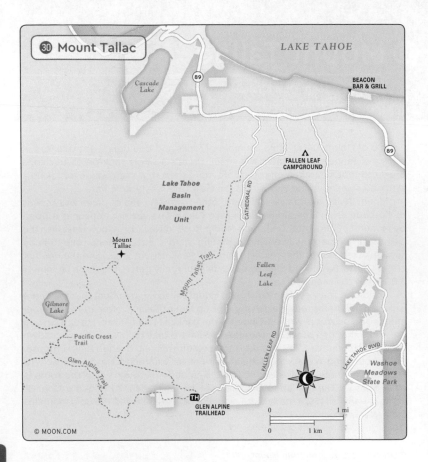

BEST ACTIVITY: HIKE MOUNT TALLAC

Mount Tallac towers over Lake Tahoe and its surrounding basin, where the lake and sky seem to merge into a cobalt-blue spectacle. This popular trail (and the trailhead parking) can be jammed on summer weekends. Yet once you set off, the crowds disperse and you can make the experience your own. Plan to make a day of it.

The **Glen Alpine Trailhead** (11.6 miles round-trip, 7.5 hours) is located south of Fallen Leaf Lake and is your best starting point (see *Insider's Tip*). From this trailhead the hike to the top is a one-way tromp of 5.8 miles (3.5–4 hours) with an elevation gain of 3,175 feet. The trip back is a downhill breeze. A self-service permit for day hiking is available at the trailhead.

The trek comes in three stages.

Glen Alpine Trailhead to Gilmore Lake junction
(1.7 miles)

From the Glen Alpine Trailhead, the hike starts easy and flat. On the left, you pass small but pretty Glen Alpine Falls (best seen when flush with runoff from snowmelt). The air is scented with pine duff, a familiar tang for those imprinted by Tahoe—it smells like home. For the first mile, the trail follows a rocky road that eventually transitions into a cobblestone of river rock leading to a historic camp with a few old cabins on the right. A sign

△ *trail to Gilmore Lake*

marks the entry point for the Desolation Wilderness, a threshold moment. Most hikers make quick work of the first 1.7 miles to the trail junction. Grass Lake is to the left and Gilmore Lake is to the right. Bear right for Gilmore Lake, where the trail surface improves dramatically.

Gilmore Lake
(2.6 miles)

From the Gilmore Lake junction, it's a steady climb out of the canyon for 2.6 miles to Gilmore Lake. Fortunately, trail builders installed enough switchbacks to keep the grade just right. It is common to see tons of wildflowers here, even in early August, with lots of lupine, mule's ear, paintbrush, and rafts of corn lilies. The creeks are flush with clear, cold water and harbor miniature waterfalls. In late spring (during snowmelt and ice-out), mosquitoes can be a problem; bring bug juice.

You'll pass a series of trail junctions (paths lead left to Susie and Heather Lakes); continue ahead toward Gilmore Lake. As you top a crest, pretty Gilmore Lake—the largest lake in the area—is revealed before you. The lake sits nestled in a basin at 8,290 feet at the foot of Mount Tallac's backside. It's a perfect stop for a rest or snack, with a confluence of trails for meeting other hikers. Backpacking (permit required) is an option here, with several flats near the trail junction with lake views.

Gilmore Lake to Mount Tallac
(1.6 miles)

On the last stretch to the summit, you'll climb 1,445 feet over 1.6 miles. Leaving Gilmore Lake, the climb is easy and the hillside is buried in greenery and wildflowers. Soon enough, the trail becomes steeper, and you'll huff and puff your way above tree line. The last 0.5 mile is the steepest as you approach the cragged rim.

As you reach the mountain crest, the Tahoe basin is unveiled before you. The trail diminishes into rock, but most hikers can scramble the route to the true summit. At the 9,735-foot top, turn west and take in the vast Desolation Wilderness, covered in granite, ice, and lakes. There is nothing else like it.

△ *Mount Tallac from Fallen Leaf Lake*

BACKPACK TO GILMORE LAKE

If you only have time to backpack to one destination near South Lake Tahoe, **Gilmore Lake** (8.6 miles round-trip, 4–5 hours) is an excellent choice. Plus, you can break up the hike to Mount Tallac by camping here overnight.

On day 1, you can hike to Gilmore Lake, then take your time and hike up Mount Tallac on day 2 for a climb of 1,445 feet over 1.6 miles. This is a classic trip in the Desolation Wilderness, with fields of wildflowers, mountain vistas, and verdant forest.

From the Glen Alpine Trailhead, follow the hike directions to Gilmore Lake, the largest lake in the area, ringed by grassy, flower-filled meadows and backed on one side by the slopes of Mount Tallac. Facing the lake, you'll see several flat areas on the left where you can set up camp within range of the creek outlet. Many people cruise by Gilmore Lake each day on their way to climb Mount Tallac, yet few take the time to hang out by the lake's sapphire waters.

Those backpacking and overnighting in the Desolation Wilderness must purchase a wilderness **permit** (www.recreation.gov) in advance and pick it up at one of four ranger stations before the hike.

BEST OVERNIGHT: FALLEN LEAF CAMPGROUND

Fallen Leaf Lake sits in a basin below high ridges at an elevation of 6,337 feet. It is three miles long, 430 feet deep (at its deepest point), and almost as blue as nearby Lake Tahoe. The campground near the north shore has 75 sites for tents, 130 sites for tents or RVs (no hookups), and six yurts. Picnic tables, food lockers, and fire grills are provided. Drinking water, vault toilets, and coin showers are available. A boat ramp, coin laundry, and supplies are nearby. Some facilities are wheelchair-accessible. Leashed pets are permitted.

Reservations (877/444-6777, www.recreation.gov, fee) are accepted. Open mid-May-mid-October.

WHERE TO EAT

If you're eating at Tahoe, a lake view can become as important as the food. That puts the **Beacon Bar & Grill** at Camp Richardson (1900 Jameson Beach Rd., South Lake Tahoe, 530/541-

INSIDER'S TIP

There are *two* trailheads for Mount Tallac, a fact that can confound newcomers to Lake Tahoe. By far, the preferred route is the suggested hike from the Glen Alpine Trailhead. Yet others see a trailhead called the "Mount Tallac Trail" on Mount Tallac Road west of Fallen Leaf Lake and figure this must be the way—and away they go.

If you hike from this second trailhead, you pay for your pleasure with a 900-foot climb in the first 1.5 miles and a total climb of 2,600 feet over the last 3 miles. It is far steeper and more challenging than the route from the Glen Alpine Trailhead.

△ *waterfall along the Glen Alpine Trail*

After you have enjoyed the summit, the trip back is a downhill glide. It is so free and easy that you have to pay attention not to miss the right turn that leads back down to Gilmore Lake and to Glen Alpine Trailhead. I've seen some hikers sail downhill past the turn on the way back and take the Mount Tallac Trail by accident. They end up at Fallen Leaf Lake, miles from where they parked.

From the Glen Alpine Trailhead, the hike to Mount Tallac can feel like gaining entry to heaven. But if you hike from the Mount Tallac Trailhead instead, you'll find out what it's like in the "other" place.

0630, www.camprichardson.com, 11:30am-8pm daily) on the map. The Beacon has been voted the "Best Outdoor Patio," the "Best Restaurant with a View," and the "Best Bartender" by the Tahoe Daily Tribune. The restaurant has lake frontage and a sweeping view of Lake Tahoe, with a short walk available on the adjacent dock.

The food and service can be uneven, though I've had sensational dinners here, once when our CBS television crew feasted for hours. Go before sunset to get the best of it.

DRIVING DIRECTIONS

To reach the Glen Alpine Trailhead: From South Lake Tahoe, take High-way 89 north for 2.9 miles to Fallen Leaf Lake Road. Turn left and drive 4.8 miles south past the Fallen Leaf Marina (the road narrows; go slow and be ready for oncoming cars). At a fork, turn left on Road 1216 (signed for Lily Lake and the Desolation Wilderness). Drive 0.7 mile to the trailhead. Parking is extremely limited, and on summer weekends all spaces fill early. To avoid the crowds, time your trip for the off-season (early spring-late May and in Sept.) or during the week.

To reach Fallen Leaf Campground: In South Lake Tahoe, at the junction of U.S. 50 and Highway 89, turn north on Highway 89 and drive 2 miles to the Fallen Leaf Lake turnoff. Turn left and drive 1.5 miles to the campground.

The closest you can come to walking on air is on the grated walkway platform surrounding the fire lookout perched on a crag atop the Sierra Buttes.

The Sierra Buttes are a series of towering crags that loom above the Yuba River Canyon, with Sierra City on one side and the Sardine Lakes and the Lakes Basin Recreation Area on the other. The Sierra Buttes top out at 8,587 feet and seem to poke a hole in the sky. Reaching the top takes a hike of 2.5 miles with a climb of 2,400 feet, a little over an hour or so. The trek is highlighted by a stairway with 176 steps that jut into open space in a few spots. Here the hike becomes an act of faith.

All of this is crowned by a view that extends for hundreds of miles everywhere you look. On that grated walkway, you look down and into the open air below, towering over Upper and Lower Sardine Lake directly below. You might get dizzy. Some people get a sense of spatial disorientation. For most, it's rapture.

The first time I hiked the Sierra Buttes, I worried about the summer heat and the potential number of people at the stairs. I left shortly after dawn and was there by early morning. Guess what? It was cold and nobody else was around. Since then, I depart around 9am (on weekdays) and usually meet only a few folks, coming and going, and never worry about sharing the stairs. Popular weekends may get crowded, but an early start can solve that. Hiking is best June-October, when the trail is most likely to be free of snow.

▽ *Sardine Lakes from Sierra Buttes Lookout*

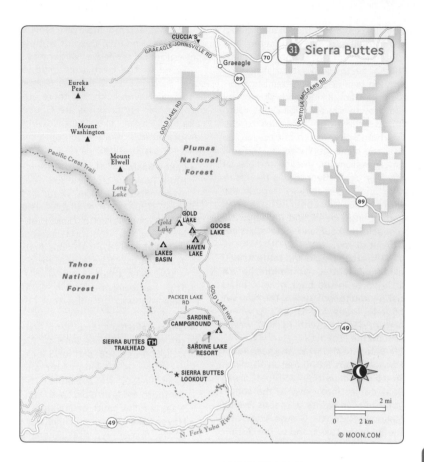

CUCCIA'S

GRAEAGLE-JOHNSVILLE RD

Graeagle

70

89

PORTOLA MCLEARS RD

Eureka
Peak ▲

GOLD LAKE RD

Plumas
National
Forest

89

Mount
Washington ▲

Pacific Crest Trail

Mount
Elwell ▲

Long
Lake

Gold
Lake

GOLD LAKE

GOOSE
LAKE

LAKES
BASIN

HAVEN
LAKE

Tahoe
National
Forest

PACKER LAKE
RD

GOLD LAKE HWY

SARDINE
CAMPGROUND

49

SIERRA BUTTES
TRAILHEAD TH

SARDINE LAKE
RESORT

★ SIERRA BUTTES
LOOKOUT

N. Fork Yuba River

49

0   2 mi

0   2 km

© MOON.COM

BEST ACTIVITY: SIERRA BUTTES TRAIL

Atop the 8,587-foot **Sierra Buttes** (5 miles round-trip, 3.5 hours), the view from the lookout station is one of the best you can get with a short hike. But that's not what will stay with you for years. What you will remember is how the metal stairways extend into space and the small, grated walkway around the lookout that juts out into the air. This is where you get the one-of-a-kind sensation that you are walking on air. It's one of the most spectacular day hikes in California.

Plan for a one-way hike of 2.5 miles with a climb of about 2,400 feet. From the parking area and trailhead near the Pacific Crest Trail, the

△ *Sierra Buttes lookout tower*

trail starts at 6,200 feet as an old jeep road. You'll pass by a designated OHV route on your right at about 1.5 miles, then begin to climb. After making your way up to a ridge, the trail becomes a single-track hiking path shaded by old-growth whitebark pine. The route follows the ridge and rises to the southern spine of the buttes. As you rise, the climb gets steeper. The trail emerges from the treeline and hits an old jeep road. Bear left as the route rises and carves its way through the lower buttes. You continue up the trail and around a bend, and suddenly the pinnacle, lookout, and metal stairs are in front of you.

The stairs jangle and rattle as you climb 150 feet up; you might hear a little voice in the back of your head daring you to look down. The final set of stairs feeds you to the top where a grated deck (with railing) wraps around the lookout.

Below to the west, the Yuba River Canyon drops 5,000 feet in 10 miles. To the distant north, 10,457-foot Lassen Peak comes into view. To the south, you can scan across gorgeous French Meadows Reservoir, Grouse Ridge, and the Bowman Lakes, and to the distant snowy crest of the Crystal Basin on the edge of Tahoe. Below to the east are the Sardine Lakes. As you stand there, perhaps daring to look straight down past your boots into the open air, you may realize you've never experienced anything like this anywhere.

EXPLORE THE LAKES BASIN RECREATION AREA

The Sierra Buttes are the gateway to the **Lakes Basin Recreation Area** (also known as the Gold Lakes Basin), which offers great hiking, camping, and trout fishing.

From Highway 89 in Graeagle, the Gold Lake Highway stretches 17 miles south past national forest speckled with plenty of flat-water lakes for paddling, fishing, and low-speed boating, plus campgrounds and lodges. Canoe,

kayak, boat, and mountain bike rentals are available nearby. Despite all this, the region has the feel of wilderness.

Some of the best lakes include Lower Sardine Lake, Gold Lake, Goose Lake, and Haven Lake, but there are many more. My favorites are Goose Lake and Haven Lake. The following campgrounds offers a jumping-off point for exploration:

- **Lakes Basin** has 11 sites. Reservations (www.recreation.gov, fee) are accepted. Drinking water and vault toilets are available. The campground is on Gold Lake Highway, nine miles south of Graeagle.
- **Gold Lake** has 37 first-come, first-served sites. There is no drinking water. Vault toilets are available. The campground is on Gold Lake Highway, 10 miles south of Graeagle.
- **Goose Lake** has 13 first-come, first-served sites, some with picnic tables, fires rings, and food lockers. There is drinking water, and vault toilets are available. The campground is on Gold Lake Highway, 12 miles south of Graeagle.
- **Haven Lake** has four primitive, first-come, first-served sites. There is no drinking water, and a portable

△ *Lower Sardine Lake*

A series of small resorts with **cabin rentals** are available in the Lakes Basin Recreation Area. Both Sardine Lake Resort and Salmon Lake Lodge provide two of the prettiest cabin settings in the state. Some cabins may be booked long in advance; your best hope is to get on the cancellation lists (which I have successfully done) to secure a spot.

★ **Sardine Lake** (Sardine Lake Resort, 530/862-1196, www.sardinelakeresort.com)

★ **Packer Lake** (Packer Lake Lodge, 530/862-1221, www.packerlakelodge.com)

★ **Salmon Lake** (Salmon Lake Lodge, 530/852-0874, www.salmonlake.net)

★ **Gold Lake** (Gold Lake Lodge, 530/836-2350, www.goldlakelodge.com)

★ **Long Lake** (Elwell Lakes Lodge, 530/836-2347, www.elwelllakeslodge.com)

toilet is available seasonally. The campground is on Gold Lake Highway, 12 miles south of Graeagle.

All campgrounds are open in summer only; fees vary. A high-clearance vehicle is advised in order to reach Goose and Haven Lakes. For more information, contact the **Plumas National Forest** (Beckwourth Ranger District Office, 23 Mohawk Hwy., Blairsden, 530/836-2575, www.fs.usda.gov).

BEST OVERNIGHT: SARDINE CAMPGROUND

Sardine Campground (Tahoe National Forest, Yuba River Ranger District North, 530/288-3231, www.fs.usda.gov/tahoe) is a great staging area to climb the Sierra Buttes. The campground is in the Tahoe National Forest near Sand Pond, about a mile from Lower Sardine Lake. Lower Sardine Lake is a jewel below the Sierra Buttes, one of the prettiest settings in California. A great hike is routed along the shore of Lower Sardine Lake to a hidden waterfall (in spring) that feeds the lake. Ambitious hikers can explore beyond to Upper Sardine Lake.

There are 29 sites for tents or RVs up to 22 feet. Picnic tables and fire grills are provided, and vault toilets are available. Leashed pets are permitted.

Reservations (877/444-6777 or www.recreation.gov, fee) are accepted. Open June-October.

There's also the small **Sardine Lake Resort** (530/862-1196, www.sardinelakeresort.com), which rents cabins and has a small store and restaurant (see Insider's Tip).

WHERE TO EAT

After climbing the Sierra Buttes in the morning, and then launching a canoe and catching a few trout at Lower Sardine Lake in the afternoon, we booked it down the Gold Lake Highway to Graeagle to celebrate. If you spend any time in Plumas County, you'll discover the woodsy little joint the locals call **Cuccia's** (545 Mohawk Hwy., Graeagle, 530/336-2121, www.ilovecuccias.com, 5pm-close Tues.-Sun.), which serves the best food around. The menu is on the Italian side, with dishes that include Caesar salad, chicken scaloppini, specialty pizzas, and seafood options from scampi fettuccine to mahi mahi. After climbing the Sierra Buttes, you deserve a reward. This is where you get it.

CAMPFIRE STORIES

There are a few places that can give you the sensation of "walking on air." I felt this phenomenon when I scaled the South Tower of the Golden Gate Bridge in San Francisco. The catwalk around the bridge's South Tower is similar to the walkway around the Sierra Buttes lookout; look down and you'll peer straight into the open air to the ocean water 750 feet below. I felt a bit lightheaded and shaky atop both the Golden Gate and the Sierra Buttes.

I'm a certified pilot. I fly complex, high-powered aircraft, but from a pilot's seat, I've never felt anything other than rock-solid. The Sierra Buttes, on the other hand, is like taking a trip into another dimension. It gets me every time.

△ *"Stairway to Heaven"...Sierra Buttes Lookout*

DRIVING DIRECTIONS

From Truckee, take I-80 exit 188A for Donner Pass Road/Truckee/Highway 89 and drive 0.3 mile to Donner Pass Road. Turn left and drive 0.2 mile to a traffic circle. Take the second exit to stay on Donner Pass Road. Continue 0.2 mile to another traffic circle and take the third exit onto Highway 89. Drive 27.4 miles north to Highway 49. Continue west onto Highway 49 and drive 12.9 miles to the Gold Lake Highway. Turn right and drive 1.3 miles to Packer Lake Road. Turn left and drive 0.3 mile to a junction (straight for Sardine Lake). Turn right (still on Packer Lake Road) and drive 2.6 miles; the Packer Lake turnoff is on the right. To reach the trailhead for the Sierra Buttes, continue straight for 1.9 miles. The paved road then becomes dirt (OK for cars) for 2.7 miles. The signed parking area is on the left at the trailhead.

㉜ Crystal Basin Recreation Area

530/644-2324 | Eldorado National Forest, Placerville District | www.fs.usda.gov

The Crystal Basin Recreation Area is a magical place that fronts the ridge for the Tahoe Basin and Desolation Wilderness. The area gets its name from the high granite slopes and crest, which rise above tree line and look like crystal when covered with frozen snow. The high peaks of the Crystal Range overlook the Tahoe basin and its multitude of lakes. This 1,000-square-mile swath of land provides some of the state's best camping, boating, day hiking, and fishing.

Union Valley Reservoir is the centerpiece of this area, set amid an array of beautiful lakes, big and small, that includes Ice House Reservoir, Wrights Lake, and Loon Lake.

Timing is everything in the outdoors, and so it is at Crystal Basin. On peak summer weekends (July 4-late summer), it seems like every campground is full. After all, the main road in is paved and makes for easy access for any vehicle— just throw your camping gear in the car, pop a kayak on top, and head off. Most folks head to Union Valley, the biggest of the lakes with a variety of lakeside campgrounds plus three boat ramps.

The best season for camping is mid-July-August; campgrounds typically sell out on weekends in summer, so book a site well in advance. The best fishing is early in the season, usually late April for Ice House Reservoir, early May for Union Valley Reservoir, and June for Loon Lake. The whole place is virtually abandoned in fall.

▽ *Ice House Reservoir*

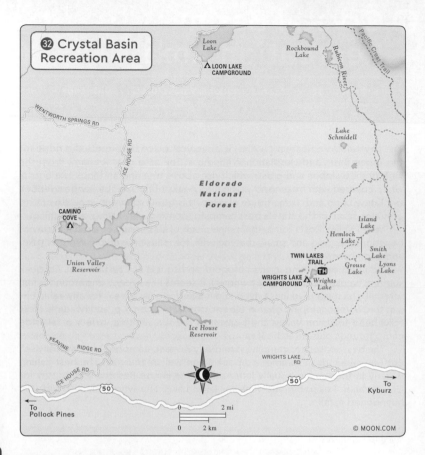

BEST ACTIVITY: FISHING ON UNION VALLEY RESERVOIR

Union Valley Reservoir sits at an elevation of 4,900 feet in the heart of the Crystal Basin. The 3,000-acre lake is in a beautiful area that is the essence of woods and water. There are nine campgrounds and three boat ramps (Jones Fork, West Point, and Yellowjacket). Most folks use one of the campgrounds as a base, then boat, fish, or hike all day. Boating and water sports are popular in summer when the cool, clean water can be refreshing. The reservoir provides good fishing, with some large (but elusive) trout attracting top anglers. The fishing is best just after ice-out in the spring and when cold weather arrives in fall.

In summer, there is often an evening bite for trout at dusk, what we call "The Witching Hour," with an additional short burst at dawn. The few who fish for kokanee salmon troll with downriggers to get into the summer thermocline. There are several feeder streams located up each of the lake's two arms; the fishing is typically better in these areas for all species.

Get away from the boat traffic and find the cooler freshwater entering the lake from its feeder creeks. The rainbow trout always seem reliable here, and you might pick up a nice brown or brook trout while you're at it. Union Valley produces some of the largest Mackinaws in the state (including fish in the 15- to 25-pound range), but it doesn't give up its secrets easily. Fortunately, the Department of Fish and

△ Wrights Lake

Wildlife stocks Union Valley with both rainbow trout and kokanee salmon fingerlings.

BEST OVERNIGHT AT UNION VALLEY: CAMINO COVE

Camino Cove (Placerville Ranger District, 530/644-2324, www.fs.usda. gov/eldorado) has long been my favorite campground at Union Valley Reservoir. The campground is located on a peninsula at the north end of the lake. It's absolutely beautiful, a tree-covered landscape with sweeping views of the Crystal Basin. This is a primitive, do-it-yourself site with no facilities. There are 32 sites for tents or RVs (no hookups). Fire rings are provided, and vault toilets are available. There is no drinking water, and garbage must be packed out. A swimming beach is nearby and a boat ramp is 1.5 miles away at West Point. Some facilities are wheelchair-accessible. Leashed pets are permitted. Reservations are not accepted; all sites are first-come, first-served. There is no fee for camping. Open early May-October.

HIKE WRIGHTS LAKE TO SMITH LAKE

Small and pretty Wrights Lake is situated 25 miles east of Union Valley Reservoir in the Crystal Basin. It's an hour's drive to reach the region's best day hike (or simply camp here instead). A self-service **permit** for day hiking is available at the trailhead.

At the head of Wrights Lake, the **Twin Lakes Trail** (6.2 miles, 3 hours, moderate/difficult) leads 3.1 miles one-way with a 1,700-foot climb to Grouse Lake, Hemlock Lake, and finally Smith Lake, a stunning beauty at 8,700 feet. Despite the relentless climb, this hike is a favorite, with one hit after another from start to finish.

From the trailhead parking area at the end of Wrights Lake Road, the Twin Lakes Trail arcs north past a meadow, then enters a pine and fir forest interspersed with stretches of granite. The trail leads 1.3 miles to the boundary of the Desolation Wilderness and a trail junction. Turn right onto Grouse Lake Trail for the 0.8-mile hike to pretty **Grouse Lake,** a heart-pumping climb.

The lakes get progressively prettier as you go, but the ascent gets

On one trip in the Crystal Basin in late September, I put my canoe in at Loon Lake (nobody was around), then paddled up to Pleasant Lake (still nobody around) and had my pick of any site at the boat-in campground. You don't need to be a billionaire to own a piece of paradise. You just need the right timing and it can be yours.

Loon Lake is the last of the chain of lakes in the Crystal Basin, located at the end of Ice House Road. At the head of Loon Lake, you can launch a kayak and then paddle to the far end of the lake where a peninsula extends left to create an opening through to Pleasant Lake. Pleasant Lake is about one-quarter (600 acres) the size of Loon Lake and is peppered with rocks near its north shore. A boat-in/hike-in **campground** (10 sites, first-come, first-served, www.fs.usda.gov, June-Oct., free) is available midway along the eastern shoreline. (As you head up the lake, look for it on the right past a shoreline point and tucked in a cove.) There is no drinking water, but a compost toilet is available. A campfire permit is required.

Pleasant Lake is a great launch point for wilderness hikes. You can hike four miles —with no kill-me, eat-me climbs—and reach Bucks Island Lake and Rockbound Lakes, located just inside the border of the Desolation Wilderness.

The **Loon Lake Campground** has forested sites and a boat ramp near the south shore of Loon Lake. While there are no lake views, it is private and quiet. There are 53 sites for tents or RVs. Drinking water and vault toilets are available. Some facilities are wheelchair-accessible. Leashed pets are permitted. Reservations (877/444-6777, www.recreation.gov, fee) are accepted. Open mid-June-mid-October.

To reach Loon Lake: From U.S. 50, turn left on Ice House Road and drive 26 miles (route becomes Forest Road 3) to the fork with Loon Lake Road. Turn left and go 3 miles to reach Loon Lake's north shore.

△ Loon Lake

steeper, too. Tiny **Hemlock Lake** (at 2.6 miles) is only 0.5 mile from Grouse Lake and features a spectacular rockslide on one shoreline with scrawny hemlock trees on the other. Gorgeous **Smith Lake** (at 3.1 miles) lies near tree line, a 1,700-foot climb from the trailhead. As you ascend, turn around for views of both Wrights Lake and Ice House Reservoir.

Backpackers can camp at **Grouse Lake;** look for wood posts that indicate designated campsites. Hardier types should head uphill for **Hemlock** and **Smith Lakes.** Smith Lake lies at 8,700 feet and it's a stunner. Note that backpackers must purchase a Desolation Wilderness **permit** (www.recreation.gov) in advance and pick it up at one of four ranger stations before the hike.

BEST OVERNIGHT: WRIGHTS LAKE CAMPGROUND

Wrights Lake Campground (Placerville District, 530/644-2324, www.fs.usda.gov/eldorado) can be your base camp for this hike, with options to kayak, canoe, and swim in 65-acre Wrights Lake. There are 67 sites for tents or RVs (no hookups) and 15 equestrian sites. Picnic tables and fire grills are provided. Drinking water and vault toilets are available. Some facilities are wheelchair-accessible. Leashed pets are permitted.

Reservations (877/444-6777, www.recreation.gov, fee) are accepted and may be required in July and August. Open late June-mid-October.

WHERE TO EAT

After roamin' and ramblin' in the Sierras, brother Rambob found **Bricks Eats & Drinks** (482 Main St., Placerville, 530/303-3480, https://bricksonmainstreet.com, 11am-8:30pm Sun.-Thurs., 11am-9pm Fri.-Sat.) and lassoed me into our first dinner there. What a fun time! The menu spans a broad spectrum, with flavorful salads and entrées, plus plenty of craft brews. (We'd stay away from the fish-and-chips, though.) With all kinds of burgers and beers, Bricks killed it for a couple of hungry cowboys. Bricks Eats & Drinks has a dedicated following among U.S. 50 travelers, and that includes Rambob and me.

DRIVING DIRECTIONS

From Placerville, take U.S. 50 east for 20 miles to the junction with Ice House Road (also called Soda Springs-Riverton Road). To reach Union Valley Reservoir, turn left onto Ice House Road (route becomes Forest Road 3) and drive 16 miles to Union Valley Reservoir on the left.

To reach Wrights Lake: Turn left onto Ice House Road (becomes Forest Road 3) and drive 10.5 miles to the junction with Ice House Road/Wrights Lake Road. Turn right onto Wrights Lake Road. As you approach Wrights Lake, you will pass the Wrights Lake Equestrian Camp and arrive at a junction on the right (still Wrights Lake Road) near the foot of the lake. Turn left and continue on Wrights Lake Road for 1.2 miles to the parking area and trailhead at the head of the lake.

~ Chapter 7 ~

SAN FRANCISCO BAY AREA

In the center of San Francisco Bay, Angel Island offers eye-popping views everywhere you turn. On a bright, blue-sky day, the views stretch across the bay to San Francisco, the Golden Gate Bridge, Alcatraz, and the Marin Headlands. This is the Bay Area's backyard, with an array of first-class getaways that include biking the Perimeter Road, hiking to the top of Mount Livermore, and camping overnight in one of the park's 10 walk-in campgrounds.

Angel Island has a profound history that spans its origin as a site for Native peoples, to a Civil War outpost, and, from 1910-1940, as an immigration center and then a detainment camp for Japanese Americans during World War II.

Nobody gets here by accident—access is only by boat. Scenic ferry rides are available from San Francisco and Tiburon, while private boats and kayaks can dock in Ayala Cove. The views, history, and the adventure just to get here make this a world-class destination regardless of age, background, or outdoor experience. Everyone is drawn by the chance of magical moments in this spectacular setting.

The ferry runs daily Apr.-Oct. and on weekends only Nov.-Mar. It's best to visit spring through fall.

▽ *My wife Denese takes in the view of the Golden Gate Bridge from Angel Island.*

BEST ACTIVITY:
BIKE THE PERIMETER TRAIL

The **Perimeter Trail** (5 miles) is a service road that rings Angel Island and offers fantastic views via an easy bike ride.

Visitors can bring a bike on the ferry or rent a mountain bike near the ferry landing at Ayala Cove. The **bike rental shed** (415/435-3392, http:// angelisland.com, $15/hour or $60/ day) is on the left, facing the shore from the dock.

Start by biking past the **visitors center** and then turn left. From here, it's a short climb up a few switchbacks to the Perimeter Road. Ride the loop counterclockwise as it undulates through a series of small hills and drops. The first stop is **Camp Reynolds,**

a Civil War-era barracks with a great view of the Golden Gate Bridge. The road then passes above Point Blunt as it points toward San Francisco for a fantastic view of the city waterfront and high-rises. Bear left, passing Fort McDowell and the East Garrison; a gorgeous and secluded beach is hidden in a cove below the garrison. The road continues on the loop past the **U.S. Immigration Station** (open Wed.-Sun., tours available, 415/435-5537) and China Cove with views of the East Bay waterfront and foothills before turning back to Ayala Cove. Along the way, benches sit perched at lookouts, and the views, of course, are sensational. The bench with the best view of the Golden Gate Bridge is inscribed with the words "Live The Life You Love."

INSIDER'S TIP

The first time I kayaked to Angel Islands was for a show on CBS. We launched from Sea Trek Beach in Sausalito and paddled over to Angel Island, then we climbed Mount Livermore for a boat-and-hike adventure. It was such an electric experience that I've repeated it several times since. Now you can do it too.

To kayak to Angel Island, choose a day when the forecast calls for light winds and the difference between high and low tides is benign (which means there is little tidal surge). The trip starts from Sausalito with a paddle across Richardson Bay, a trip that is easy, flat, and fast. As you emerge from Richardson Bay, you'll enter the big waters of San Francisco Bay with a crossing of Raccoon Strait. (Stay clear of the

△ colorful kayaks on the bay

ferryboats and the freighters.) On a calm day, it's a euphoric paddle to the west-facing shore of Angel Island. Turn left and parallel the shore into Ayala Cove for one of the best boat-and-hike adventures anywhere.

Trail notes: Cyclists age 18 and under must wear helmets. Bikes rentals are due back by 3pm weekdays and 3:30pm weekends. Bikes are not permitted on the North Ridge Trail to the Mount Livermore summit.

HIKE MOUNT LIVERMORE

The hike to the top of **Mount Livermore** (4.5 miles, 2 hours) provides one of the best urban views in the state. From the ferry landing at Ayala Cove, walk to the visitors center for a park map and brochure. Then follow the Perimeter Road for a short distance to the junction with the **Sunset Trail.** Turn left and climb a series of graded switchbacks up the south flank of Summit Ridge. After about two miles, you will reach a junction with the **North Ridge Trail.**

Turn here and climb the final push to emerge at the top at 788 feet. The big views include Golden Gate Bridge, San Francisco waterfront, Marin Headlands, Raccoon Strait, Sausalito, Bay Bridge, East Bay hills, and Alcatraz.

BEST OVERNIGHT: ANGEL ISLAND CAMPGROUNDS

Angel Island has four walk-in campgrounds and each is unique. On the east side of the island, the **East Bay** and **Sunrise** sites feature pretty sunrises and protection from wind, and offer the shortest route to the top of Mount Livermore. On the west side of the island, the exposed **Ridge** sites enjoy night views of the Golden

△ *view of the Golden Gate Bridge from Angel Island*

Gate Bridge. Also on the west side is the **Kayak Camp** boat-in site, which accommodates groups. There are 10 campsites total in the park.

From the Ayala Cove ferry landing, reaching the campsites requires a walk of 1-2 miles. Campers must bring and carry all gear with them to their campsite (most treat it like a mini-backpacking trip). It's a dream to be camping wilderness-style in the middle of an urban center of eight million people. At night, bring a flashlight and hike to the top of Mount Livermore on a dark, moonless night. The lights of the Golden Gate Bridge against the black night sky look magical. At each turn, the city's prominent landmarks are lit and glowing like the Emerald City.

Picnic tables, barbecues, and food lockers are provided. Drinking water, pit toilets, and garbage service is available. Wood campfires are not permitted; only charcoal is allowed. Some facilities are wheelchair-accessible.

Reservations (800/444-7275, www.reservecalifornia.com, fee) are accepted and can fill six months in advance. Campers must show reservation vouchers to the ferryboat operator and then check in at the Ayala Cove kiosk (415/435-5390). Open year-round.

WHERE TO EAT

The **Angel Island Café** (Ayala Cove, 415/435-3392, www.angelisland.com, open daily Apr.-Oct., hours vary) is like a miniature United Nations—you'll meet and hear visitors from around the world here. The chicken Caesar salad is a 10, done exactly right and by the book. Rare for a state park, beer, wine, and dessert are all included on the full menu, an unexpected bonus.

DIRECTIONS

Ferry trips to Angel Island are available year-round out of Tiburon and San Francisco.

Tiburon: The **Angel Island Tiburon Ferry** (415/435-2131, www.angelisland-ferry.com, $15 round-trip) provides daily service from Tiburon April-October and on weekends November-March. Purchase tickets onboard (cash only) for the 12-minute ferry ride.

To get to Tiburon, cross the Golden Gate Bridge north on U.S. 101. In Marin, take exit 447 for Highway 131 toward Tiburon Boulevard/East Blithedale

CAMPFIRE STORIES

*L*owe Shee Miu first set foot on Angel Island in 1928. She had arrived from China to start a new life with her husband in America. She was 17 years old, pregnant with her first child, and didn't speak a word of English. Some 70 years later, Low Shee shared her memories with two of her children, Lily Au, 64, and Victoria Lowe, 68, and her granddaughter, Patty Au. Patty and her husband, Paul Sakuma, have been close friends of mine for nearly 40 years.

I spent a day at Angel Island with Patty, and she shared her family history with me. She told me how Low Shee Miu was detained at Angel Island (then known as "The Ellis Island of the West") and eventually released to join her husband in Oakland. Their descendants, the "three generations of Mius," as Patty calls them, all became educated, employed in a variety of professions, and are now raising new generations of Americans. Her return to Angel Island was part of an unofficial gathering she called an "homage to our ancestors."

Avenue. Drive east for 0.3 mile to Tiburon Boulevard/Highway 131. Turn right on Tiburon Boulevard and drive 4.3 miles to the Tiburon Ferry. Pay parking lots are on the left.

San Francisco: The **Blue & Gold Fleet** (Pier 41, 415/773-1188, www.blueandgoldfleet.com, $10 round-trip) provides service from downtown San Francisco daily. Ferry tickets are available online; reservations are not required. The ride to Angel Island takes about 25 minutes; the return ride is 45 minutes.

It's also possible to connect to Pier 41 from the East Bay. The **San Francisco Bay Ferry** (415/773-1188, www.sanfranciscobayferry.com) provides service from Alameda (Main Street), Oakland (Jack London Square), and Vallejo.

Big Basin Redwoods State Park is a forested basin in the heart of the Santa Cruz Mountains. It extends west over ridges and down canyons to emerge along Waddell Creek and out to the coast at Rancho del Oso.

This is one of the best state parks in California for year-round camping and hiking. For most, the centerpiece of the park's 18,000 acres and 80 miles of trails is the hike to Berry Creek Falls, a 10.5-mile round-trip hike that passes three waterfalls: Berry Creek Falls, Silver Falls, and Golden Falls. One of my favorite spots on Earth is the brink of the Silver cascade, where you can reach out and touch the passing water, then turn and walk a few steps to the final chute of the Golden cascade where white water flows over golden sandstone.

Big Basin is also the center cut for the 34-mile Skyline-to-the-Sea Trail, which spans Castle Rock State Park through Big Basin Redwoods to Rancho del Oso. It's a great one-way hike (with a shuttle) and a world-class backpacking trek in winter, when the waterfalls are flush and other mountain destinations are locked up by snow.

There's a moment of irony at Big Basin Redwoods State Park. On weekends, the parking lot fills and it can seem like people are everywhere within a mile radius of the park headquarters (see *Insider's Tip*). As hikers disperse into the park's giant old-growth redwoods, the waterfalls, ridgetop views, and trail camps begin to emerge and the numbers of people lessen, providing some of the best backpacking around.

Same park, two worlds.

▽ *Berry Creek Falls*

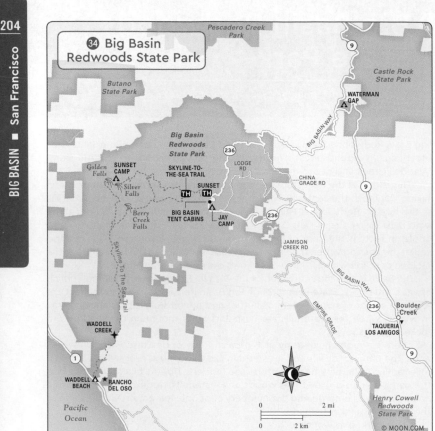

BEST ACTIVITY: BERRY CREEK FALLS

The hike to **Berry Creek Falls** (12.5 miles round-trip, 5–6 hours) and its succession of waterfalls is one of the prettiest spots in California. From the main parking lot across from the park headquarters, walk west past an amphitheater to the trail along Opal Creek. Turn right and walk a short distance to a bridge; cross over and walk upstream to the **Sunset Trail** (on the left). Follow the Sunset Trail as it climbs out from the basin floor amid big redwoods. After crossing the Middle Ridge Fire Road, cruise downhill for a short distance to the **Sunset Connector Trail.** Turn left as the trail leads down past the headwaters of

Kelly Creek and to the **Skyline-to-the-Sea Trail.** From here, it's a nice, easy cruise down to Waddell Creek Canyon and Berry Creek. A signed right turn leads a short distance to **Berry Creek Falls** and a viewing platform. Berry Creek Falls is a 70-foot waterfall framed by a canyon and complete with ferns, redwoods, and the sound of rushing water. Even when the flows are reduced to a trickle, it is still a gorgeous mosaic of silver water across the rock face.

A mile upstream from Berry Creek Falls is **Silver Falls,** a 60-foot free fall. The trail is cut into the sidewall of the plunge basin and rises up to the brink. At the brink, rock steps are cut into the canyon, with a woven wire safety rail. Just upstream past the brink is the final cascade of **Golden Falls,** which looks like a giant waterslide. One of the golden cascades looks like a miniature Aztec temple (my brother Rambob calls it Aztec Falls).

Continue ahead as the trail climbs to a service road near **Sunset Camp.** (Do not miss the right turn off the service road to Sunset Trail.) From here, the Sunset Trail meanders through a remote section of the park, in and out of chaparral and forest, before looping back into redwoods and returning to park headquarters.

Trail notes: Heavy rains have plundered a section of the Skyline-to-the-Sea Trail, with slides and hundreds of downed redwoods across the route. It may never be reclaimed. A detour is in place to get you around it.

BACKPACK THE SKYLINE-TO-THE-SEA TRAIL

The **Skyline-to-the-Sea Trail** (31.6 miles one-way, 3 days) is one of the most worshipped trails in the Bay Area, complete with primitive trail camps. Whenever we hike it, we always start with a group high five and then shout, "Down!" That is because you start at Castle Rock State Park at 3,000 feet and then drop all the way down to the

sea. You get fantastic views, redwood forests, waterfalls, and trail camps. (In winter, there are no services.)

Day 1: Waterman Gap
(9.6 miles)

From the trailhead at Castle Rock State Park, take the Saratoga Gap Trail to the Waterman Gap trail camp (water is available) for a first-day hike of 9.6 miles. In the first 2 miles, you will cross an open rock face that leads past the foot of Goat Rock. As the landscape opens up, you get fantastic views of Big Basin and Monterey Bay. You then drop down into the forested headwaters of the San Lorenzo River, pass an old homestead, and continue through mixed forest. Camp at Waterman Gap.

Day 2: Jay Camp
(9.5 miles)

The logical plan for the second day is to hike 9.5 miles from Waterman Gap to Jay Camp at Big Basin headquarters. Once you cross Highway 9, you will pass the boundary for Big Basin Redwoods. For a few miles the route roughly parallels the park's access road. Then it breaks off, passes an open sandstone face with great westerly views, traces a narrow ridge, and drops into a lush

△ *Waddell Beach, end of the Skyline-to-the-Sea Trail*

redwood canyon with a stream. Only Skyline-to-the-Sea hikers typically travel this area, so by seeing this landscape you join a select club. Eventually the trail emerges at the bottom of Big Basin and you camp at Jay Camp, near park headquarters. Although this camp is not a backcountry experience, the convenience of restrooms, coin showers, drinking water, and a small store is well received.

Day 3: Waddell Beach
(12.5 miles)

On the last day, you face a hike of 12.5 miles from park headquarters to the finish. Start by heading out of the basin floor amid giant redwoods, following the trail description for the hike to Berry Creek Falls. After taking in the waterfalls, the Skyline-to-the-Sea Trail heads west to the coast. It's a breeze as you cross over Waddell Creek on several temporary bridges (usually installed in late April). The trail widens onto a service road and passes several trail camps. Arrive at the coast, where you have a vehicle parked, and share a moment of exultation with your hiking partners: You have completed one of the great coastal backpack trips in California.

BEST OVERNIGHT: BIG BASIN TENT CABINS

Your best bet for a good night's sleep is in one of the 36 tent cabins in Big Basin's Huckleberry Loop, about a mile from headquarters. Each tent cabin comes with a wood-burning stove, a seating area, and a padded platform for sleeping (bring linens or sleeping bag and a pillow).

The park also has multiple campgrounds, with 31 sites for tents or RVs, 67 sites for tents only, 36 walk-in sites, two bike-in sites, 40 hike-in sites, and four group sites within the park. Picnic tables, food lockers, and fire grills are provided. Drinking water, pit toilets, restrooms with flush toilets and coin showers, a dump station, firewood, and groceries are available. Some facilities are wheelchair-accessible. Leashed pets are allowed in campsites and on paved roads.

Reservations (800/444-7275) are accepted for the tent cabins. Campground reservations can be made online (www.reservecalifornia.com, fee). Open year-round.

WHERE TO EAT

At age 91, my dad's last trip to Big Basin Redwoods was topped off when he picked **Taqueria Los Amigos** (13070 Hwy. 9, Boulder Creek, 9am-9pm daily) for dinner. Whenever he ordered the chile relleno, no matter how hard he tried, he always mangled the pronunciation. We loved him for that. The tacos are also awesome (get them with the verde sauce), but be sure grab some extra napkins to clean up afterwards. The place may not look like much, but we've always hit the bull's-eye here.

DRIVING DIRECTIONS

From the coast: From Half Moon Bay, take Highway 1 south for 50 miles to Santa Cruz. At the junction with Highway 9/River Street, turn left onto Highway 9 and drive 12 miles to Boulder Creek. At the stoplighted intersection with Highway 236/Big Basin Way, turn left and drive 9.9 miles north to Big Basin Redwoods (park on left). A state park entrance fee is charged.

From the south: From the South Bay, take Highway 85 north to the exit for Saratoga Avenue. Take that exit for 0.3 mile, turning west on Saratoga Avenue. Drive 1.9 miles into Saratoga (the road becomes Big Basin Way). Continue on Big Basin Way (which becomes Highway 9; continue straight across Skyline/Highway 35) for 13.4 miles to Highway 236 on the right. (RVs and trailers not advised; continue to Boulder Creek). Bear right on Highway 236 and drive 8.2 miles on the narrow, twisty road to the parking lot on the on right. Park headquarters are on the left.

INSIDER'S TIP

As in love, timing is everything. The best time to hike to the Big Basin Red-woods waterfalls is **mid-March-late April,** when the stream flows are high, the waterfalls are flush, and longer days offer more sunlight hours. Others prefer the warm days of **May, June, and July,** when the temporary bridge over Waddell Creek is up and they can hike the Skyline-to-the-Sea Trail. Families fill the campgrounds and tent cabins on **summer weekends** (late May-early Sept.), when an advance reservation is a necessity.

A wildcard is **winter:** Trail use is low and the campgrounds are wide open (if a bit wet). I once convinced the district superintendent to open the trail camps in winter (minimum-impact, pack-it-in, pack-it-out), and even with the shorter days, cold nights, and likely rain, it is my favorite time to visit. There's no people, a pristine landscape, and vibrant waterfalls.

The best way to **avoid the crowds** at Big Basin? Bike and hike to Berry Creek Falls in reverse. Start from the coastal outpost at **Rancho Del Oso** (Hwy. 1, 18.6 miles north of Santa Cruz). From here, the round-trip trek to Berry Creek Falls is 15 miles; 12 miles by mountain bike and 3 miles on foot. At Rancho del Oso, the ride starts out easy and flat on the Skyline-to-the-Sea Trail. The trail then rises and falls over a series of short hills and, 6 miles in, you'll arrive at a bike rack. Lock your bike up here, then hike 0.5 mile to Berry Creek Falls. You can continue 1 mile up the canyon to Silver Falls and the Golden Cascade.

When my son Kris was 11, we did this bike-and-hike as his first major trek. I still savor the moment.

△ a section of the Golden Cascade

A few years ago, an editor asked me to rate my favorite Bay Area parks. Since I've been to them all, I created a system: I rated 275 recreation destinations in 10 categories and graded each category 1–10. When I added up the results, Del Valle Regional Park came in No. 2 (just behind Point Reyes National Seashore).

This is why: You can fish, boat, camp, hike, bike, swim, and picnic, and most of it is top-shelf.

Del Valle Reservoir is set in a long, deep canyon in remote southern Alameda County and covers 750 acres with 16 miles of shoreline. This is one of the few lakes in the Bay Area that provides camping with lake views, a small marina with rental boats, and a boat ramp. An excellent mountain bike ride starts north of the marina and runs along the lake. Two swimming beaches are located near campgrounds, and are popular in summer. A trailhead near the Lichen Bark Picnic Area provides access to the Ohlone Wilderness Trail and Rocky Ridge. The trail spans 28 miles through the Sunol Wilderness and past Mission Peak, with overnight camps available. The park spans nearly 5,000 acres, and with the adjacent Sunol-Ohlone Wilderness, Mission Peak, and watershed lands, it is one of the biggest contiguous wildland areas in any metropolitan area in America.

▽ *Del Valle Regional Park*

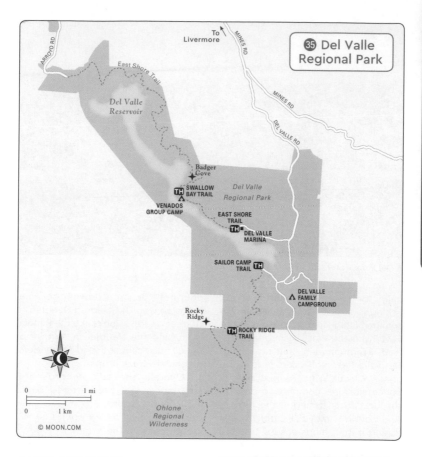

㉟ Del Valle Regional Park

To Livermore

East Shore Trail

Del Valle Reservoir

MINES RD

MINES RD

DEL VALLE RD

ARROYO RD

Badger Cove

TH SWALLOW BAY TRAIL

VENADOS GROUP CAMP

Del Valle Regional Park

EAST SHORE TRAIL
TH DEL VALLE MARINA

SAILOR CAMP TRAIL **TH**

DEL VALLE FAMILY CAMPGROUND

Rocky Ridge

TH ROCKY RIDGE TRAIL

0   1 mi
0   1 km

© MOON.COM

Ohlone Regional Wilderness

BEST ACTIVITY: BOATING AND FISHING

Del Valle Reservoir is one of the best lakes for boating in the Bay Area; the five-mile lake is big enough for everybody. The small **Del Valle Marina** (925/449-5201, www.rocky-mountainrec.com, last boat rented at 4:45pm, rates vary) has a boat ramp and rents boats with motors as well as fishing boats with steering wheels, party-style pontoon boats, rowboats, and canoes and pedal boats (Apr.-Oct. only). Or bring your own boat (all boats must be certified dry and mussel-free) and launch. Personal watercraft or fast boats with tubers, wakeboarders, or water-skiers are not allowed, and a 10-mph limit keeps it

△ *a fisherman holding a giant 13.5-pound largemouth bass caught at Lake Del Valle*

△ *Del Valle Reservoir*

calm for low-speed sports. Kayak fishing is popular, as is swimming in summer. Lifeguards are posted at the East Swim and West Swim beaches.

Fall through winter and into spring, Del Valle Reservoir takes part in the annual "Trout Wars," where several concessionaires compete to provide the best trout fishing in the region. And trout is what you'll catch. A daily fishing permit helps ensure that the lake is stocked about every week.

I have several favorite spots.

When using bait, I anchor at the head of the lake on the eastern edge of the historic river channel. With a depth finder, scan the lake bottom until you find the river channel, where the bottom drops off a submerged ledge. The edge of this ledge is the best fishing spot. I use a two-hook rig, Power Nuggets, and a nightcrawler for bait. This is your best bet for a chance at the five-trout limits.

For the big fish, I troll offshore of Swallow Bay. After launching from the marina, turn right. You will pass a shoreline point that extends well into the lake on your right; just beyond is Swallow Bay. Approach the dam on the right (the corners of the dam are off-limits). What works best is to troll a gold/black jointed Rapala (15–20 feet

deep) set up on a downrigger line behind a Cop Car-colored Needlefish (10 feet deep). It looks like the Rapala is chasing the Needlefish. With this trick, I once caught 5- and 7-pounders on back-to-back drops.

Overall, the lake records are amazing: A 40-pound striped bass, a 30-pound catfish, a 17-pound rainbow trout, and a 14½-pound largemouth bass. In the summer months, the water warms and the trout fishing slows. Bass, catfish, and bluegill offer the best fishing until October.

HIKE THE OHLONE TRAIL TO ROCKY RIDGE

The trek to 2,426-foot **Rocky Ridge** (4.8 miles round-trip, 3 hours) is a hate-love hike: First you hate, then you love.

The trailhead for the Ohlone Trail is located near the Lichen Bark Picnic Area (past the campgrounds near the southwest shore of the lake). From the picnic area, walk about one mile south on the Sailor Camp Trail to the sign-in box near the trailhead. This sign-in is your **day-hike permit**.

The hike starts out easy on a service road through oak woodlands with some steep "butt-kicker" stretches

INSIDER'S TIP

If this is your first trip, get a good feel for Del Valle by mountain-biking along the **East Shore Trail** (3.6 miles round-trip), a great, easy bike trail. The East Shore Trail trailhead is located north of the boat launch. It follows a service road along the east side of the lake with gorgeous views for 1.8 miles to Venados Group Camp.

At Venados Group Camp, you can turn right on the **Swallow Bay Trail** (10 miles) for a more challenging ride—a rhythmic climb up around Badger Cove followed by a drop to Swallow Bay. There are several places to stop and catch your breath and take in the pretty lake views. The trail continues north, venturing inland for a spell with rises, drops, and more rises, before descending to Heron Bay with just enough hills and views to spike your interest.

Bicycle rentals are available at **Livermore Cyclery** (2752 1st St., Livermore, 925/455–8090, www.livermorecyclery.com, 9:30am-6pm Mon.-Sat., 10am-5pm Sun.).

△ *East Shore Trail*

that will let you know what kind of hiking condition you are in. The trail climbs 1,700 feet over 2.4 miles; one 1.5-mile stretch has a 1,600-foot ascent, with most of the climb in direct sun. If you hike it on a hot day, this is all hate, no love. Instead, pick a cool spring morning, best in the years after a wet winter, when the bright sun hits the saturated soils.

When you finally emerge atop Rocky Ridge, take an east-facing seat for a spectacular view across Del Valle Reservoir below and across to Cedar Mountain and the southern flank of the Diablo Range. When ready, turn west toward Wauhab Ridge. In perfect years, with saturated soils and a hot afternoon sun, the goldfields here can span miles, one of the best blooms in California.

BEST OVERNIGHT: DEL VALLE FAMILY CAMPGROUND

Lakeside campsites are so rare in the San Francisco Bay Area that Del Valle's campgrounds have great appeal and are in high demand. **Del Valle Family Campground** has 150 sites for tents or RVs (including some with full or partial hookups) and four equestrian sites. There are two types of campsites: Phase 2 sites are in an open area close to the water; the more wooded Phase 4 sites are inland. There are also two walk-in group sites, as well as seven cabins available for rent. Picnic tables and fire grills are provided. Drinking water, restrooms with showers and flush toilets, a dump station, a marina, boat rentals, seasonal campfire programs, swimming beaches, and a boat launch are available. Some facilities are wheelchair-accessible. Leashed pets are permitted.

Reservations (888/327–2757, www.reserveamerica.com, fee) are accepted. Open year-round.

WHERE TO EAT

A lot of people are liable to drive right on by **South Smokin' BBQ** (2271 S. Vasco Rd., Livermore, 510/940-3929, noon-7:30pm Fri.-Sat., noon-6pm Sun.), and that's a shame. South Smokin' serves the kind of mouth-watering Texas-style barbecue that's perfect after a day on the lake or on the trail. Choose from tri-tip, pulled pork, chicken, or ribs with all the fixins', pulled right off the grill and presented in a clamshell container.

There's an unspoken bond that you never mess with another guy's barbecue. The best suggestion is to stand back and let owner Tim do his thing. You can't go wrong.

DRIVING DIRECTIONS

From I-580 in Livermore, take exit 52A for Portola Avenue/North Livermore Avenue and drive a short distance to Portola Avenue. Turn left and drive 0.8 mile to North Livermore Avenue. Turn right onto North Livermore Avenue and drive 2.5 miles through downtown Livermore. The road veers left becoming Tesla Avenue; continue 0.5 mile east to Mines Road. Turn right onto Mines Road and drive 3.5 miles south to Del Valle Road. Continue straight on Del Valle Road (Mines Road veers left) and drive 3.1 miles south to the **park entrance** (7000 Del Valle Rd., Livermore, 7am-6pm daily, $6 parking) and **visitors center** (9am-6:30pm Sat.-Sun. June-Sept.).

Pay the entry fee at the kiosk, then drive a short distance to a fork. At the fork, turn right for the marina and boat ramp or turn left for the campsites and swimming beaches.

CAMPFIRE STORIES

*O*ne spring we held a "Fish With Tom" contest where we took young-sters out for their first fishing trip. We had about 4–5 kids on the boat, which was anchored at the head of Del Valle Reservoir. In order to have enough fishing rods, I had to borrow my son Jeremy's trout rod—it was his first rod, the one I gave him when he was a boy.

During the contest, I looked over and saw a six-year-old boy getting a bite. The kid looked shocked, then confused, and then he threw the fishing rod—Jeremy's fishing rod—into the lake, where it sank to the bottom.

I cast out many times to try to snag it, but came up with zilch. Then I tried to troll to snag it and came up empty, too. What would I tell Jeremy?

After the fish stopped biting, we moved about a quarter mile down the lake. About two hours later, another eight-year-old started acting like he had a monster on the line. It took forever to get it in. As the kid reeled in the line . . . there was Jeremy's lost fishing rod! On the line was the fish that had apparently dragged the rod a quarter mile to our new spot. It seemed unbelievable, but a trout had brought that rod home.

△ *fishing at Del Valle Reservoir*

36 Los Vaqueros Reservoir

925/371-2628 | Brentwood and Livermore |
www.ccwater.com/losvaqueros

You could search across the country and not find another place like the Los Vaqueros watershed. This is some of the fastest-developing wildland habitat, with an enormous carrying capacity of food, shelter, and water to support the region's fish and wildlife. Yet the watershed has plenty of recreation options for people, too, with 55 miles of hiking trails and service roads that include 12.5 miles of mountain biking and equestrian trails.

At the center of this fish and wildlife paradise is the Los Vaqueros Reservoir, the largest lake in the San Francisco Bay Area. Its rich aquatic food chain supports trout, striped bass, largemouth bass, and many other species of fish. I took a survey with three of the state's most traveled anglers: Dan Bacher of the Fish Sniffer, Bill Karr of *Western Outdoor News,* and Bob Simms of KFBK-1530-Radio. They picked Los Vaqueros Reservoir as the No. 1 up-and-coming fishing lake in California (Bacher picked it No. 1 overall).

Surrounding the gorgeous lake are 20,000 acres of emerald grasslands, rolling amber foothills, and thick oak woodlands home to sensational numbers of migratory golden and bald eagles (in winter) and hawks, falcons, kites, and owls year-round.

The best time to visit is late winter-early spring, when the hills are green, the views from the trail are clear, the lake levels are high, the trout fishing is at its best, and the numbers of migratory raptors are at their highest.

▽ *Los Vaqueros Reservoir*

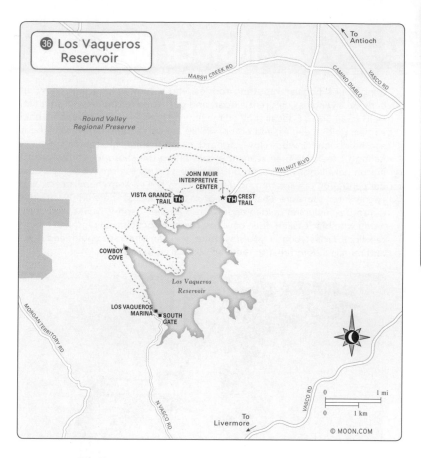

36 Los Vaqueros Reservoir

BEST ACTIVITY: FISHING

A rich aquatic food chain, high stocks of trout, catfish, largemouth bass, and bluegill, and a steady inflow of striped bass pumped in with the water from the Delta ensure long-term fishing greatness. The marina rents boats for three activities: fishing, wildlife-viewing, and scenic touring. No water sports or personal boats are permitted on the lake.

The best fishing is out of the South Gate (Vasco Road near Livermore), where a marina and two fishing piers are located at the south end of the reservoir.

The best fishing is for trout in late winter and spring. I like to use bait (like Power Nuggets) at South Cove, Oak Point, or Cowboy Cove. The lake has high water clarity, which makes using lightweight, low-visibility line a must (for trout, I use 6-pound ultra-green and 4-pound fluorocarbon leaders).

In the fall (Sept.-Nov.), fishing for striped bass can be sensational. Schools of striped bass will chase baitfish on the surface; it's possible to catch-and-release 20, 30, or more stripers in a siege. Troll Hair Raiser-style or Worm-Tail jigs, and then, when you get a bite, stop and cast to the school. Advanced fly fishers with silver streamers can have a ball with scads of 15- to 18-inch stripers.

The **Los Vaqueros Marina** (9990 Los Vaqueros Rd., Byron, daily trout permit) sells fishing permits and rents several styles of boats. The king of the fleet are the 16-footers with electric

INSIDER'S TIP

Bring your binoculars, spotting scopes, and a camera lens, then show up early on a windless day, rent a boat, and get ready for the time of your life. Field scout Steve Goodall showed me how he mastered **photographing** bald eagles, golden eagles, and other wildlife at Los Vaqueros. He rents a boat and heads into Cowboy Cove, or north of the marina, into the West Fork of Kellogg Creek. He then scans the oaks along the shore for eagles perching on bare limbs or peering out from nests. This region has the greatest concentration of wintering golden eagles in the western hemisphere, and each winter, there are a half dozen or so active nests. There are 19 varieties of raptors, including golden eagles, bald eagles, osprey, hawks, and owls, along with black-tailed deer, coyotes, foxes, bobcats, wild pigs, and mountain lions. From a boat, if you stay quiet, you can often see eagles and deer, and remain a non-threat to them as you watch the show.

△ osprey at Los Vaqueros

motors that look like jet drives. They are far more powerful than your typical electric motor.

In the spring and early summer, the conditions are marginal due to high winds that howl through the valley. The marina may put a wind-hold on all rentals until calmer, safer conditions prevail.

HIKE THE VISTA GRANDE TRAIL

The best hiking is out of the North Gate on the **Vista Grande Trail** (2.6-mile loop, 1.5 hours). First stop at the **John Muir Interpretive Center** (19 Walnut Blvd., Brentwood, 9am-4pm Sat.-Sun.) where you can park, use the restrooms, and pick up a trail map. Start at the trailhead for the Crest Trail, which ascends 1.2 steep miles west to a ridge merging onto the Vista Grande Trail. Turn left and hike south toward the Los Vaqueros Dam. Your payoff is a spectacular panorama across the reservoir. The views extend across the adjoining Morgan Territory and beyond to the flank of Mount Diablo.

△ *Mount Diablo as seen from the summit of Round Valley Regional Preserve*

To complete the loop, descend about 1.5 miles east, past the dam, to return to the John Muir Interpretive Center.

BEST OVERNIGHT: ROUND VALLEY REGIONAL PRESERVE

One of the Bay Area's least-known backpacking trail camps is in adjacent **Round Valley Regional Preserve** (19450 Marsh Creek Rd., Brentwood, 888/327-2757, 8am-5pm, free). From the Marsh Creek staging area on Marsh Creek Road, it's a 3.6-mile (one-way) hike to the tent-only sites. Amenities include picnic tables and a restroom. Bring your own drinking water or a water filter (non-potable water is on-site).

Backpacking reservations must be made at least five days in advance. For information or reservations, contact the **East Bay Regional Park District** (888/327–2757, option 2, www.ebparks. org, 8:30am-4pm Mon.-Fri.).

WHERE TO EAT

Livermore is not exactly in the wilderness, but for an hour or two at the **First Street Alehouse** (2106 1st St., Livermore, 925/371–6588, 11am-11:30pm Mon.-Wed., 11am-midnight Thurs.-Fri., 9am-midnight Sat., 8:30am-10:30pm Sun.) you can feel like you've left at least some of the world behind. The interior of the brewpub is open and woodsy with high ceilings and a huge collection of more than 6,000 beer cans lined along a high shelf. That enthusiastic spirit extends to the 28 beers on tap and the constantly rotating elixirs available. The menu includes high-quality burgers and the usual fried fare, as well as an array of salads for those yearning for something healthier.

DRIVING DIRECTIONS

To reach the South Gate: From I-580 in Livermore, take the exit for Vasco Road (east of Livermore). On North Vasco Road, drive 4.5 miles into the hills to Los Vaqueros Road at the crest. Turn left and drive to the South Gate entrance ($6/vehicle) and park at the marina.

To reach the North Gate: In Antioch, take Highway 4 east and merge left onto the Brentwood Bypass. Continue on the bypass (past Oakley and Brentwood) to Walnut Boulevard. Turn right on Walnut Boulevard and drive one mile to the entrance gate ($6/vehicle). Park at the John Muir Interpretive Center.

CAMPFIRE STORIES

M any of the best wildlife encounters are a surprise. So it was for us at Los Vaqueros. On one fall trip, we rented a boat and trolled out from Cowboy Cove, heading toward the dam adjacent to the shoreline. We'd hook up (often with a little guy, a 14- to 15-incher) and stop the boat, then pull out our casting rods and fly rods. We'd cast to the school, using Worm-Tails, Ratteltraps, and large blue/silver Kastmasters, and even sail out a Blanton-tied streamer with a No. 7 fly rod, rigged with sink-tip line. We'd catch-and-release.

In an intuitive moment, I felt a shadow, looked up, and saw a bald eagle sail right overhead. The eagle had sighted the same school of small stripers that we were casting to. It sailed down with its talons forward and, without slowing, plucked a 12-inch striped bass out of the water. Just as fast, the eagle sailed off to perch in an oak along the shore. I pulled out my binoculars and watched that eagle eat the whole fish one beakful at a time.

For us, it was a magical encounter. For the eagle, it was just another day of living at Los Vaqueros.

△ bald eagle in flight at Los Vaqueros

The flanks of Montara Mountain span from the San Mateo coast at Moss Beach east across the ridge to San Bruno and Woodside, and from Pacifica south to Half Moon Bay. The mountain rises 1,898 feet to tower over one of the largest contiguous urban wildlands in the nation: San Pedro Valley County Park in Pacifica, Sweeney Ridge, the 23,000-acre Crystal Springs watershed, McNee Ranch, Rancho Corral de Tierra, and miles of greenbelt.

I lived at the foot of Montara Mountain for 15 years and have climbed it perhaps 1,000 times from every direction. I've explored every road, trail, and route, including the adjacent off-limits Crystal Springs watershed. (In my novel, The Sweet Redemption, I used a hidden concrete bunker as the site of a crime. Some locals got a smile out of that.)

More than anywhere, this is the place I go to find peace, world-class views, and one of the best hikes in the Bay Area. On virtually any weekday morning, I can find a trail without another soul.

The best time to visit is any time—it's good year-round—but it's different in each season. During the first warm days of spring, the air is clear and the views north from San Pedro Ridge are spectacular. When the summertime fog takes over the coast, you can hike up Montara Mountain and emerge 1,200 feet above the fog line into bright blue skies. In fall, the days are warm with excellent clarity. And in winter, Brooks Falls starts to flow. After a heavy rain, the waterfall turns into a five-deck stream for a day or two.

▽ *en route to the trailhead for the Montara Mountain Trail*

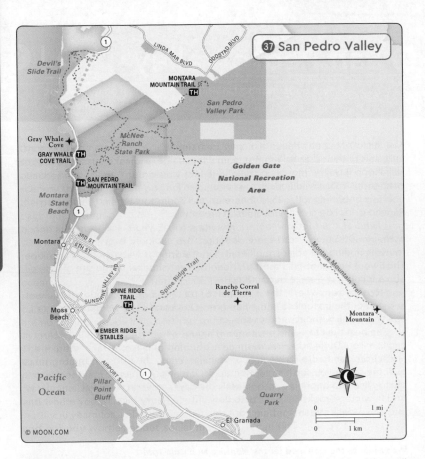

37 San Pedro Valley

BEST ACTIVITY: MONTARA MOUNTAIN TRAIL

You can carve your own personal slice of heaven on the **Montara Mountain Trail** (7 miles round-trip, 3 hours). The trailhead is on the southwest side of the parking lot in San Pedro Valley Park. From the signed trailhead, hike 1.3 miles uphill through a eucalyptus grove to the junction with the Brooks Creek Trail (you'll take this trail on the way back).

Continue hiking 0.4 mile southwest on the Montara Mountain Trail as it rises above tree line to a spur (which leads a short distance to a rock outcrop along San Pedro Ridge for a sensational coastal view north).

At the top of a sub-ridge, the trail enters McNee Ranch State Park. Turn left to follow Montara Mountain Road, a service road, southeast for the final 1.1-mile push to the 1,898-foot summit.

△ *Gray Whale Cove*

△ *view from the trail out of McNee Ranch to Montara Mountain*

(There's a fenced antenna station off to the side.)

Atop the actual pinnacle, the views are absolutely stunning in all directions. On a clear spring day, you can see across the Pacific Ocean to the Farallon Islands and into miles of the adjacent Crystal Springs watershed. Look downslope to the southeast for a glimpse of gorgeous Pilarcitos Lake.

For the return trip, hike back down the service road and turn right onto Montara Mountain Trail. At the fork with the Brooks Creek Trail, bear right. In 0.7 mile, look south across the gorge for Brooks Falls, a connected series of narrow, silver-tasseled waterfall tiers in a chaparral-covered canyon. The falls are 175 feet tall from top to bottom, including breaks. At peak flow, there can be up to five strands, though there never seems to be enough water, even after heavy rain.

Continue 0.3 mile north on the Brooks Creek Trail to return to the parking lot.

EXPLORE NEARBY PARKS

McNee Ranch State Park

Along Highway 1 north of Montara, a service road marked by a yellow pipe gate is the access point for **McNee Ranch** (Montara State Beach, 650/726-8819, www.parks.ca.gov, 8am-sunset daily) at the foot of Montara Mountain. At the gate, turn left to hike the **San Pedro Mountain Trail** (3 miles round-trip, 1.5 hours) as it tracks along the coastal ridgelines. It's an easy-to-moderate climb that leads to an overlook of the ocean and **Gray Whale Cove.**

Note: There is parking for only a few cars at the entrance road. Park instead on the west side of Highway 1 and then return on foot to the gate.

Alternately, drive 0.9 mile on Highway 1 and park at the Gray Whale Cove trailhead. Look for the trailhead at the south end of the parking area. The **Gray Whale Cove Trail** (3 miles round-trip, 1.5 hours) climbs into McNee Ranch and rises a few hundred feet to a coastal ridge near San Pedro Road for a great ocean view.

I've always loved sitting in this spot, taking in the expanse. Directly below, you'll see a line of cars on Highway 1 where drivers push, push, push, as if trapped in a bubble, unaware of the natural beauty that surrounds them.

Rancho Corral de Tierra

I've probably hiked the trail from **Moss Beach to Spine Ridge** (6 miles round-trip, 2.5 hours) more than any other, exploring the routes on top in every direction. After parking on Etheldore Street, look for the trailhead at the Ember Ridge Stables. Walk past the stables and Pigs Pond to an old dirt road on the left that connects to Spine Ridge.

The Spine Ridge Trail climbs up a hill, then crests and narrows, venturing up Spine Ridge to the flank of Montara Mountain; some spots are steep, others are eroded. As you climb, the slopes on either side plunge into remote valleys. Near the ridge, turn around for a panorama across Pillar Point Harbor and the coast.

BEST OVERNIGHT: SAN FRANCISCO RV RESORT

Contrary to the name, **San Francisco RV Resort** (700 Palmetto Ave., Pacifica) is not in San Francisco. It is in Pacifica, about six miles north of San Pedro Valley Park. Perched on a flat spot just above the ocean, there are 150 paved sites with full hookups for RVs. Though there is too much asphalt and the RV sites are a bit close together, the proximity to the beach (via the Esplanade Beach Overlook Trail) compensates, as do the dramatic ocean sunsets.

This place doesn't lack for amenities: restrooms with showers, a heated swimming pool and hot tub, a playground and clubhouse, plus laundry facilities, Wi-Fi, and a convenience store. Some facilities are wheelchair-accessible. Leashed pets are permitted. **Reservations** (877/570–2267, www.sanfranciscorvresort.com, fee) are recommended. Open year-round.

WHERE TO EAT

In a converted railroad car on the east side of Highway 1, **Gorilla Barbecue** (2145 Hwy. 1, Pacifica, 650/359–7427) is a can't-miss deal for hungry hikers. Order the meat combo sampler with ribs, tri-tip, pulled pork, and chicken (extra barbecue sauce on the side is a must). It's located in the Vallemar section of Pacifica (south of Sharp Park and north of Rockaway Beach), near the lone stoplight at Reina Del Mar Avenue.

You might wonder, "What are the hours for Gorilla Barbecue?" The answer is that they are open until they sell out. Get there before they do.

DRIVING DIRECTIONS

From San Francisco, take I-280 south for 10 miles to Daly City. At the split with Highway 1, bear right for Pacifica and drive south for 7.2 miles. Get in the left lane and turn left at Linda Mar Boulevard. Drive slowly for 1.9 miles. At Oddstad Boulevard, turn right and drive a short distance to the park **entrance** (600 Oddstad Blvd., Pacifica, 650/355–8289, https://parks.smcgov.org, 8am-close). A visitors center is open 10am-4pm weekends and holidays. There is a vehicle entry fee of $6.

To reach McNee Ranch State Park: From San Francisco, take I-280 south for about 10 miles to Daly City and the split on right for Highway 1/Pacifica. Bear right on Highway 1 and continue south 11 miles (through Pacifica and past Devil's Slide) and emerge at Montara State Beach on the right, McNee Ranch on the left.

Note: At the trailhead entrance, marked by a yellow pipe gate at the service road, there is space for four or five cars; most park at Montara State Beach and walk the short distance to the trailhead.

To reach Rancho Corral De Tierra: Drive as above to Montara State Beach, then continue south on Highway 1 for 1.2 miles to Moss Beach and Etheldore Street. Turn left on Etheldore and drive 0.8 mile to Ranch Road on the left. Park along Etheldore in the area, and then walk up Ranch Road to Ember Ridge Stables and the trailhead/road on the right.

CAMPFIRE STORIES

*O*n a cool spring day at McNee Ranch, I hiked up San Pedro Road with my dog Rebel. At a junction, the road split and a series of utility poles ran down the slope to the left. Near the power poles, an unmarked path led downhill through chaparral to the remains of an old concrete army bunker that had been dug into the mountain during the Cold War.

It was near the bunker that Rebel disappeared.

For a moment, I was petrified. I thought about the potential loss of the best pal I'd ever known. Yet I could hear the barely discernable panting of his breath nearby. I followed the sound, swept aside some brush, and found Rebel at the bottom of a 10-foot-deep hole, where he was sitting next to a fawn.

About 10 feet away from me, a doe was watching our every move. Apparently, the fawn had fallen into the hole (a dry well shaft dug during the military era), and Rebel had jumped right in after it. The hole was too deep to reach Rebel, so I hiked back out to the ranger's office and we returned with a ladder and a blanket.

I first pulled Rebel out and gave him a hero's hug. The ranger then climbed down into the hole, wrapped the fawn in a blanket, and carried it up the ladder, releasing the fawn to its mother.

Out there on the flank of Montara Mountain, in a long-forgotten dry well shaft, 'ol Rebel had saved the life of a fawn.

△ *That's Rebel and me. In this photo, he was 17.*

415/388-2070 | Marin | www.parks.ca.gov

At 2,571 feet, the East Peak of Mount Tamalpais in Marin County provides one of the best views around. A trip here feels powerful and never fails to stir the soul. To the south, the flank of Mount Tam plunges to Richardson Bay, with views of Sausalito and across San Francisco Bay. From the East Peak lookout, you can see the San Francisco waterfront, the Golden Gate Bridge, and miles of coast and ocean. To the east is San Pablo Bay and the shore of the East Bay with Mount Diablo on the horizon. To the north are miles of the Marin watershed, with Lagunitas and Bon Tempe Lakes directly below. Even when fog socks in the coast, the view here is still spectacular, and the sunsets are among the best anywhere.

Mount Tamalpais State Park provides more than 50 miles of trails for hiking and biking, which in turn link to a network of 200 miles in adjoining parks and watershed lands. As you explore, you will discover a mixed landscape of redwood groves, oak woodlands, lush canyons, and grasslands.

Several major trailheads—Pantoll, Bootjack, and Rock Spring—line the Panoramic Highway, the main road through the state park. Pantoll and Bootjack also have walk-in tent sites, while Rock Spring provides access to the West Point Inn, with turn-of-the-19th-century vintage lodging and pancake breakfasts. The East Peak summit is the crown jewel of a visit to Mount Tamalpais State Park and where many first-timers start their adventure.

▽ *view of the Bay, San Francisco, and the coast from the Mount Tam summit*

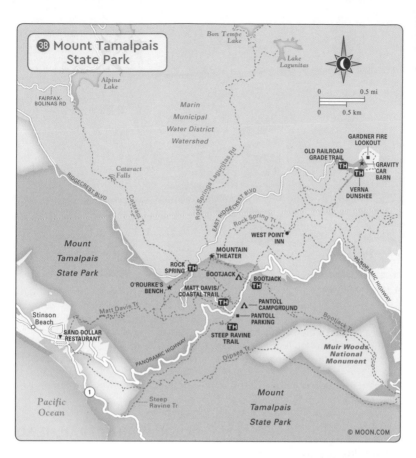

STOP 1:
PANTOLL TRAILHEAD

Your first stop on the Panoramic Highway is at the Pantoll Ranger Station and Campground. The large parking lot (fee) fills quickly on summer weekends, so arrive early to grab a spot. From the Pantoll Trailhead, several adventures await.

Steep Ravine Trail
(3.4 miles round-trip, 1.5 hours)

This is one of the few hikes best done during a rainstorm. That is when the divine spirit of nature will baptize you. When wet, this gorgeous canyon is one of the prettiest walks anywhere. From Pantoll, the trailhead is at the far west end of the parking area. From

△ *Steep Ravine Trail*

△ *wooden bridge on the Dipsea Trail*

here, you descend quickly, including down a section with wood steps, into the lush canyon. You'll arrive at the bottom of the ravine at pretty Webb Creek. The trail follows Webb Creek, crossing the stream eight times in all. Redwoods tower over you, and at times, the forest canopy closes off the sky. In some spots, ferns line the canyon walls. In less than a mile, you'll reach a drop-off with a ladder, and in high flows, this brink produces a small but pretty waterfall.

The trail continues to a historic dam, 1.7 miles in, downstream of the junction with the Dipsea Trail (580 feet elevation). It's a fine picnic site. Look close and you might see small fish in the pool. Head back when ready for a climb of 920 feet in 1.7 miles.

Matt Davis/Coastal Trail
(6.4 miles round-trip, 3 hours)

From the Pantoll parking lot, cross the Panoramic Highway north for the Matt Davis Trailhead. The Matt Davis Trail leads 1.6 miles west into the woods, generally where you contour along the foothills to a trail junction (1,540 feet elevation) with the Coastal Trail. Here you turn right onto the Coastal Trail (Bolinas Ridge Trail on maps) and climb 280 feet over the course of 1.6 miles to the Willow Camp Fire Road (1,820 feet). The final stretch provides a series of jaw-droppingly beautiful coastal views. Return the way you came.

STOP 2: ROCK SPRING TRAILHEAD

From the Pantoll parking lot, drive north across Panoramic Highway and make a sharp left turn onto Pantoll Road. (If you are heading west on Panoramic Highway, without the stop at Pantoll, you'll veer right onto Pantoll Road.) Pantoll Road heads north to connect with Ridgecrest Boulevard en route to the East Peak of Mount Tam. The curvy road offers multiple stops and hikes.

O'Rourke's Bench
(0.6 mile round-trip, 0.5 hour)
Park at the Rock Spring Trailhead and cross Ridgecrest Boulevard. Look for the trail to O'Rourke's Bench on the south side of the road (near the junction with Pantoll Road). From here, it's an easy 0.3-mile walk to a stone bench with a plaque that reads:

🐾 INSIDER'S TIP

This is the coolest cheap sleep in California. The **West Point Inn** (Old Stage Rd., 415/388–9955, http://westpointinn.com, Tues.-Sun., from $50) is perched at 1,785 feet on the flank of Mount Tam. It was built in 1904 and remains much the same as the day it opened, with no electricity and a kitchen that runs on propane. The inn has seven rooms and five cabins; guests bring their own camping gear, food, and perhaps an instrument. (I've stayed with groups that have booked the entire inn; most folks brought instruments and we played into the night.) A stay at the inn includes a communal kitchen, a members' lounge, a front parlor (open to the public), and a covered deck with picnic tables.

West Point Inn also hosts a **pancake breakfast** (9am-1pm, $10) on Mother's Day, Father's Day, and the second Sunday of each month May-October. Volunteers who work the event spend the night prior at the inn for free.

Access is via a two-mile walk (or bike ride) from most trailheads. If you are part of a group that is staying overnight, you may be allowed access to a service road to the facility, which means you can bring all your gear in by vehicle.

Reservations are accepted online. Nonmembers can make reservations up to 90 days in advance; members (apply in person, $20 fee) can make reservations up to 120 days in advance. Sunday-night stays are for members only.

"Give me these hills and the friends I love. I ask no other heaven.

To our Dad O'Rourke, in joyous celebration of his 76th birthday, Feb. 25th, 1927.

From the friends to whom he showed this heaven."

From this perch at 2,040 feet, coastal hills and valleys plunge at your feet to the Pacific Ocean for amazing views.

Return to the trailhead and cross Ridgecrest Boulevard for the 0.25-mile spur trail to **Mountain Theater (**www.mountainplay.org), a 3,750-seat open-air amphitheater on the southeast side of Mount Tam that hosts popular theatrical performances in summer.

Walk across the bench seats to the east side and look for the **Rock Spring Trail** (3 miles round-trip, 1.5 hours) for an easy downhill glide of about 200 feet to the **West Point Inn** (see Insider's Tip).

Laura Dell Loop
(2.5 miles round-trip, 1.5 hours)

The Laura Dell Trail provides the easiest route to Cataract Falls, a series of cascades that rushes down a beautifully wooded canyon set in the northwest slopes of Mount Tamalpais. Walk down the fire road 0.7 mile to the Laurel Dell picnic site, then turn left on the Cataract Trail for a 1-mile descent into the steep canyon to see Cataract Falls. Continue along the Cataract Trail to the High Marsh Trail. Turn right on the High Marsh Trail, hike onward, and turn right at any of the next three trail intersections to return to the Laurel Dell Trailhead. Of the three choices, the second makes the best return loop, as the short cutoff will put you within a few hundred yards of the trailhead.

STOP 3:
EAST PEAK OF MOUNT TAM

Mount Tam is one of those rare spots that projects a feeling of power—standing on its highest point, you can sense that power flowing through you. The hike on the

Verna Dunshee/Mount Tam Summit Trail
(0.4 mile, 1 hour)

The Mount Tam Summit Trail to the East Peak is very short, yet it climbs 330 feet to an elevation of 2,571 feet. The East Peak parking lot is right at the foot of the summit trail. The Verna Dunshee/Mount Tam Summit Trail starts on wooden slats as it arcs up the north flank of the peak. Look below (to your left) to see Bon Tempe Lake. The trail circumnavigates the peak counterclockwise. As you near the summit, climb a rock staircase to the Gardner Fire Lookout (closed to the public), which sits perched on the summit. The Gardner Fire Lookout is the classic fire lookout station: a square building perched on the summit with spectacular long-distance views in every direction. If you're lucky, a docent or ranger might allow visitors on the deck to take in the views. You can still rock-hop around the base of the lookout, admiring the views in every direction. When ready, return the way you came (avoid the illegal trails down, as they cause erosion and potential slides).

A volunteer-staffed **visitors center** (11am-4pm Sat.-Sun., www.friendsof mttam.org) and the **Gravity Car Museum** (noon-4pm Sat.-Sun.), which showcases the railroad history of Mount Tam, are located near the parking lot and trailhead. Free astronomy programs are hosted here in summer by the **Friends of Mount Tam** (www. friendsofmttam.org, Sat. evening Apr.-Oct., dates vary).

MOUNTAIN BIKE THE OLD RAILROAD GRADE

The **Old Railroad Grade** (13.2 miles one-way with shuttle ride) is a rite of passage for mountain bikers. Start at the parking lot for East Peak. Look for the dirt road/trailhead just down the road on the left. From here, it is 1.4 miles with a descent of 450 feet to West Point Inn. The route continues with a drop of 2,100 feet to a lower trailhead at the end of Blithedale in

△ west flank of Mount Tamalpais

Mill Valley. Because the Old Railroad Grade follows a historic rail line—not too steep, but requires a steady grind—ambitious riders will instead start in Mill Valley and ride to the top, then sail back down (26.4 miles).

You can get there via shuttle provided by the **West Marin Stagecoach** (415/526-3239, www.marintransit.org), which provides rides to recreation sites and destinations around Mount Tam.

BEST OVERNIGHT: PANTOLL AND BOOTJACK CAMPGROUNDS

Two excellent campgrounds are located off Panoramic Highway. **Pantoll** is one of the prettiest campgrounds in the Bay Area, with 16 walk-in tent sites nestled under a forest canopy on the western slopes of Mount Tamalpais. The landscape is a mix of redwood groves, oak woodlands, and grasslands, with drop-dead views of the ocean. Pantoll is the trailhead for several day hikes, including the Steep Ravine Trail and the Matt Davis/Coastal Trail. A ranger station is at the parking lot.

The **Bootjack** tent sites on the north side of the highway are not quite as sheltered as those at Pantoll. Sites are wooded and there is a day-use area nearby. The Bootjack Trailhead provides access to the Matt Davis Trail to West Point Inn and the nearby Old Stage Road.

A short walk (100 feet-0.25 mile) is required to all campsites. Picnic tables, food lockers, and fire grills are provided. Drinking water, flush toilets, firewood (fee), and Wi-Fi (Pantoll only) are available. Leashed pets are permitted at campsites only.

Reservations are not accepted at either campground. All sites are first-come, first-served. Open year-round, weather permitting.

WHERE TO EAT

On a warm afternoon after a long hike, I love to relax on an outdoor patio with the scent of the ocean in the air. That's what you get at the **Sand Dollar Restaurant** (3458 Hwy. 1, Stinson Beach, 415/868-0434, www.stinsonbeachrestaurant.com, 3pm-9pm Mon. and Thurs.-Fri., 11am-9pm Sat.-Sun.) in addition to great drinks, oysters on the half shell, a decent menu, and the big-time mud pie for dessert. On crowded weekends, the experience can be quite different. Come early or late in the day, or come on a weekday in the late afternoon for plenty of room and sunshine.

DRIVING DIRECTIONS

From San Francisco, cross the Golden Gate Bridge and take U.S. 101 north for 4 miles to Marin and the exit for Highway 1/Stinson Beach. Exit onto Highway 1 and continue west for 1 mile (under U.S. 101) to the stoplight at a T intersection for Shoreline Highway/Highway 1. Turn left on Shoreline Highway and drive 2.6 miles to the Panoramic Highway. Bear right on Panoramic Highway and drive 5.3 miles to Pantoll Road (at the junction, continue straight). Bear right on Pantoll Road and drive 1.4 miles to a Y-split in the road at Rock Spring and Ridgecrest Boulevard. Bear right and drive 3.5 miles to the parking lot at the foot of the East Peak lookout.

The park is open 7am-sunset. Parking fees are enforced at the East Peak, Pantoll, and Bootjack Trailheads (cash or check only), and the lots fill fast. On weekend mornings, plan to be at the trailhead by 9am in order to secure a parking spot.

CAMPFIRE STORIES

*O*n an evening drive up Mount Tam, we saw that the fog line had dropped down to the roadway. "Looks like this is no evening for the sunset," I said.

Then, at about 2,000 feet, we broke through the top layer of fog and let loose a huge cheer of relief. We kept driving to the summit and made the short hike to the top, then took a perch and looked to the west. Below us, the stratus stretched across the horizon like a sea of fog. What happened next is the kind of thing that makes you feel lucky to be alive.

The sun dipped below that fog layer and sent refracted yellows, oranges, and pinks through 50 miles of fog. It was a kaleidoscope, and each minute the colors changed, over and over, until the sun finally buried itself beneath the horizon and the fog turned gray.

I've watched thousands of sunsets into fog since then, hoping for another glimpse of the phenomenon. But it's never happened. Just that once.

△ *Mount Tam Summit Lookout Station*

Some places are special, with an aura that calls to you, drawing you back again and again. Fall in love with Point Reyes and you'll always hear its call.

Point Reyes National Seashore is an arched peninsula 30 miles north of San Francisco that spans 71,000 acres fronted by the Pacific Ocean and backed by wilderness.

The hiking trail system is one of the best anywhere. Trek through old-growth forests up to valley ridges along the Coast Trail. Follow sculpted beaches to panoramas of Drakes Bay. Climb along the bluff top of Chimney Rock or watch a waterfall plunge into the ocean at Alamere Falls.

Then spend the night on the coast at one of four great trail camps where the sound of the ocean waves will lull you to sleep.

▽ *wildflowers blooming at Point Reyes National Seashore*

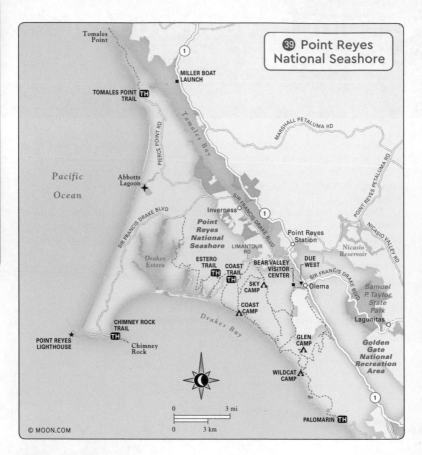

39 Point Reyes National Seashore

BEST ACTIVITY: BACKPACK THE COAST TRAIL

The **Coast Trail** (16.1 miles one-way, 2–3 days with shuttle) provides an extended tour of Point Reyes with the chance to stop at trail camps along the way. This trip is just long enough for lingering hikers to spend the weekend.

Bring a hiking partner who can double as a shuttle driver so that you can leave a car at each end of the trail. Pack a backpacking tent (advised against coastal moisture) and a backpacking stove.

Reserve your campsite(s) online in advance (www.recreation.gov). Pick up your **camping permit** (required) from the **Bear Valley Visitor Center** (10am-5pm Mon.-Fri., 9am-5pm Sat.-Sun. Mar.-Oct., 10am-4:30pm Mon.-Fri., 9am-4:30pm Sat.-Sun. Nov.-Feb.) and you're ready to start your trip.

Day 1: Coast Camp
(2.8 miles)

From the trailhead near the Point Reyes Hostel (Limantour Road), start the trip by hiking north-south to keep the wind at your back and out of your face. Hike 2.8 miles south along a pretty creek that attracts wildlife at dusk. The trail is easy and relatively flat. As you approach the ocean, you'll have a view of the coastal foothills.

The first night is at **Coast Camp,** set on an open ocean bluff above Santa Maria Beach. There are 12 individual and two group hike-in sites.

△ *Drakes Estero*

Day 2: Wildcat Camp
(7.8 miles)

From Coast Camp, hike 7.8 miles south along the Coast Trail to **Wildcat.** This breeze of a walk passes Sculptured Beach (2 miles), a beach with tidepools and sculpted rocks, then past Kelham Beach (3.5 miles) to a 0.2-mile spur for Arch Rock (4.4 miles), with plenty of time left for a side trip to Alamere Falls.

Hike south on Wildcat Beach for one more mile for a view of **Alamere Falls,** a rare waterfall that pours over a cliff, onto a beach, and then into the ocean.

Spend the second night at the popular **Wildcat Camp,** sited on a grassy meadow above remote Wildcat Beach. There are five individual sites and three group sites, each separated and secluded by high brush.

Day 3: Palomarin Trailhead
(5.5 miles)

Close out your last day with a great hike past a series of freshwater lakes. From Wildcat, hike south on the Coast Trail past Wildcat Lake, then little Ocean Lake. After climbing a short ridge, the Coast Trail continues south, past hidden Crystal Lake and skirting

above pretty Pelican Lake en route to the northern shore of Bass Lake.

The trail veers southwest up a coastal hill, topping out at 563 feet, then laterals down a canyon and back to the ocean bluffs heading south. In about one mile, you'll arrive at the Palomarin Trailhead where your shuttle car awaits.

WILDLIFE WATCHING

Point Reyes is a wildlife paradise with one of the largest Tule elk herds in California and plentiful sightings of elephant seals, harbor seals, whales, deer, bobcats, and foxes. Following are the best spots:

Harbor Seals

The **Estero Trail** (2.5 miles round-trip) is routed through pines and cypress to emerge at a bridge at the inlet of Home Bay on Drakes Estero. Extend the hike 1.3 miles to a ridge for sweeping views of the surrounding water. It's another 1.4 miles south to secluded Sunset Beach (7.8 miles round-trip). Drakes Estero is home to the largest colony of breeding harbor seals in Point Reyes.

Trailhead: Sir Francis Drake Boulevard
Directions: From Bear Valley Visitor Center, drive to Bear Valley Road.

Turn left and drive 1.7 miles to Sir Francis Drake Boulevard. Turn left and drive 7.6 miles to the access road (on the left) for the Estero Trail.

Elephant Seals

Walk along the knife-edge of the headlands' **Chimney Rock Trail** (2.8 miles round-trip), with Drakes Bay on one side and the Pacific Ocean on the other. The cliff-top lookouts provide views of Chimney Rocks and the Farallones. December-March, look for elephant seals from the Elephant Seal Overlook near Chimney Rock above Drakes Bay. The numbers are usually not very high, but in late winter, there may be small harem.

Trailhead: Sir Francis Drake Boulevard. In winter, access is via shuttle bus from Drakes Beach (weekends Jan.-Apr.).

Directions: From Bear Valley Visitor Center, drive to Bear Valley Road. Turn left and drive 1.7 miles to Sir Francis Drake Boulevard. Turn left and drive 17.6 miles to the Point Reyes Lighthouse. Turn left and drive 0.9 mile to the Chimney Rock Trailhead.

Bird-Watching

This easy walk skirts the shore of gorgeous **Abbotts Lagoon** (3.2 miles round-trip), then is routed across sand dunes toward the beach. This is a diverse habitat matrix that can support waterfowl that require freshwater, migratory shorebirds, and songbirds that love the mix of coastal grasslands and a pond.

Trailhead: Pierce Point Road

Directions: From Bear Valley Visitor Center, drive to Bear Valley Road. Turn left and drive 1.7 miles to Sir Francis Drake Boulevard. Turn left and drive 5.6 miles to Pierce Point Road. Bear right and drive 3.3 miles to the trailhead for Abbotts Lagoon.

Whales

In winter, there may be no better place to watch migrating whales than from the lookout at **Point Reyes Lighthouse** (0.8 mile round-trip, 0.5 hour). The trail descends 308 steps to a bluff-top lookout that fronts the historic Point Reyes Lighthouse, with prospects to see the puff-of-smoke spouts of passing gray whales. On a good day, you might see

△ elephant seals near Chimney Rock Trailhead

△ red-tailed hawk spotted on the Tomales Point Trail

INSIDER'S TIP

Tomales Bay is among the most unusual places in Northern California: a long, narrow bay cut by the San Andreas Fault, one of the earth's most feared earthquake fault lines. Because Point Reyes shields the bay from north winds, these quiet waters are ideal for boating. One of the best ways to make this paradise feel like yours alone is by booking one of the **boat-in campsites** nestled along the shore of Tomales Bay.

Along the western shore of Tomales Bay, from Indian Beach in Tomales Bay State Park north toward the tip of Tomales Point, about 15 dispersed boat-in campsite are set within small, sandy coves along the base of steep cliffs.

Most boaters launch from the **Miller Boat Launch** (23240 CA-1, Marshall, www.marincountyparks.org, fee), on the east side of Tomales Bay. Paddle across the bay to the campsites on the west shore. (Go early to beat the wind, and time your paddle between the tides so that you don't have to fight the currents.)

Pit toilets are available at Marshall Beach and Tomales Beach; otherwise, boaters must bring portable toilets. There is no drinking water, no wood gathering, and garbage must be packed out.

Permits (800/444-7275, www.recreation.gov, fee) are required; twenty permits are issued daily. Reserve your campsite online in advance (www.recreation.gov), and then pick up your permit in person at the Bear Valley Visitor Center (10am-5pm Mon.-Fri., 9am-5pm Sat.-Sun. Mar.-Oct., 10am-4:30pm Mon.-Fri., 9am-4:30pm Sat.-Sun. Nov.-Feb.).

Overnight parking for boat-in campers is available at the Tomales Bay Resort and at the Miller Boat Launch. Overnight parking for boat-in campers is prohibited within Point Reyes National Seashore (i.e., along the Pierce Point and L Ranch Roads and at the Marshall Beach Trailhead) and Tomales Bay State Park.

5-10 whale spouts, and if you're lucky, a breech or tail salute.

Trailhead: Sir Francis Drake Boulevard. In winter, access is via shuttle bus from Drakes Beach.

Directions: From Bear Valley Visitor Center, drive to Bear Valley Road. Turn left and drive 1.7 miles to Sir Francis Drake Boulevard. Turn left and drive 17.6 miles to the Point Reyes Lighthouse.

Tule Elk

The **Tomales Point Trail** (6 miles round-trip, 3.5 hours) extends to Tomales Point with views of the ocean to the west and Tomales Bay to the east. The route is intersected by game trails and offers great wildlife-watching for herds of tule elk.

Trailhead: Pierce Point Ranch

Directions: From Bear Valley Visitor Center, drive to Bear Valley Road. Turn left and drive 1.7 miles to Sir Francis Drake Boulevard. Turn left and drive 5.6 miles to Pierce Point Road. Bear right and drive 9 miles to Pierce Point Ranch and park.

BEST OVERNIGHT: TRAIL CAMPS

The trail camps at Point Reyes National Seashore are a hot ticket that are in high demand. **Reservations** (800/444-7275, www.recreation.gov, fee) are mandatory, and scoring one involves planning ahead. You have to work the system, watching for the first dates available in order to book a reservation. (Hint: Saturday nights go fast.) Weekdays during the shoulder seasons (spring-late May and early Sept.-winter) offer the best weather, and plenty of sites are usually available.

- **Coast Camp:** From the Laguna Trailhead (Limantour Road, near the Point Reyes Hostel), it's a 1.8-mile hike south on the Laguna Trail. There are 12 individual and two group sites. Also accessible via the Coast Trail.
- **Sky Camp:** From the Sky Trailhead (Limantour Road), it's a 1.4-mile uphill hike on the Sky Trail. There are 11 individual sites and one group site.
- **Glen Camp:** From the Bear Valley Visitor Center, it's a 4.6-mile hike south on the Bear Valley Trail. There are 12 hike-in sites.
- **Wildcat Camp:** From the Palomarin Trailhead, it's a 5.5-mile hike north on the Coast Trail. There are five individual sites and three group sites.

All trail camps are open year-round. Picnic tables and fire grills are provided, and vault toilets are available at all camps. There is usually drinking water available, but be prepared to filter and treat water. Backpacking stoves are required for cooking, as wood fires are not permitted. Pack out all trash.

WHERE TO EAT

Housed in an 1865 building that was refurbished in 2019, the **Due West Restaurant** (10021 Hwy. 1, Olema, 415/663-1264, https://olemahouse. com, noon-9pm daily) is my go-to spot for dinner in the area. I'm pretty easy to please—just give me some oysters

on the half shell, fish-and-chips, and my favorite malt beverage. My wife Denese is a foodie though, and orders one of the exotic salad mixes with a glass of fine cabernet. It's located next door to the Olema House hotel.

DRIVING DIRECTIONS

From San Francisco, cross the Golden Gate Bridge and drive north on U.S. 101 for 8 miles to exit 450B for Sir Francis Drake Boulevard (toward San Anselmo). Take that exit and drive 0.4 mile, merging onto Sir Francis Drake Boulevard. In 5.7 miles, bear right at an intersection to stay on Sir Francis Drake Boulevard, continuing a total of 20.5 miles to Olema and Highway 1. Turn right and drive 0.1 mile to Bear Valley Road. Turn left and drive 0.7 mile to the Seashore Information sign and access road for Bear Valley Visitor Center. Turn left and park near the visitors center.

To reach the Coast Trailhead: From the visitors center, turn left on Bear Valley Road and drive 1.7 miles north to Sir Francis Drake Boulevard. Turn left and drive 1.3 miles to Limantour Road (signed Hostel and Limantour Beach). Turn left on Limantour Road and drive 5.9 miles west to the turnoff for the Point Reyes Hostel and the Coast Trailhead.

To reach the Palomarin Trailhead: From the visitors center, turn right on Bear Valley Road and drive 0.7 mile east to Highway 1. Turn right onto Highway 1 and drive 0.1 mile to a stop sign and the junction with Sir Francis Drake Boulevard. Continue south on Highway 1 for 9.1 miles to Olema-Bolinas Road (the sign for this road is often missing). Turn right and drive 1.8 miles to Mesa Road. Turn right onto Mesa Road and drive 4.6 miles north to the trailhead parking.

Note: Parking can be extremely limited at the Palomarin Trailhead, especially on weekends.

CAMPFIRE STORIES

The year 2018 was the "Summer of Smoke" in California, the year 1.89 million acres burned across the state. In late summer, the smoke was so thick in places that many folks couldn't even go outside.

After weeks in the smoke, I bailed from my planned mountain expeditions and headed to Point Reyes National Seashore instead. Within a matter of hours, I found redemption: clean air, clear skies, and trail lookouts with ocean views. I was like a dry sponge, soaking up the fresh air and pristine landscape of the park as it washed me clean. Point Reyes is one of the few places that can have this effect.

△ I led a group on a sunset hike to the Chimney Rock Headlands.

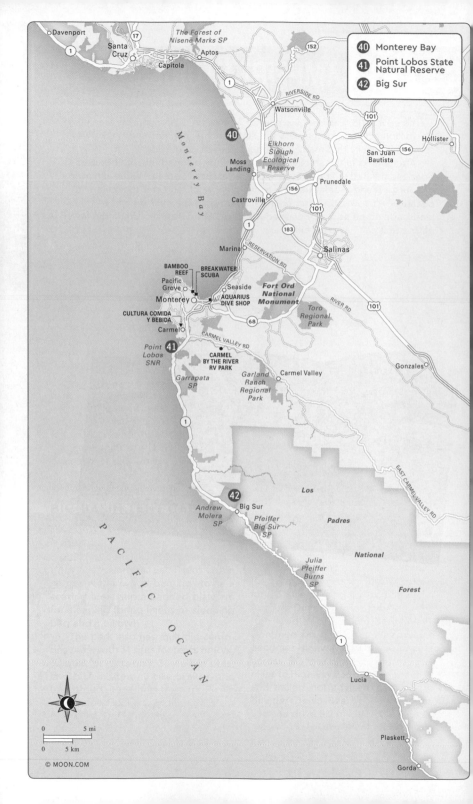

Chapter 8

MONTEREY AND BIG SUR

④⓪ Monterey Bay

831/685-6442 | Monterey | www.parks.ca.gov

Each person who gazes across Monterey Bay sees something different, something uniquely theirs that fits in their world. For most, this first treasure is the view: Monterey Bay's tourmaline waters wash against a shore of white-sand beaches and rocky outcrops with in-shore kelp beds. Venture out onto these waters on a boat, kayak, or surfboard and you can look across the sea, watching sea otters, whales, or sea lions play.

Monterey Bay stretches north from the seaside town of Monterey all the way to the surf capital of Santa Cruz. This coastline is home to a series of some of the most popular campgrounds in the state. Scenic towns line the coast, compelling travelers to cruise Highway 1 for short overnight getaways from Monterey.

Put it all together and you've got a world-class destination that you might never want to leave.

▽ *shoreline on Monterey Bay*

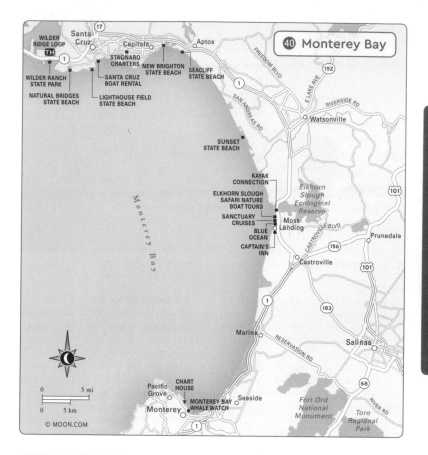

BEST ACTIVITY: WHALE-WATCHING

Monterey Bay is one of the best places for whale-watching. Within Monterey Bay, the Monterey submarine canyon rises from a depth of 1,400 feet to 800 feet within the span of one mile. Winds out of the west push plankton-rich seawater into the canyon, and when the seawater hits the underwater canyon wall, the nutrient-rich food is pushed to the surface. The upwelling produces a rich marine food chain that draws whales and marinelife from across the ocean.

In summer, it is common to sight 20–50 humpback whales on a single whale-watching trip. The first humpbacks arrive in early April and will stay as long as September. The traditional season for gray whales is winter (Jan.-Mar.). In April, you may catch a few gray whales on their annual journey north to Alaskan waters. Hundreds of dolphins, harbor porpoises, marine birds, and even a giant mola mola (a six-foot sunfish that hovers on the surface) ply these waters, too.

Monterey Bay Whale Watch (84 Fisherman's Wharf, 831/375-4658, www.montereybaywhalewatch.com) often runs 5-7 trips daily in peak season (July-Aug.). Trips range from three hours to all-day excursions. After you head out on the boat, it doesn't take long before someone spies a whale spout (and everybody shouts "thar she blows!"). Humpbacks whales, which range 40-50 feet long, will launch out of the water, turn in a half pirouette, and then crash back

△ *two otters float side by side in the calm waters of Elkhorn Slough*

into the sea. Spyhopping (when a whale pokes its head straight up), lunging to feed, swirling, and diving are common. Time it right and the ocean may seem filled with hundreds of dolphins as they hop and jump.

For all whale-watching trips, wear long pants, layers, a windbreaker, athletic shoes, a hat (with lariat), sunscreen, and sunglasses. Snacks, binoculars, and a camera can help enhance your trip. If you are vulnerable to spatial disorientation, take a pill for seasickness 30 minutes-1 hour prior to boarding.

Other whale-watching companies in the area include:

- **Blue Ocean** (831/600-5103, www.blueoceanwhalewatch.com)
- **Sanctuary Cruises** (831/917-1042, www.sanctuarycruises.com)
- **Santa Cruz Whale Watching** (831/205-2380, www.santacruzwhalewatching.com)

WILDLIFE-WATCHING

Elkhorn Slough (1700 Elkhorn Rd., Watsonville, www.elkhornslough.org, fee) is 1,400 acres of marsh and tidal flats, the precious borderline between sea and land that is home to thousands of species of birds, fish, and sea otters. **Sea otters** often cruise around on their backs, holding small rocks to their chests. (They use the rocks to break open the shells and casings of food such as sea urchins.)

Explore this natural area by booking a guided wildlife trip with **Elkhorn Slough Safari Nature Boat Tours** (7881 Sandholdt Rd., Moss Landing, 831/633-5555, www.elkhornslough.com, tours daily year-round, fee), which navigates the wetlands via a 27-foot pontoon boat. Advance reservations are required.

To explore the reserve on your own, rent a kayak from **Kayak Connection** (2370 Hwy. 1, Moss Landing, 831/724-5692) and make the easy paddle on the slough to the mouth of the harbor. Look for harbor seals and sea lions on the sandy flats at the foot of the jetty. On calm mornings, sea otters might even swim right up to your kayak, swirling, diving, and playing tag. When the incoming tide begins, turn left and cruise under the Highway 1 bridge into the estuary. Sea otters are often sighted on the right upon entering the interior estuary. Enjoy paddling for a few hours, then ride the outgoing tide back.

On one trip to Elkhorn Slough, I paddled out to the mouth of Moss

 **INSIDER'S TIP**

The coast north of Monterey is home to five gorgeous state beaches, a few coastal trails that are off the radar, and my favorite mountain bike trip anywhere: Wilder Ranch State Park.

Wilder Ranch State Park (1401 Coast Rd., 831/423-9703, www.parks. ca.gov) is located along Highway 1 north of Santa Cruz. From the parking area, cycle down to check out the historic ranch grounds, then walk your bike along the County Bike Trail, which passes through a subway under Highway 1. At a fork, turn left on the **Wilder Ridge Loop** (2 miles one-way), which rises along a series of small hills. In about 500 feet, take a spur to the left for a one-of-a-kind view across the bay. Scan south and take in the flatlands of the Salinas Valley, which make Monterey Peninsula look like an island. It's one of the coolest optical illusions anywhere. The Wilder Ridge Loop continues, meeting with the Enchanted Loop and turning back for an 8.3-mile round-trip ride.

Santa Cruz is synonymous with beach culture. Stop at **Natural Bridges State Beach** (2531 West Cliff Dr., Santa Cruz, 831/423-4609), which has a natural arch bridge and a creek, wetlands, and tidepools. Surfers should head to **Steamer Lane,** the renowned surf break near Lighthouse Field State Beach (West Cliff Dr., 831/423-4609, www.parks.ca.gov). Believe it or not, I took a surfing lesson here and sailed in on my first wave all the way to the beach. You just have to find that magic balance point deep on the board in the pocket of the break.

Santa Cruz offers fishing for salmon (best in Apr. and May), rockfish (good in summer and fall), and a rare opportunity for white sea bass in the fall. Most trips venture out of Santa Cruz with **Stagnaro's** (1718 Brommer, 831/205-2380, www.stagnaros.com) or rent a boat from **Santa Cruz Boat Rental** (15 Municipal Wharf, 831/423-1739).

About five miles east of Santa Cruz is the small community of **Capitola.** When brother Rambob and I were little kids, our dad created the Stienstra Navy and we took our first trips on rental boats out of Capitola, where we fished the kelp beds for rockfish, halibut, and white sea bass. Rent your own "Navy" vessel at **Capitola Wharf Boat & Bait** (Capitola Bay Marina, 831/462-2208, http://capitolaboatandbait.com).

Capitola is also home to **New Brighton State Beach** (New Brighton/Park Ave. exit off Hwy. 1, Capitola, 831/464-6329), which has a popular campground.

Aptos neighbors nearby Capitola along Highway 1, where several beaches offer coastal access. **Seacliff State Beach** (State Park Dr. exit off Hwy. 1, Aptos, 831/685-6500) is known for an old cement ship and RV campsites with gorgeous water views. Next up is **Manresa State Beach** (San Andreas Rd., south of Aptos, 831/724-3750), with a beautiful beachfront and campground.

Located off the same road south of Manresa, **Sunset State Beach** (Sunset Beach Rd., south of Santa Cruz, 831/763-7063) has a bluff-top campground with a short walk to the beach and great sunset views.

△ *my wife Denese and I watching the otters at Elkhorn Slough*

Landing harbor and a sea otter emerged on the surface, swirled right next to me, then dove under the boat and popped up on the other side.

BEST OVERNIGHT: CAPTAIN'S INN

I like my overnight getaways to be cozy and to feel like home. The **Captain's Inn** (8122 Moss Landing Rd., Moss Landing, 831/633–5550, https:// captainsinn.com) does that. Located about a 20-minute drive north of Monterey on Highway 1, the historic bed-and-breakfast is within walking distance of restaurants and is close to the kayak launch at adjacent Elkhorn Slough. The 10 guest rooms include nautical decor that makes a night here feel like staying on a high-end boat.

WHERE TO EAT

Sooner or later, everyone plays tourist at Monterey and that means eating on Cannery Row. The **Charthouse** (444 Cannery Row, 831/372–3362, www. chart-house.com, 5pm-9:30pm Mon.-Thurs., 5pm-10pm Fri., 4pm-10pm Sat., 4pm-9:30pm Sun.) offers big-water views that complement an expensive, first-class menu. Mouth-watering appetizers like clam chowder, lobster bisque, and crab cakes set the stage for prime rib or mahi mahi with shrimp and entrées. Chocolate fans must order the hot chocolate lava cake for dessert.

This is the kind of place where people come to celebrate birthdays, anniversaries, or just to commemorate a trip to Monterey.

DRIVING DIRECTIONS

From San Jose and U.S. 101, drive south on U.S. 101 for 49 miles. Take exit 336 and Highway 156 (signed for Monterey) for 0.4 mile, merging onto Highway 156. Drive 6.1 miles to Highway 1. Merge onto Highway 1 South and drive 11.7 miles to exit 402B (signed Del Monte/Pacific Grove). Take that exit for 0.4 mile, merging onto Del Monte Avenue, and continue 1.5 miles to Figueroa Street. Turn right and drive 100 yards to Fisherman's Wharf. Turn left and drive another 100 yards to Fisherman's Wharf parking (the road is signed). Turn right onto the access road and make an immediate left into the parking lot.

CAMPFIRE STORIES

*E*arly one summer day, my friend biologist Giancarlo Thomae and I paddled out in a kayak at dawn from Moss Landing and out into Monterey Bay. Within the first 10 minutes, we saw a dozen sea otters, 50 harbor seals, 100 sea lions, and about 50,000 terns that were feasting on a vast school of juvenile anchovies. A few miles out to sea, hundreds of dolphins began jumping all around the kayak. We stopped paddling and floated amid water dimpled with baitfish. A 40-foot humpback whale came right alongside the boat and exhaled so closely that we were nearly hit with water. Its tail jutted high in the air, propelling into a powerful dive for a feeding run.

We ended up seeing 50 whales within close range of our kayak that day. Some people pay thousands of dollars for a world-class experience like that. On a calm morning with a short paddle into Monterey Bay, we experienced it for free.

△ *A kayaker encounters a whale.*

④ Point Lobos State Natural Reserve

831/624-4909 | Carmel | www.parks.ca.gov

It's no accident that Ansel Adams lived less than 10 minutes from Point Lobos State Natural Reserve. Or that Robert Louis Stevenson also used the site as the inspiration for his novel *Treasure Island*. Point Lobos combines Adams's photographs and Stevenson's prose into a vision of what coastal beauty, wildlife, and views are at their best: gorgeous ocean views, secluded coves and beaches, frolicking sea otters, sea lions, and harbor seals, and a cliffside walk through a forest of cypress and pine trees with offshore lookouts where you might spy the spouts of passing whales.

The only problem is the ease of access. A big sign on Highway 1 announces the reserve's widely recognized name, luring spontaneous visits from those cruising the Pacific Coast Highway. On a clear Sunday, the park can fill, with cars backed up at the entrance kiosk and every parking space taken.

Here's a tip: Visit early on a weekday morning and you can make the park your own.

▽ *Whaler's Cove*

BEST ACTIVITY: POINT LOBOS PERIMETER TRAIL

The **Point Lobos Perimeter Trail** (6 miles round-trip, 3 hours) connects a number of trails to some of the park's best highlights. Get a map at the entrance station and use it to scope out the many side trips possible along the way (or trails to cut the hike short). Though this may sound complex, it's easy and beautiful.

The best starting point is the parking area for Sea Lion Point. Look for the trailhead to the Sand Hill Trail, which connects to the **South Shore Trail,** a quiet path in the southern region of the park that travels past numerous beaches and coves. Walk one mile

△ *Pinnacle Point*

△ *Cypress Grove Trail, Point Lobos*

south on the South Shore Trail to the wheelchair-accessible **Bird Island Trail** (0.8 mile). Take the short side path to Bird Island Overlook and walk down the stairs to Gibson Beach.

Return to the Bird Island Trail and head northeast on the **South Plateau Trail** (0.7 mile), hiking north across the road to the **Carmelo Meadow Trail.** Bear right on the wheelchair-accessible **Granite Point Trail** (0.2 mile) for the side trip to Granite Point. The short loop trail leads to a rocky outcrop with spectacular views toward Carmel.

Finish the loop by returning the way you came and walking west along the shore of Whalers Cove. The Granite Point Trail meets with the **Cabin Trail** near the Whalers Cabin Museum. Follow the short Cabin Trail west to a T junction with the more challenging **North Shore Trail** (1.4 miles). The North Shore Trail loops west back to the parking lot.

Visit https://pointlobos.org/plan-your-visit/ for maps and more information.

WILDLIFE WATCHING

A series of deep coves on the wind-sheltered southern shore provides excellent habitat for **sea otters.** The best spots are drop-dead beautiful China Cove, the Slot, Bluefish Cove, and Sand Hill Cove (off Weston Beach and Hidden Beach). Bring binoculars to scan for sea otters in the coves below. Camera buffs should bring a long lens, then try to get close enough for the classic photograph of a sea otter paddling on its back, its favorite rock clinging on its chest.

The main entrance road into the reserve ends at the parking area for Sea Lion Point. The trailhead for the **Cypress Grove Trail** (1 mile, 30 minutes) is located at the north end of the parking lot. Walk 0.2 mile north along the trail to the junction with Pinnacle Point. Turn left on the Cypress Grove Loop (0.6 mile) and enjoy a panorama of Carmel Bay and Pebble Beach. The trail is routed past Headlands Cove and South Point before looping back through an ancient grove of cypress. At Cypress Cove, you can occasion-

I'm not an advanced diver, but I have done enough scuba diving to know that it's the closest thing to floating or flying. One of the best dive sites on the coast is at **Whalers Cove** at Point Lobos. You will find a beach with quiet surf set in a deep half-moon cove, filled in many spots with kelp forests. (The kelp provides habitat for rockfish, lingcod, and other fish. At times, it can feel diving in Monterey Aquarium.)

Carrie Wilson of the Department of Fish and Wildlife did a night dive here and called it "the closest thing I know to heaven." She explained: "The moonlight illuminated the quiet, peaceful, underwater world and I was unafraid and truly entranced with the many fish and creatures emerging from the darkness. Only the sound of my own breathing broke the silence. Enormous stinging sea nettle jellyfishes floated by and it was mesmerizing. With every movement and burst of bubbles escaping from my regulator, bioluminescent plankton released light resembling pixie dust. I felt consumed and intoxicated with calm and peacefulness."

An advance **reservation** ($20–30 plus processing fee) is required to dive or snorkel. Make reservations online (www.parks.ca.gov, under "Point Lobos SCUBA Diving") or contact dive coordinator Samantha Shackelton (samantha.shackelton@parks.ca.gov). Each permit is for a team of two divers or snorkelers (solo diving or snorkeling is not permitted). Divers must present a valid diver certification card.

Equipment rentals are available in Monterey at **Breakwater Scuba** (225 Cannery Row, Ste. M, 831/717-4546, http://breakwaterscuba.com, 9am-6pm Mon.-Fri., 7am-6pm Sat.-Sun.), **Bamboo Reef** (614 Lighthouse Ave., 831/372-1685, www.bambooreef.com, 9am-6pm Mon.-Fri., 7am-6pm Sat.-Sun. summer), and **Aquarius Dive Shop** (2040 Del Monte Ave., 831/375-1933, www.aquariusdivers.com, 9am-6pm Mon.-Thurs., 9am-7pm Fri., 7am-7pm Sat., 7am-6pm Sun.).

---

ally spot sea otters. In spring and early summer, it's common to see the spouts of passing **gray whales** from the Pinnacle Point lookout.

BEST OVERNIGHT: CARMEL BY THE RIVER RV PARK

Carmel by the River RV Park (27680 Schulte Rd.) is on the Carmel River, minutes away from Carmel, Cannery Row, the Monterey Bay Aquarium, golf courses, and the beach. There are 35 RV sites with full hookups, each separated by hedges and flowers. Char-coal grills are provided, and restrooms with showers, cable TV, Wi-Fi, a recreational cabana, a game room with pool tables, a gas barbecue area, and river access are available. A convenience store and propane gas are nearby. Some facilities (and a bathroom) are wheelchair-accessible. Leashed pets are permitted. **Reservations** (831/624-9329, www.carmelrv.com, fee) are accepted for two or more nights. Open year-round.

WHERE TO EAT

Before he retired as the food critic for the *San Francisco Chronicle*, Michael

Bauer tipped me off on a restaurant in Carmel called **Cultura Comida y Bebida** (Su Vesino Court, Dolores Street between 5th and 6th Streets, Carmel, 831/250-7005, www.culturacarmel. com, 5:30pm-10pm daily, brunch 10:30am Sat.-Sun.). I've spent a fair amount of time in South America, and the closest thing to dinner in a Belize village in California is dining at Bebida. My favorites dishes are those where lime infuses everything, from ceviche to brick-pressed chicken edged with cilantro rice. After eating here, you might be surprised to walk out and find that you are still in California.

DRIVING DIRECTIONS

From San Francisco, take I-280 South to Daly City and exit right for Highway 1/Pacifica. Bear left on Highway 1 and continue 67 miles south to Santa Cruz. In Santa Cruz, stay in the left lane for Highway 1 South. Turn left at the signed intersection and continue 46 miles south to Carmel. Continue south on Highway 1 for 4 miles (1.9 miles south of the bridge over the Carmel River) to the park entrance on the right.

If you're coming from the inland peninsula, take U.S. 101 south from San Jose and drive 40 miles to Salinas Valley. Take the exit signed for Monterey Peninsula/Highway 156 West and merge onto Highway 156 West. Drive 6.1 miles south to Highway 1. Merge onto Highway 1 South and drive 20 miles to Carmel. Continue south on Highway 1 for 4 miles (1.9 miles south of the bridge over the Carmel River) to the park entrance on the right.

Point Lobos is open 8am-7pm daily. There is a $10 fee for parking.

㊷ Big Sur

831/667–2315 | Highway 1 south of Caramel | www.parks.ca.gov

Synonymous with rugged cliffs, rock-strewn beaches, giant redwoods, coastal streams, and scenic waterfalls, Big Sur is a bucket-list destination. The Pacific Coast Highway (Highway 1) lines the coast and provides an extended tour of this land of charm, beauty, and captivation. Campgrounds and cabins offer rustic getaways, and wildlife includes everything from sea otters to California condors.

The gateway to Big Sur is the Bixby Bridge, where you can stop at the Castle Rock Viewpoint to take in the scene. Once you pass Bixby Bridge, a procession of state parks await: Garrapata, Andrew Molera, Julia Pfeiffer Burns, Pfeiffer Big Sur, and Limekiln. You will feel your heart start to beat at what awaits farther south. Take your pick, or better yet, take your time and pick them all.

Fall is the best time to visit. The skies are clear, temperatures range in the high 60s, and visitor traffic lightens. Summer offers the worst weather; the coast can be smothered in low fog, yet 10 miles inland, the blowtorch heat can hit 100°F.

▽ *hiking in Big Sur*

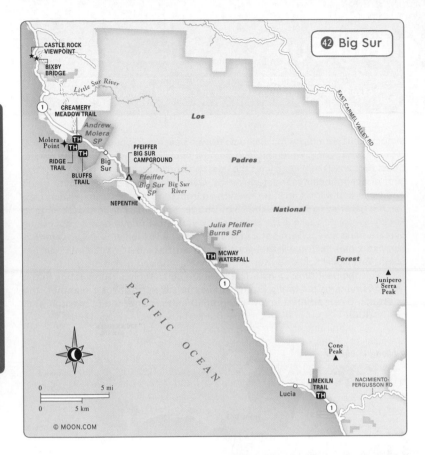

BEST VIEWS

Castle Rock Viewpoint

This is a world-class view of the Bixby Bridge and the coast south along Big Sur. The bridge crosses Bixby Creek, which feeds into a half-moon-shaped cove edged by high bluffs. Bring binoculars to peer down into the cove, where you can scan the surface for sea otters cruising around on their backs (this is their pupping ground).

Getting there: At Rio Road in Carmel (a stoplighted intersection), set your odometer to zero. Drive 13.4 miles south on Highway 1 and look for the sign for Castle Rock Viewpoint, where you can pull into one of the diagonal parking spots.

△ *Bixby Bridge*

Limekiln State Park (805/434-1996, www.parks.ca.gov) is Big Sur's best-kept secret. The **Limekiln Trail** (1.8 miles round-trip, 1 hour) is routed along Limekiln Creek for 0.5 mile to the park's limekilns, which were used to make limestone bricks and cement in the 1880s. Beyond the kilns, a fork off the main trail leads to Limekiln Falls, a gorgeous 100-foot waterfall that cascades over a limestone face. In late winter and early spring, when flush with water, you may get your boots wet while rock-hopping your way to the plunge pool. Your reward is an unforgettable experience.

If you want more, the trail continues to Twitchell Flats and beyond to Stony Ridge and Cone Peak for long-distance ocean views.

△ *hiking along Limekiln Creek*

Limekiln State Park has 24 **campsites** near the beach and in the redwoods. Picnic tables and fire grills are provided, and drinking water, restrooms with showers and flush toilets, and firewood are available. Some facilities are wheelchair-accessible. Leashed pets are allowed, except on trails. Parking is limited. **Reservations** (800/444-7275, www.reservecalifornia.com, fee) are accepted. Open year-round.

McWay Falls Overlook

McWay Falls is the postcard-perfect waterfall that pours over a cliff onto a beach and then flows out into the sea. The curved beach is protected by cliffs, with a massive rock outcrop jutting up from its southern side; there is no access to the actual beach.

Getting there: McWay Falls is on Highway 1, 36 miles south of Camel. The best view is from an unsigned dirt pullout on the shoulder (if you reach the entrance to Julia Pfeiffer Burns State Park, you have gone a 0.5 mile too far). Look for an opening between the trees on the edge of the bluff.

Wheelchair-accessible option: In **Julia Pfeiffer Burns State Park** (Hwy. 1, 831/667-2315 or 831/649-2836, www.parks.ca.gov), the Overlook Trail (1 mile round-trip, 1 hour) is paved to handle the high traffic to the falls. It's routed 0.5 mile through a tunnel under Highway 1 to a bench with similar eye-popping views. (The trail beyond the bench is closed due to damage from winter storms.)

BEST HIKE: BLUFF TRAIL

In their eagerness to reach the heart of Big Sur, people often cruise right by the best coastal hike in the region. **Andrew Molera State Park** (Hwy. 1, 831/667-1112, www.parks.ca.gov) is

△ *McWay Falls, Julia Pfeiffer Burns State Park*

parks.ca.gov) is one of the most popular campgrounds in California. There are 189 sites for tents or RVs and trailers, and the adjoining Big Sur Lodge offers 62 cottages. Picnic tables and fire grills are provided, and drinking water and restrooms with flush toilets and showers are available. Some facilities are wheelchair-accessible. Leashed pets are permitted in the campground and on paved trails only.

Reservations (800/444-7275, www. reservecalifornia.com, fee) are a necessity. Open year-round.

WHERE TO EAT

Sooner or later, everybody who cruises through Big Sur ends up eating at **Nepenthe** (48510 Hwy. 1, Big Sur, 831/667-2345, 11:30am-10pm daily). For many, it feels just right: under the neck tie-and-big money scene at Ventana, but a cut above the old hippy retreats. Choose a clear day and dine outdoors on the deck to take in the sunset with a cold brew or glass of your favorite wine. I've gorged on the BLT with shrimp and tons of fries (I know, I know, may not be your thing). Though I hear stories claiming otherwise, I've never been disappointed.

DRIVING DIRECTIONS

There are few physical addresses in Big Sur. Your best bet is to set the odometer to zero in Carmel and match your mileage to the stops below. At the intersection with Highway 1 and Rio Road in Carmel, start tracking your miles as you head south on Highway 1:

- Garrapata State Park is 7 miles south.
- Bixby Bridge is 13 miles south.
- Andrew Molera is 19 miles south (2 miles north of the town of Big Sur).
- Pfeiffer Big Sur is 26 miles south (2 miles south of Big Sur).
- Julia Pfeiffer Burns is 37 miles south (13 miles south of Big Sur)
- Limekiln is 52 miles south (27.7 miles south of Big Sur).

home to the **Bluff Trail** (2 miles round-trip, 2 hours), which overlooks miles of beach, coast, and ocean, with world-class views.

From the trailhead, hike along the Creamery Meadow Trail for a short distance to the Big Sur River. Cross over the footbridge and hike one mile to the junction with the Ridge Trail. Turn left and continue 100 yards to the connection with the Bluff Trail on the right. A series of stacks and outcrops rise along the shore, and a deep cove feeds the Big Sur River and its lagoon as the trail curves to the north to Molera Point. The breathtaking view extends out to sea.

BEST OVERNIGHT: PFEIFFER BIG SUR STATE PARK

At Big Sur, the campgrounds come in a variety of settings: small hideaways in the redwoods, with some near the Big Sur River and others in the forest. Reservations are needed far in advance. **Pfeiffer Big Sur State Park** (Hwy. 1, mile marker 47.2, 831/667-1112, www.

CAMPFIRE STORIES

$\mathcal{T}$hanks to a captive breeding program, condors (once almost extinct) have been reestablished, and there are now 463 condors living in the vicinity of Big Sur and the neighboring Ventana Wilderness.

For a CBS television segment, it was my job to find, film, and tell the story of the California condor and its recovery. Our crew showed up and, after two days, the best we could do was capture distant shots of condors hovering over Ventana Ridge more than 10 miles away. They looked like little black specks against the sky. After lunch at Nepenthe, we drove south and rounded a curve where an unbelievably giant California condor sat perched on the post of a guardrail along a pullout on the shoulder. A layer of fog hung right below. We filmed the giant condor for half an hour and then, as if in a movie, it lifted off, braced its wings, and angled in and out of the surface layer of fog. It was an incredible stroke of luck and produced an amazing film.

Then the fog lifted and we saw that a dead whale had washed up on the beach below. That's why the condor was there. The scavenger swooped down and landed on the whale for its own lunch.

△ *California condor*

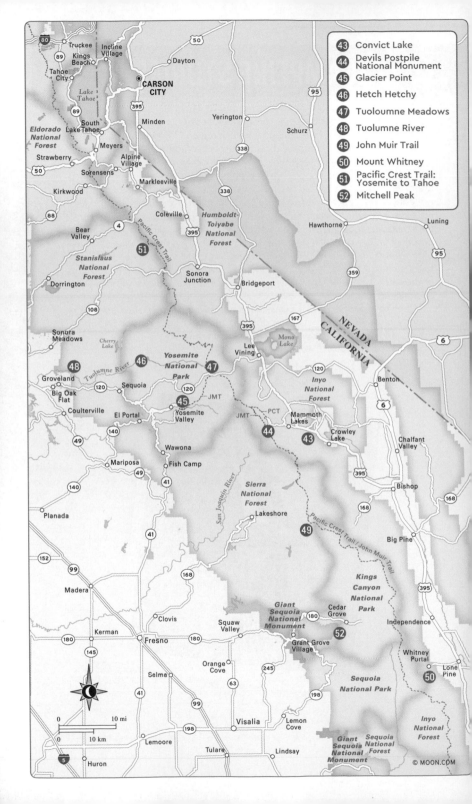

43	Convict Lake
44	Devils Postpile National Monument
45	Glacier Point
46	Hetch Hetchy
47	Tuoloumne Meadows
48	Tuolumne River
49	John Muir Trail
50	Mount Whitney
51	Pacific Crest Trail: Yosemite to Tahoe
52	Mitchell Peak

© MOON.COM

~ Chapter 9 ~

YOSEMITE AND EASTERN SIERRA

㊸ Convict Lake

800/992-2260 | Convict Lake Resort | www.convictlake.com

At 7,583 feet, Convict Lake is a mountain shrine framed by a wall of wilderness peaks, fronted by a conifer-lined shore, and bordered by the John Muir Wilderness. The fishing and hiking is outstanding here, and the scenery is off-the-charts beautiful. In fall, aspens coat the surrounding basin in brilliant yellows and golds—a world-class artist could not paint a prettier picture.

Convict Lake has excellent trout fishing (especially in April), a small marina with boat rentals, a pretty resort with cabin rentals, a nearby campground, and a trailhead for spectacular hikes. The trail up the canyon opens anytime late May-early July. The resort's peak season is summer, yet it's fall when Convict Lake truly shines and when a visit here will be hard to forget. The aspens turn the basin into a kaleidoscope of colors, and hiking here feels like walking through a painting.

▽ *Convict Lake*

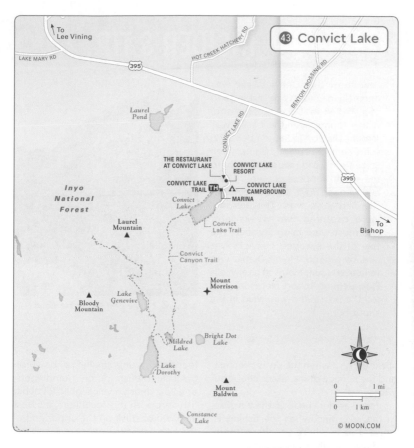

BEST ACTIVITY: FISHING

Anglers who love natural beauty, lots of trout, and a chance for a trophy can practice their religion at Convict Lake. The fishing here can be outstanding, with lots of fish and a sprinkling of giants. High levels of trout stocks jump-start the success.

The legal hours for trout fishing are defined as one hour before sunrise until one hour after sunset. Here's a tip: Time your trip during a new moon, when the skies will be at their darkest. This is when the trout are most likely to feed (during a legal fishing time). If you plan to target big browns and rainbows, plan to fish at both dawn and dusk in shaded areas and near

△ fishing Convict Lake

Few know that Convict Lake was originally named "Lake Diablo" and that 12,268-foot Mount Morrison, which looms over the basin, was "Mount Diablo." In September 1872, some convicts escaped from Carson State Prison and made their way to the south. A posse cornered them here, engaging in a shoot-out that the bad guys won. The convicts were captured two weeks later and most were hung. By then, the tale of the escaped convicts was already legend. Mount Diablo was renamed Mount Morrison after Wells Fargo agent Robert Morrison, who led the posse and was killed in the shoot-out.

△ Convict Lake and Mount Morrison

structures, or when the sky is overcast and the surface of the lake is chopped with wind.

Many anglers head to the left side of the lake, and when the fishing is good, this is where you'll see them lined up. Shoreliners, welcome to the club. Anglers will rig here with a single hook and a split shot and a chartreuse Power Nugget for bait, toss it out, and wait for a bite. Bring lawn chairs, prop your rod up alongside, and take in the grandeur of the Sierra backdrop while waiting for the fish to bite. Don't sweat the line of anglers. All that bait in the water brings the fish right up, almost like a chum line.

In the early summer and early fall, when the weather is cold and fishing pressure is low, huge rainbow trout and brown trout can be caught by trolling with a technique I call the "cat-and-mouse." Off downrigger lines, I run a large Cop Car-colored Needlefish, AC Plug with plastic tail, or a jointed black-gold Rapala on lines usually 25 feet deep. Just above, at 15

feet deep, I run a smaller rainbow-colored Needlefish, purple Humdingers, or a Sparklefish. I've caught a lot of big fish here with this technique. It's best at dawn or dusk on the upper end of the lake near the outlet creek and the shoreline drop-offs.

A last note: At dusk, the big browns can emerge. A few times I've seen how "zip trolling" (zigzagging with a Speedy Shiner) can entice a big one during the last half hour of legal fishing time.

Convict Lake Resort operates a **marina** (760/934–3800, sunrise-sunset daily late Apr.-Nov. 15) and boat ramp off Convict Creek Road. Fishing boats are available for rent; reservations are required. The lake speed limit is 10 mph, good for small boats with trolling motors, kayaks, or canoes.

HIKE THE CONVICT CREEK TRAIL

This is one of the best treks in the Eastern Sierra. From the trailhead at

△ *Convict Creek Trail*

the north shore of Convict Lake, the **Convict Creek Trail** (6 miles round-trip, 3.5 hours) is routed along the side of the lake to climb west past aspens into Convict Creek Canyon. The trail is steep with little shade outside of a few aspens. The big views start as you hike above Convict Lake Basin. As you near the canyon, look east across the desert and west to Convict Creek Canyon above, framed by a granite rim. About 1.5 miles in, you'll have to scramble to get around a few short sections of trail with some washouts. At 3 miles in, you arrive at the Convict Creek crossing, the "end of the road" for most day hikers.

Convict Creek is impassable in high water, except in late summer when the crossing is usually an easy rock-hop. For a 15-mile round-trip day hike (or a great overnighter), follow the trail as it continues steeply up the canyon and disappears in spots due to past washouts. As it enters the John Muir Wilderness, you'll arrive at a series of alpine lakes above tree line at 10,000 feet. The first lake is **Mildred Lake,** (4.9 miles one-way), a payoff destination for the ambitious day

hiker. Beyond Mildred Lake, the route becomes faint and hard to follow. A 2,750-foot climb leads to **Lake Dorothy** (7.5 miles one-way) at 10,275 feet, the largest lake in the basin and known for its rare, white-sand beach. It's 1 mile farther to **Lake Genevieve** (7.5 miles one-way) at 10,000 feet.

Trail notes: The trail past Convict Creek is hard to follow, and the crossing *should not be attempted in high water*. Attempts to install a bridge at this crossing have met with washouts from early summer snowmelt. For a report on creek conditions, call Lara Kaylor at the **Mammoth Lakes Welcome Center** (760/924-5500, 8am-5pm daily). Overnight visits require a **permit** (www.recreation.gov) and a bear-proof container. Campfires are not permitted above 10,000 feet.

BEST OVERNIGHT: CONVICT LAKE RESORT

Over the years, **Convict Lake Resort** (2000 Convict Lake Rd., Mammoth Lakes, 800/992-2260, www.convict-lake.com) has transformed from a fish camp in the 1920s to a full-service

△ Convict Lake

resort with cabin rentals, a restaurant, bar, store, and small marina that rents boats. The rustic 28 cabins and three lodges are open year-round and come with fully equipped kitchens, beds and linens, private baths, heating, and free Wi-Fi. Pets are welcome, and horseback rides are available. The place often fills in summer and offers a sensational setting to watch meteor showers.

If the resort is full, try nearby **Convict Creek Campground** (Inyo National Forest, www.fs.usda.gov, closed in winter), located about 0.5 mile south of the resort. The stark desert setting along Convict Creek has 85 sites for tents or RVs (no hookups). Picnic tables, fire grills, and bear boxes are provided. Drinking water, flush toilets, and a dump station are available. Showers are available at the resort. Some facilities are wheelchair-accessible. Leashed pets are permitted.

Reservations (877/444-6777, www. recreation.gov, mid-Apr.-Oct., $25) are accepted.

WHERE TO EAT

The biggest surprise at **The Restaurant at Convict Lake** (Convict Lake Resort, 760/934-3800 ext. 2 for reservations, 5:30pm-close daily) is the top-shelf menu, decent pricing (on the high end), a pretty woodsy interior with high ceilings, a gorgeous setting, and a full bar. This is no low-end grill. Take your pick from a variety of continental cuisine—lamb, grass-fed steaks, seafood, pastas, and pizza in summer—plus an array of appetizers and drinks. An adjoining lounge offers the same menu, plus sports across four TVs. When small-craft pilots fly in to nearby Mammoth Lakes Airport, this is where they eat.

DRIVING DIRECTIONS

From Lee Vining at the junction of Highway 120 and U.S. 395, take U.S. 395 south for 31 miles (5 miles past Mammoth Junction) to Convict Lake Road, adjacent to Mammoth Lakes Airport. Turn right (west) on Convict Lake Road and drive 3 miles to Convict Lake. For the resort and cabins, turn right; for the campground, turn left.

CAMPFIRE STORIES

*O*n a cool fall evening, just as dusk was overtaking Convict Lake, I spotted a 20-pound brown trout just ahead of my canoe. It rolled on the surface of the lake like a whale. In the moment, it felt like cannons were firing in my chest. In perfect silence, I approached and then passed over the fish and nearly stopped breathing. Just as I envisioned my lure in front of that giant trout, I said, "Now." A second later, my rod went off—a fish had struck the lure and it felt like the switch thrown for an electric chair. I set the hook so hard that the poor little 6-inch trout I'd *actually* hooked came flying out of the water 20 feet through the air.

I let it go and, as it swam away, we both appeared a bit dazed. Maybe it was heading to the trout chiropractor to treat a sprained neck.

△ *Convict Lake*

44 Devils Postpile National Monument

888/466-2666 | Mammoth Lakes | www.visitmammoth.com

Devils Postpile National Monument contains one of the best examples in the world of an unusual hexagonal, columnar jointed rock. From the Postpile, trails lead to Rainbow Falls, a breathtaking 101-foot cascade that produces rainbows in its floating mist, and then expands out into the surrounding Ansel Adams Wilderness where the John Muir and Pacific Crest Trails meet and then join to become one.

This area was a playground for John Muir and Ansel Adams. Everywhere you turn, high Sierra granite beauty and pristine gem-like lakes and streams surround you. Trailheads, campgrounds, and peaks line up one after another. From Agnew Meadows, the John Muir Trail leads north to the outlet of Thousand Island Lake (9,833 feet), backed by the stegosaurus-like rim of the Minarets and topped by Banner Peak (12,942 feet) and nearby Mount Ritter (13,149 feet). From Upper Soda Springs, the John Muir Trail trips south along the San Joaquin River and past Minaret Falls toward Reds Meadow Resort.

The road from Mammoth Lakes heads west over Minaret Pass and down the other side to a series of adventures that are among the best in California. No matter what you choose, you may feel the presence of Muir and Adams every step of the way.

▽ Devils Postpile National Monument

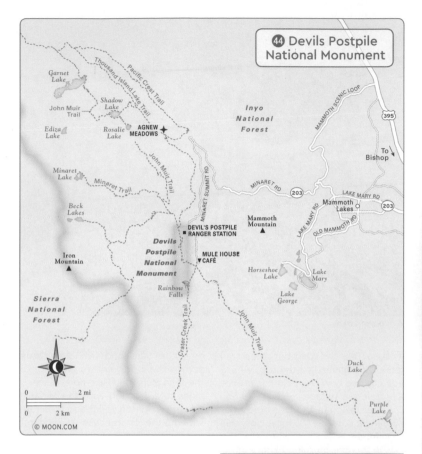

BEST ACTIVITY:
HIKE TO RAINBOW FALLS

The first time you lay eyes on 101-foot **Rainbow Falls** (5 miles round-trip, 3 hours), the tall, wide, and forceful waterfall comes as an awesome surprise. Most first-time visitors see it during a trip to the Devils Postpile, the fascinating pillar of volcanic rock columns left from a lava flow nearly 100,000 years ago. You get to see both on one of the best short hikes in California.

From the Devils Postpile Ranger Station (shuttle stop 6), walk 0.4 mile south to view the **Devils Postpile** lava columns. The columns rise together to form a massive pillar of columnar rock. A pile of eroded rubble lies at

△ *Rainbow Falls at Devils Postpile National Monument*

△ *Minaret Lake*

its base. Take the short but steep trail (about 15 minutes) to the top, where you can see how the columns create a mosaic-like surface.

After taking in this geologic phenomenon, continue 2.5 miles downhill to **Rainbow Falls.** Plan to arrive at the falls in the late morning or mid-afternoon; this is when the sun refracts in the mist, creating a prism effect that often results in a spectacular rainbow. Two overlook areas across from the brink of the falls offer an excellent view, or hike down a refurbished staircase to a plunge pool at the base of the falls for an even better vantage point.

BACKPACK TO MINARET LAKE

Minaret Lake (16 miles round-trip, 2 days) sits nestled at 9,735 feet in granite below the glacial-carved Minarets. The trail to get there is a 2,400-foot climb over eight miles. It might be the closest thing to falling in love.

From the Devils Postpile Ranger Station, hike south to cross a bridge over the San Joaquin River. Once across the bridge, turn right onto the John Muir Trail. Hike north for two miles to a junction with the Minaret Lake Trail. Tighten your pack, then turn left onto the Minaret Lake Trail and get ready for a climb.

The trail ascends along Minaret Creek, eventually rising above tree line in the last mile, an hour-long butt-kicker of a hike. The trail skirts the Minaret Lake outlet, tracing the line of the north shore, before arriving at the lake. There are several good lakeside campsites. Make camp, grab a seat, and fall in love: The panorama includes miles of high-country rims topped by 12,264-foot Clyde Minaret and 12,205-foot Ken Minaret Peaks.

Trail notes: A wilderness **permit** is required. Reserve one online in advance (www.recreation.gov, fee). Permits can be picked up in person at the **Mammoth Lakes Welcome Center** (2500 Main St., Mammoth Lakes, 760/873-2483, www.fs.usda.gov/inyo, 8am-5pm daily summer, 8:30am-4:30pm daily winter).

△ *out of Agnew Meadows trailhead*

(You can also hike to Minaret Lake from Upper Soda Spring Campground. Just hike south on the Pacific Crest Trail, then turn north on the John Muir Trail. The distance is about the same as from the ranger station.)

BEST OVERNIGHT: AGNEW MEADOWS

This is a camp best used as a launching pad for a backpacking trip or day of fly-fishing for trout. It is set at 8,400 feet along the Upper San Joaquin River. Near camp, you can connect to either the River Trail or the John Muir Trail. On the JMT, this is the best launch point south for the seven-mile (one-way) hike to Thousand Island Lake, a beautiful lake sprinkled with islands set below Banner Peak and Mount Ritter.

The campground consists of standard sites and four group sites. The group sites are set up for 10–20 people; we'll book it for our group of typically 6–8 and use it as a base for fishing and day hikes. Picnic tables, fire grills, and bear-proof food lockers are provided.

Drinking water and vault toilets are available. Supplies can be obtained at the Reds Meadow Resort store. Some facilities are wheelchair-accessible. Leashed pets are permitted.

Reservations (877/444-6777, www. recreation.gov, fee) are required for the group sites. Standard sites are first-come, first-served with self-registration. A $10 per vehicle day pass is required to drive into Reds Meadow/ Agnew Meadows. Open July-mid-September, weather permitting.

WHERE TO EAT

Reds Meadow Resort (1 Reds Circle, Mammoth Lakes, 760/934-2345, www. redsmeadow.com, 7am-7pm daily, dinner reservations required before 4pm) is a rustic mountain resort with pretty A-frame cabins, horseback riding, a general store, and the **Mule House Café,** a landmark on the John Muir Trail. After two weeks of eating trail food while backpacking the JMT from Whitney, eating here feels like dining at The Ahwahnee in Yosemite.

⬤ INSIDER'S TIP

On the Upper San Joaquin River, you get the rare chance to catch the "Grand Slam" of high Sierra trout fishing: rainbow, brook, brown, and golden trout, all on the same day.

Plan to drive in at first light (before 7am) in order to beat the required shuttle bus. Past the entrance station, there's a deep bend in Highway 203. Turn right here onto Agnew Meadows Road and drive the access road to **Agnew Meadows Campground.** Park and hike a spur down to the **River Trail,** which provides access to the Upper San Joaquin River at roughly 8,500 feet. In most summers, the river dwindles to a large creek. Hike upstream in complete stealth, staying low and keeping any shade off the water. Sneak-fish with a fly rod, floating line, and 9-foot leader, and make short, precise casts. My go-to patterns are the Prince Nymph, Copper John, Hare's Ear, and caddis when there's a surface hatch, and the near-guaranteed winner, Royal Coachman. Hit it right and you can have a 20-fish Grand Slam day. Though the fish aren't large, the high Sierra landscape makes this one of the best fly-fishing trips in California.

Note: If you turn left and walk downstream, there is about a mile or so of good fishing, but then you'll start running into people from the downstream campgrounds of Soda Springs and Pumice Flat.

I remember staring at the ice cubes in my glass of water, not quite believing how anyone could take ice for granted. Then a bacon cheeseburger was placed in front of me. It may sound like standard fare, but that first bite is impossible to describe.

DRIVING DIRECTIONS

Devils Postpile is west of Mammoth Lakes in the Eastern Sierra. From US 395 near Mammoth Lakes, take the exit for Highway 203. Turn west on Highway 203 and drive 4 miles through the town of Mammoth Lakes to Minaret Road (Highway 203). Turn right onto Minaret Road and drive 4.5 miles to the shuttle bus terminal adjacent to Mammoth Mountain Ski Area. Purchase an access pass and board the shuttle bus here.

SHUTTLE BUS

Reds Meadow Road (closed in winter) into Devils Postpile is only open to private vehicles before 7am and after 7pm (with a $10 entrance fee), unless you are staying at Reds Meadows Resort or are camping. All other visitors must take the **Reds Meadow Shuttle Bus** (www.nps.gov/depo, hours and times vary seasonally, $8 adults, $4 children ages 3–15), which leaves from the Mammoth Mountain Main Lodge (Minaret Rd.), where parking is usually available.

The shuttle bus stops at Agnew Meadows (shuttle stop 1), Upper Soda Springs (shuttle stop 3), Minaret Falls (shuttle stop 5), Devils Postpile Ranger Station (shuttle stop 6), Rainbow Falls Trailhead (shuttle stop 9), and Reds Meadow Resort (shuttle stop 10).

CAMPFIRE STORIES

*O*n one trek into the Ansel Adams Wilderness, past Thousand Island Lake at the foot of Banner Peak and Mount Ritter, we took photos with an old 35mm camera and black-and-white film. While we were there, we felt the shadow of John Muir and Ansel Adams everywhere we went. When we printed up the photos, it was like looking at microfiche from a time machine. This was affirmation that no outdoor adventure is about your accomplishments. It's not about how far you hiked, how fast, what mountain you summited, or how big a fish you caught. The greatest reward of the outdoors is how it makes you feel. Looking at those black-and-whites was one of the great lessons on how the wilderness can transform your life.

△ *Mount Ritter and Banner Peak*

⑮ Glacier Point

209/372-0200 | Yosemite National Park | www.nps.gov/yose

There may be no better sight than the view from 7,214-foot Glacier Point. From the parking lot at Glacier Point, it is a short walk downhill to the leading edge of the overlook. Directly across the open air is 8,839-foot Half Dome, rising up like nature's perfect sculpture. To the left of Half Dome, you can see Tenaya Canyon, the least-known wildland in Yosemite. Across is a view of Yosemite Falls and below, in the Merced River Canyon, is Vernal and Nevada Falls. Beyond is several hundred square miles of Yosemite's wilderness backcountry.

As you drive in on Glacier Point Road (closed in winter), you will pass three of the park's best trailheads, all of which offer day hikes with views in summer (in winter, these become snow treks). These include Sentinel Dome (incredible view of Yosemite Falls), Taft Point (breathtaking drop, incredible view of El Capitan), and Dewey Point (directly across from El Capitan), and the starting point for one of Yosemite's greatest one-way hikes with a bus shuttle, the Panorama Trail Loop (past three waterfalls).

Most of Glacier Point Road closes November-June. The best time to come here is in the peak of summer (July-Sept.), when finding a parking spot may be difficult. But there is a relief valve for this pressure-cooker. From Yosemite Valley, take the park's shuttle bus to Glacier Point instead, and then hike the Panorama Trail back to the Valley.

▽ *You have to hike off the Pohono Trail in order to get to this spot in Glacier Point.*

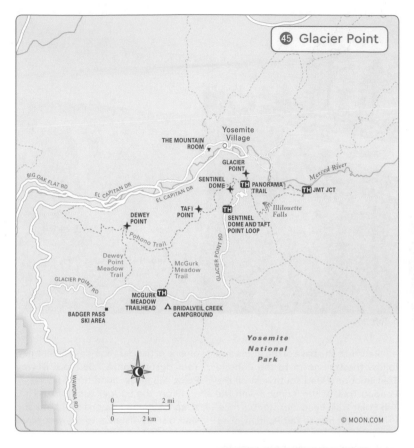

THE MOUNTAIN ROOM

Yosemite Village

GLACIER POINT

SENTINEL DOME

TH PANORAMA TRAIL

TH JMT JCT

Merced River

BIG OAK FLAT RD

EL CAPITAN DR

EL CAPITAN DR

DEWEY POINT

TAFT POINT

TH

SENTINEL DOME AND TAFT POINT LOOP

Illilouette Falls

Pohono Trail

Dewey Point Meadow Trail

McGurk Meadow Trail

GLACIER POINT RD

GLACIER POINT RD

MCGURK MEADOW TRAILHEAD **TH**

A BRIDALVEIL CREEK CAMPGROUND

BADGER PASS SKI AREA

Yosemite National Park

WAWONA RD

0   2 mi

0   2 km

© MOON.COM

BEST ACTIVITY: SENTINEL DOME AND TAFT POINT LOOP

Take one trailhead, add two hikes, and you've got the **Sentinel Dome and Taft Point Loop** (4.9 miles round-trip, 3–4 hours). From the Sentinel Dome and Taft Point Trailhead on Glacier Point Road, head northeast on the Sentinel Dome Trail. The hike to 8,122-foot **Sentinel Dome** (1.8 miles round-trip, 1 hour) provides the park's best view of Yosemite Falls below. The easy walk is nearly flat over the mile-long trail to the base of the dome. Everybody breaks off-trail to trek up to the top of the polished granite dome (about 100 yards or so) for the panorama of Yosemite Valley.

△ *view from the Sentinel Dome Trail*

△ Taft Point

Return to the base of the dome and follow the trail north to the Pohono Trail junction. Head southwest on the Pohono Trail. At the junction with the Taft Point Trail, head west for 0.5 mile.

The short hike to **Taft Point** involves a small climb. The payoff is a cliff-top brink where you can peer over the edge into Yosemite Valley thousands of feet below. As you arrive at the south rim, you first pass a series of fissures—deep cracks in the leading edges of granite. Just beyond is 7,503-foot Taft Point. Standing at the edge and peering thousands of feet down is awesome and surreal, with stunning views of all the valley landmarks.

Return via the Taft Point Trail for 1.1 miles back to the joint trailhead.

DEWEY POINT

Snowshoe in Winter

When you set off from the **Badger Pass Ski Area** (Glacier Point Rd., 209/372-1000, www.travelyosemite.com, mid-Dec.-Mar.) with a pair of snowshoes or cross-country skis, you are launching off on one of the best one-day winter treks. Your destination is 7,385-foot **Dewey Point** (9.8 miles round-trip, 5 hours).

From the Badger Pass parking lot, strap on your crampons or Yaktrax and walk a short distance to snow-covered Glacier Point Road (where snowplow operations stop). Turn right and snowshoe 1.4 miles east up Glacier Point Road toward Summit Meadow. Look for a sign on the left: a gold triangle with the number 18. This is the **Dewey Point Meadow Trail.**

Turn north here and trek 2.5 miles to a junction signed for the **Dewey Point Trail.** (Trail markers on the trees help keep you on track.) Descend 1 mile and emerge from forest at Dewey Point. Perched directly across the valley is the 7,573-foot vertical monolith of El Capitan. To the right is Cathedral Spire. The views extend beyond Yosemite Valley to Half Dome and across to Clouds Rest, miles of snow-bound wilderness.

For the return trek, hike back along the **McGurk Meadow Trail** to Glacier Point Road. (The **Dewey Point Ridge**

△ *foggy morning at the Bridalveil Campground*

Trail is best hiked on the way in. It requires an additional climb and is longer, plus you get views west to a silhouette of Mount Diablo).

Hike in Summer

The **McGurk Meadow Trailhead** (8 miles round-trip, 4–5 hours) is on Glacier Point Road, north of Bridalveil Campground. (Look for a parking pullout on the left shoulder.) The McGurk Meadow Trail is routed through pristine McGurk Meadow and along Bridalveil Creek; this is one of the prettiest off-the-radar sites in Yosemite. In 1.9 miles, turn left (west) on the Pohono Trail, which ventures 2.1 miles to Dewey Point and its overlook of El Capitan.

BEST OVERNIGHT: BRIDALVEIL CAMPGROUND

Set in the forest at an elevation of 7,200 feet, **Bridalveil Campground** (off Glacier Point Rd.) is the closest campground to Glacier Point. Though the campground does not have views of Yosemite Valley, it does have access to some of the best day hikes in the park. There are 110 sites for tents or RVs (no hookups), three equestrian sites, and two group sites. Picnic tables, fire rings, and bear boxes (mandatory) are provided. Drinking water and flush toilets are available. Leashed pets are permitted, except in the group sites.

Reservations (800/444-6777, www.recreation.gov, fee) are accepted for the group sites. Individual sites are first-come, first-served. A park entrance fee is required. Open July-early September.

WHERE TO EAT

There is nowhere to eat along Glacier Point Road, so you'll have to drive 45 minutes into Yosemite Valley.

In Yosemite Valley, dining at The Ahwahnee is out for most of us since it requires "proper attire" (and, if you've been camping for a week, a shower as well). If you still want a first-class dinner and your appearance is at least passable, head to **The Mountain**

The **Panorama Trail** (8.3 miles one-way, 6–8 hours) is one of the greatest one-way hikes (with a shuttle bus). From Yosemite Valley, take the Glacier Point Tour bus (see *Driving Directions*) to Glacier Point. From Glacier Point, locate the trailhead for the Panorama Trail. The Panorama Trail plummets 1,300 feet (4,000 feet total) down switchbacks past Illilouette Fall (at 2 miles) before climbing 800 feet out of the canyon to the ridgeline. You'll descend again 600 feet to the junction with the John Muir Trail at the top of 594-foot Nevada Fall, with a sensational view of Liberty Cap. To continue into Yosemite Valley, turn right on the Mist Trail, which is routed 2.9 miles past Nevada Fall, the Emerald Pool, and 317-foot Vernal Fall. A shuttle stop (and a restroom) await at the Happy Isles Trailhead.

Room Restaurant (Yosemite Valley Lodge, 9006 Yosemite Lodge Dr., 888/413–8869, www.travelyosemite.com, 5pm-10pm daily). The restaurant's towering glass windows frame a view of Yosemite Falls, the perfect setting for top-shelf steaks, seafood, and salads.

DRIVING DIRECTIONS

From Yosemite Valley, drive out of the valley on Northside Drive. In 4.8 miles, you'll reach a fork with Southside Drive; get in the left lane. Turn left on Southside Drive and continue 0.9 mile (stay right) to a fork with Highway 41S/Wawona Road. Bear right on Highway 41 and drive 9.2 miles south to Glacier Point Road. Turn left onto Glacier Point Road and drive 5.1 miles to Badger Pass, 7.8 miles to the turnoff for Bridalveil Campground, 13.2 miles to the Sentinel Dome and Taft Point Trailhead, or 16 miles to the parking area and restrooms at Glacier Point. If you wait for a few minutes, parking spots may open up.

Note: Glacier Point Road will close in 2021 in order to rebuild the 10 miles of road from Badger Pass to Glacier Point.

Shuttle bus option: Late May-October, the **Glacier Point Tour bus** (888/413–8869, www.travelyosemite.com, departs 8:30am and 1:30pm, $28.50 one-way, $57 round-trip) shuttles visitors from the Yosemite Valley Lodge to Glacier Point. Purchase tickets in advance online or at any Yosemite tour desk.

CAMPFIRE STORIES

*O*n a winter trek to Dewey Point, we were gearing up for the trip at the Badger Pass parking lot when a guy strolled by who couldn't understand all the equipment we had brought with us: cross-country skis, three pairs of different-size snowshoes, multiple sizes of crampons, and two sets of Yaktrax. "It's like golf," I told him, "you need a club for every shot." He appeared skeptical. I explained that the snowshoe trek to Dewey Point is my favorite winter trip anywhere. Yet every time we've gone, the conditions have varied radically, from three feet of powder (where we had to break trail with giant snowshoes) to a hardened ice cap where we could walk in hiking boots with Yaktrax and ski poles.

Here's the deal: Match your gear with the conditions. Select the size of snowshoe according to snow conditions (and not your weight): the softer the snow, the larger the snowshoe (to keep from postholing). On ice, wear Yaktrax. On iced-over steep slopes, wear crampons, where the steeper the slope, the longer the points. A few other things: Never snowshoe in a cross-country ski trail. Wear synthetics, a fleece layer, and a Gore-Tex shell. Apply sunscreen, and wear polarized sunglasses and high-quality snow gloves.

The guy, it turned out, was unconvinced. "I think you just like having a lot of stuff."

△ *Dewey Point*

Some call Hetch Hetchy John Muir's "heaven and hell." Muir fought hard against the damming of Hetch Hetchy, considered a second Yosemite Valley. He lost the battle against the dam in 1913 and passed away the following year. Many said he died of a broken heart. But Muir's hell can be heaven for today's hikers and backpackers.

From the top of 403-foot O'Shaughnessy Dam, the water plunges straight down, feeding into the Tuolumne River. The reservoir's cerulean-blue water spans for miles and is surrounded by towering granite landmarks. To the right, massive Kolana Rock (5,772 feet) looms over the lake. To the left, a mini El Capitan rises nearly vertical. Just beyond, look for the lower tier of Wapama Falls. At 6,197 feet, Hetch Hetchy Dome juts up at a 45-degree angle. On a far ridge is 7,730-foot Smith Peak, a stark mountaintop against the sky.

The dam is the launch point for one of the park's great day hikes: the trail to Wapama Falls. Backpackers can take off on a 25-mile loop into the wilderness via Lake Vernon and Mount Gibson down to Rancheria Falls and the headwaters of Hetch Hetchy.

At 3,783 feet, Hetch Hetchy experiences the park's warmest temperatures. Spring arrives early, and hiking access is often good in March and April. Access to the high-country wilderness opens in late May and early June. By mid-July-August, it's very hot.

Every day in summer, 20,000 people jam into the 7.5-square miles of Yosemite Valley. But quiet Hetch Hetchy sees only a fraction of that. For today's visitors, Muir's hell can be a hiker's heaven.

▽ *Hetch Hetchy Reservoir*

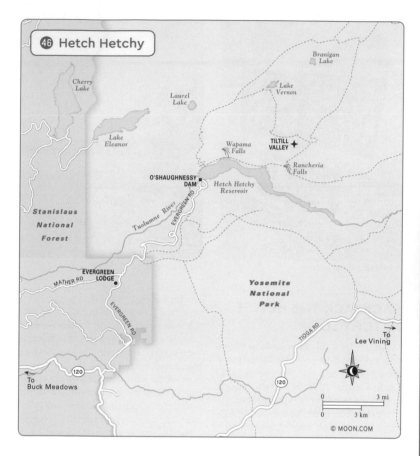

BEST ACTIVITY: HIKE TO WAPAMA FALLS

The trail to **Wapama Falls** (5 miles round-trip, 2 hours) is a great and easy walk with a world-class payoff: Memorable views of granite domes and mountain peaks without the herds of people you find on the trails in Yosemite Valley.

From the O'Shaughnessy Dam, a paved path extends across the top of the dam and through a 500-foot tunnel. As you emerge out the other side of the tunnel, you're met with a sweeping view of the Hetch Hetchy Reservoir, one of the best spots for a photo. The undulating trail is etched into the granite wall in spots, and wide and treed in others, for 2.4 miles to the lower chute of Wapama Falls where a metal bridge extends over Falls Creek. This is a great spot to take a seat, have lunch, and peer at the lower cascade.

When flying my plane over Hetch Hetchy, I can look down and see its entire 1,400-foot length. From the brink of the falls, the water free-falls into a gorge, stair-steps twice, and then emerges to feather out in a wide, white flume before crashing into the rocks near the bridge.

Note: During peak flows and in years of heavy snowmelt, the waterfall can flood the bridge and the park will close the trail at this point. Hikers trying to cross in hip-deep water have been swept away and have drowned.

△ *hiking trail signpost*

△ *Lake Vernon*

BACKPACK THE HETCH HETCHY LOOP

I love this trip. This **25-mile loop** offers the opportunity to camp at pristine Lake Vernon and visit Rancheria Falls, with a stop at little-known Mount Gibson, one of my favorite spots.

While I do love this trek, completing it in two days might be too ambitious for some. You can ease the miles by extending the trip with overnights at Laurel Lake on the way in and at Tiltill Valley (fair) or Rancheria Falls (excellent) on the way out.

An advance **reservation** (www. yosemiteconservancy.org, $5/person, $5/reservation) and a wilderness **permit** are required.

Day 1: O'Shaughnessy Dam to Lake Vernon
(8.6 miles)

From Hetch Hetchy, hike 1 mile from the O'Shaughnessy Dam (3,900 feet) to the cutoff for the Beehive Trail on the old Lake Eleanor Road (look on the left, past the tunnel). The trail climbs steeply, switchbacking 1.8 miles north out of Hetch Hetchy. It's a butt-kicker (a 2,700-foot elevation gain overall),

so stop often to enjoy the great views. At a trail junction, turn right and hike 3.3 miles northeast to Beehive Meadows, a lush, often swampy, meadow with wildflowers galore. From Beehive Meadows, hike 2 miles on the signed trail to the foot of Lake Vernon (6,568 feet). You'll emerge from the forest and into a glacial-carved valley of granite, ice, and streams. Gorgeous Lake Vernon is set in an alpine landscape. At the fork in the trail at the foot of the lake, head left for the best campsites, about 0.5 mile in.

Day 2: Lake Vernon back to trailhead
(14.9 miles)

From Lake Vernon, return to the trail fork at the foot of the lake and turn left. The trail crosses the outlet creek of Lake Vernon, then turns left to rise for a panorama of the lake amid the granite backdrop. The trail is clear and well-signed at all junctions.

Turn right (south) and climb steeply toward the forested flank of 8,412-foot Mount Gibson (2 miles), with sensational views across the lake and miles of Yosemite high country. As the trail eases, you'll enter a virtual Garden of Eden, a flourishing matrix of meadows, wildflowers, creeks, and trees. I swear I felt the imprint of Muir here. At one point, I took a seat against a tree and let the feelings touch me to the core.

The trail eventually emerges to reach a series of long, exposed switchbacks that plunge down to Tiltill Valley (6.8 miles). Overall, expect a 1,200-foot climb then a 4,000-foot descent.

You'll reach a major junction in Tiltill Valley. At a clearing near Tiltill Creek, many hikers stop for lunch before deciding whether to camp or to continue the trek. From this trail junction, the backpacker camp at **Rancheria Falls** (reservation and permit required in advance) is only 2.8 miles south.

From Tiltill Valley, the trail climbs up a short sub-ridge then steeply descends, entering the Grand Canyon of the Tuolumne. At a signed trail junction for Rancheria Falls, turn left to arrive at a series of trail camps. Just beyond is pretty Rancheria Falls and a series of excellent swimming holes.

Turn west at Rancheria Falls to follow the trail along a terraced wall above the lake for an easy 5.3 miles past Wapama Falls back to the trailhead.

BEST OVERNIGHT: EVERGREEN LODGE

Evergreen Lodge (33160 Evergreen Rd., Groveland, 209/379-2606, www.evergreenlodge.com) is located within a mile of the Hetch Hetchy entrance station, which means it is only an eight-mile drive to Hetch Hetchy. That alone makes it a winner, but there's more. Evergreen Lodge has 88 gorgeous redwood cabins in five different styles, and each has a balcony. There are also 16 custom camping sites. Set in the forest, the surrounding property is very secluded yet upscale. This is a full-service resort, with a restaurant, tavern, and general store. Its close proximity to Camp Mather, and its popular ice-cream cones, is an additional bonus.

WHERE TO EAT

On my backpacking trips in the Yosemite wilderness, it doesn't take many days in the backcountry before I start dreaming of the restaurant at **Evergreen Lodge** (33160 Evergreen Rd., Groveland, 209/379-2606, www.evergreenlodge.com, 7am-10:30am, noon-3pm, and 5pm-9pm daily). Waiting at the end of any Yosemite trip is this top-notch restaurant and bar. I always get the buffalo burger with cheddar cheese, which borders on awesome, but you really can't miss. It's a little pricey, but that's what you get when you're in a world-renowned tourist destination. The last time I was here, I heard four different languages at five tables, and saw smiles all around.

DRIVING DIRECTIONS

From San Francisco, cross the Bay Bridge (stay in the right lane) heading east. At the split with I-580, bear right on I-580 East and drive 46 miles to I-205 East. Merge onto I-205 and drive 14 miles to I-5 North. After a brief merge, drive 2 miles to the exit for Highway 108/120 (Manteca/Sonora). Take that exit, turning right on Highway 108/120. Stay on Highway 108/120 at all signed junctions. In about 100 miles, Highways 120 and 108 split; turn right to stay on Highway 120 for 20 miles to Groveland. From Groveland, continue east on Highway 120 for 22 miles to Evergreen Road (signed for Hetch Hetchy). Turn left on Evergreen Road and drive 7.4 miles to Hetch Hetchy Road. Turn right on Hetch Hetchy Road and drive 9 miles to the dam and trailhead. There is a parking lot just up the road.

The Hetch Hetchy entrance is open seasonally sunrise-sunset. There is no park access once the gated Hetchy Hetchy Road entrance has closed.

CAMPFIRE STORIES

*O*ne summer night at Emeric Lake in the Yosemite backcountry, our group had three bears at our campsite at once. Across the lake, another camper starting banging on a pot and yelling, "Get away bears!" The three bears in our camp reared up, looked at each other for a moment, and then went running around the lake headed for the sound. It turned out that banging on that pot was like ringing the dinner bell. By the time we arrived to help scare them off, 11 bears had been drawn to the camp, that pot still banging away. Shortly thereafter, Yosemite required backpackers to use bear-proof food canisters when in the wilderness. The collective impact was a game-changer.

The Hetch Hetchy entrance station (8am-5pm) rents **bear-proof food canisters** ($5/week, $95 deposit, first-come, first-served, call 209/379-1922 to confirm availability). Pick one up on your way in.

△ *black bear in Yosemite*

Tuolumne Meadows can change the way you feel. When you stand along the Tuolumne River and take in the wall-to-wall meadows that lead to granite slopes high above, you can feel what John Muir felt. This valley was part of his church—a shrine.

Above Tuolumne Meadows, the Lyell Fork runs off the flank of 13,305-foot Mount Lyell (the highest point in Yosemite) and pretzels its way through the upper meadow to merge with the Tuolumne River. Downstream of the park campground, the Tuolumne River gains in strength, edged by more expansive meadows and surrounded by a horizon of mountain rims with landmark peaks. Eventually the river flows over Tuolumne Falls and into its emerald plunge pool.

Tuolumne Meadows is home to the best trailhead in the Sierra Nevada. The array of opportunities include easy day hikes, challenging high-alpine treks, and backpacking expeditions past waterfalls along the Grand Canyon of the Tuolumne. And all of it is easily accessible from the largest campground in Yosemite National Park.

▽ *Tuolumne Falls*

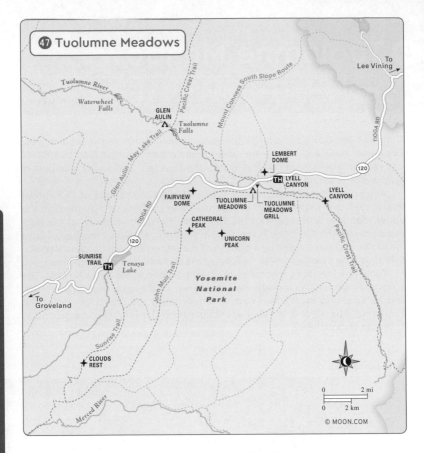

Here are a few tips:

- Plan your visit for the height of summer, when Tioga Pass Road (Highway 120) is open.
- Try to come on a weekday in order to avoid the weekend summer crowds.
- Make campground reservations up to six months in advance (or pray for a first-come, first-served site).
- Get an early morning start on the trail for the best chance at solitude.
- Backpackers: Reserve wilderness permits (and bear kegs) in advance.

Even without all that, a trip to Tuolumne Meadows can be one of your best experiences at a national park. You could put on a blindfold, twirl in a circle, and then stop, point, and look. No matter which direction you face, there's a world-class hike waiting for you.

BEST EASY DAY HIKES

Lembert Dome

The hike to **Lembert Dome** (2.8 miles round-trip, 1.5 hours) can make anyone feel like a mountaineer, yet this is an easy trip with a fair elevation gain. The Lembert Dome parking area and trailhead is located a short distance east of Tuolumne Meadows on Tioga Road (look for the Lembert Dome/Soda Spring/Dog Lake/Glen Aulin turn on the left). From the trailhead (vault toilets are nearby), the trail arcs around the back of the dome and then up. You

△ Lembert Dome

can make up your own route to the top, climbing 850 feet to the dome at 9,450 feet. The view of Tuolumne Meadows and the surrounding peaks, highlighted by Unicorn Peak to the south, is unforgettable.

Glen Aulin

The Lembert Dome parking lot (also signed for Dog Lake/John Muir Trail/ Pacific Crest Trail) is also the starting point for the hike to **Glen Aulin** (11 miles round-trip, 6–8 hours), an easy cruise with only an 800-foot elevation gain on the way back (though it feels fairly flat). Follow the dirt road from the Lembert Dome parking lot west toward Soda Spring. As you near Parson's Lodge, veer right on the signed trail to Glen Aulin. You'll walk through lodgepole pine forest, then move closer to the Tuolumne River and get incredible views of Cathedral and Unicorn Peaks, as well as Fairview Dome. After three miles, cross the Tuolumne River on a footbridge and in another mile you'll reach the first stunning drop of **Tuolumne Fall,** a 100-foot,

churning freefall that pours cold and clean into a large plunge-pool basin.

Backpacking option: Turn the hike from Glen Aulin into a backpacking trip to **Waterwheel Falls** (18 miles round-trip, 2–3 days) and the Grand Canyon of the Tuolumne. Spend the first night at the **Glen Aulin High Sierra Camp** (reserve at www.travelyosemite.com, open seasonally). From Glen Aulin, it's three miles with a descent of 1,500 feet into the leading edge of the Grand Canyon of the Tuolumne and California Falls, LeConte Falls, and Waterwheel Falls. Short spurs provide access to the best views, but Waterwheel is the showstopper: The river hydraulics make the falls look like a rotating circle of water.

An advance **reservation** (www.yosemiteconservancy.org, $5/person, $5/reservation) and a wilderness **permit** are required for overnight stays in the backcountry. Pick up your permit in person at the **Tuolumne Meadows Wilderness Center** (off Tioga Rd., one mile east of the visitors center, late May-mid-Oct.), which also

△ *Glen Aulin trail*

You'll have a 2,300-foot climb over 14 miles. Those who have completed it will tell you that each step on the final mile qualifies as one of the greatest hours of their lives.

The trailhead is the Sunrise Trail, located at the foot of Tenaya Lake. The trail ascends steadily for the first 4 miles, descends steeply for 0.5 mile, then climbs again more moderately. Keep the faith—the first 2.5 miles from the trailhead are the toughest.

The final climb is along a knife-edge ridge with plummeting drop-offs. On top at 9,931 feet, you get a view across the backside of Half Dome and beyond into Yosemite Valley. Miles of wilderness peaks, the Clark Range, and down Tenaya Canyon are in your scope.

Note: Do not take this trip lightly. It is an extreme physical challenge.

sells maps and rents bear canisters ($5/week with $95 deposit).

Lyell Canyon via the John Muir Trail

From Tuolumne Meadows, the trail south along **Lyell Canyon** (6 miles round-trip, 3 hours) follows the John Muir/Pacific Crest Trail along the Lyell Fork of the Tuolumne River. To reach the Lyell Fork, cross the Dana Fork on a footbridge less than 0.5 mile from the parking lot. Then after 0.5 mile, cross the Lyell Fork on a second footbridge and head left along the river's south side. A third bridge takes you across Rafferty Creek and into Lyell Canyon. About 3 miles upstream, the shade hits the river and you get a sweeping view from the canyon to 13,114-foot Mount Lyell, the highest point in Yosemite. On its sloping face sits the Lyell Glacier.

BEST BUTT-KICKER HIKE: CLOUDS REST

The hike to **Clouds Rest** (14 miles round-trip, 8 hours) is as epic as climbing Half Dome, but with far fewer people elbowing you along the way.

BEST OVERNIGHT: TUOLUMNE MEADOWS

At 8,600 feet elevation, **Tuolumne Meadows** (Tioga Rd., summer only) is Yosemite's largest campground. It serves as a base for stellar day hikes, as well as fishing and wilderness expeditions. With 304 sites for tents or RVs, neighbors are guaranteed—as are food-raiding bears (bear-proof lockers are provided). Camp hosts are on-site to ensure quiet time in the evenings. The campground also has seven group sites, four horse sites, and a backpacker trail camp (permit required, cash only) that is heavily used by Pacific Crest Trail thru-hikers. Drinking water, flush toilets, an amphitheater, and a dump station are available. Some facilities are wheelchair-accessible.

Reservations (877/444-6777, www.recreation.gov, $26) for half the sites are accepted; the remaining sites are first-come, first-served. The campground is usually open June-late September, but access depends on when Tioga Road is plowed. In high-snow years, the campground has remained closed until August.

When hiking at high elevation, the first rule is to make sure your body is acclimatized to the thin air: 1) Take your time. 2) Camp a night (or two) at higher elevations before you start to hike or climb. 3) Drink a ton of water and stay hydrated.

At high elevations, the oxygen level in your bloodstream can drop to a low level, which causes **hypoxia** (headaches, dizziness, and rapid heartbeat). If you don't return to a lower elevation, this can turn into **altitude sickness** (or worse, cerebral or pulmonary edema).

Those who live at sea level or low elevations are the most vulnerable, but even athletic and fit hikers are susceptible. Ibuprofen can relieve the early symptoms of headache, rapid heartbeat, and dizziness. If your heart rate becomes too high (i.e., the Red Zone), stop and rest until it returns to normal (i.e., the Green Zone).

So take your time. Get used to the high elevations. Hydrate. And don't push too hard. If you experience any symptoms, stop and give your body a chance to catch up with your ambition.

WHERE TO EAT

Tuolumne Meadows Grill (Tioga Rd., 209/372-8426, 8am-6pm daily June-mid-Sept.) is a legend among PCT hikers, who drop their packs to line up for a breakfast of scrambled eggs, biscuits, and sausage or bacon (best earlier in the day, not always so good later). For these folks surviving on freeze-dried dinners and energy bars, a hot burger and fries or a chicken sandwich can make their day. The blue-chip winner? An ice-cream cone.

Over the years, I've waited in line here with PCT thru-hikers, have run into guys like world-class mountaineer Josh Helling, and then, 10 minutes later, met Fred and Ethel Finkelbaum from Iowa traveling in their RV. Though we maintain separate orbits in life, we all found the same landing spot here.

DRIVING DIRECTIONS

Tuolumne Meadows is accessible in summer only. (The road is closed in winter.) From the west, follow Highway 120 east to Groveland and drive 24 miles to the Big Oak Flat entrance station (park entrance fee required) for Yosemite National Park. Continue south on Big Oak Flat Road (Highway 120) for 7.7 miles to Crane Flat. Turn left onto Tioga Road (Highway 120) and drive almost 39.5 miles to Tuolumne Meadows.

From the east, at the junction of U.S. 395 and Highway 120, follow Highway 120 west for 11 miles to the Tioga Pass entrance (park entrance fee required). Continue 8.5 miles west to Tuolumne Meadows.

For information (and bathrooms), visit the **Tuolumne Meadows Visitor Center** (on Tioga Rd., hours vary daily late May-late Sept.).

From Yosemite Valley: Set your odometer to zero. From Yosemite Valley Lodge, drive out of the valley on Northside Drive for 4.8 miles to a fork (stay right). Continue ahead onto El Portal Road and drive 0.9 mile to Big Oak Flat Road (signed for Highway 120/Tioga Road). Turn right and drive 9.5 miles to Crane Flat and the junction with Tioga Road. Turn right on Tioga Road and drive almost 40 miles to Tuolumne Meadows.

CAMPFIRE STORIES

*O*ut of Tuolumne Meadows, we hiked up Lyell Fork, and about four miles in, I remember the excitement as we peered up at Mount Lyell and the Lyell and Maclure Glaciers. For my Emmy-winning PBS special, *The Mighty T: The Tuolumne River: From Glacier to Golden Gate,* this was our destination. In a few days, Peter Devine of the Yosemite Conservancy and I climbed the face of Lyell. With ice axes, crampons, and rappelling gear, we traversed the glacier and, about midway on its face at about 13,000 feet, found a large hole in the ice. We were able to actually climb inside the glacier. I took a seat, and with my water bottle, captured drops of water from inside the melting glacier. It was the sweetest-tasting water on Earth.

In the weeks that followed, we then traced the path of that water in its course down the Tuolumne River to the Golden Gate Bridge and San Francisco. Near Fort Point, at the southern foot of the bridge, I turned on a faucet, filled my water bottle, and drank the same symbolic drops of water from the Tuolumne River.

△ *atop Maclure Glacier*

The Tuolumne River (the "Mighty T") is one of the most renowned white-water rivers for rafting. The prize stretch features 30 miles of legendary runs, rapids, and falls from the put-in near Cherry Creek downstream to Don Pedro Reservoir. This pool-and-drop river has a series of Class IV rapids and just enough breaks to allow you to catch your breath; yet it also features Clavey Falls, a Class V cascade with a series of foaming, frothing chutes and ladders.

There are two primary runs. The Upper T runs from the put-in at Cherry Creek to Meral Pool near Lumsden Campground. The Main T runs from Meral Pool to Wards Ferry above Don Pedro Reservoir. Each run has sections with Class V rapids (you'll need an expert at the oars) and prime scenery with wilderness-like settings. Note that the section from Cherry Creek to Clavey Falls shows evidence of the 2015 Rim Fire.

Prime rafting season is in summer; the season usually starts after May. (In wet years, the runs can be too high to attempt prior to May.)

▽ *rafting the Tuolumne River*

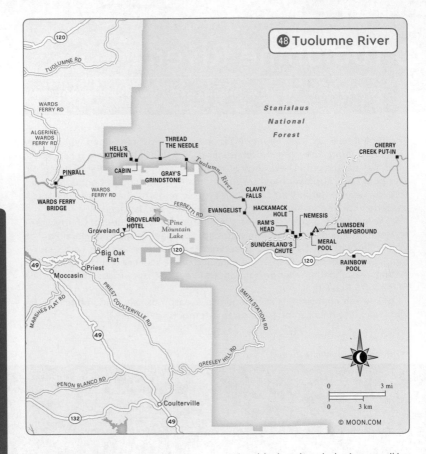

48 Tuolumne River

THE MAIN T: MERAL POOL TO WARD'S FERRY

The **Main Tuolumne,** or the "Main T," includes one of the most fun rapids in California—Pinball—and one of the most terrifying, Clavey Falls. This 18-mile run is rated Class IV with 40 named rapids. It should be run only with expert guides.

From the put-in at Meral Pool, downstream from Lumsden Campground, rafters float downstream to Ward's Ferry above Don Pedro Reservoir. From Meral Pool, the first five miles encounter several Class IV rapids and drops, including Nemesis, Sunderland's Chute, Hackamack Hole, Ram's Head, and Evangelist. The ride is exciting and

enjoyable, but the whole time you'll be anticipating the pending confrontation with Clavey Falls. You know it's coming. You know it's waiting. Then, finally, you round a bend and there it is. Before you even realize it, you are plunging down through the white water like a snow-ball in hell. Some people surrender and portage, but this is the one that nobody forgets.

Past Clavey Falls, the last 9 miles are peppered with more Class IV rapids: Gray's Grindstone, Thread the Needle, Cabin, and Hell's Kitchen. At 0.5 mile upstream of the take-out, you arrive at Pinball, one of the most enjoyable rapids on the run.

Pinball is located just above the take-out at Ward's Ferry and Don Pedro Reservoir. It ends the trip on an

INSIDER'S TIP

Rafting companies cooperate with the San Francisco Water Department to negotiate releases from Cherry Lake and Hetch Hetchy Reservoir in order to develop a flow that is ideal for rafting throughout the summer. Even when river levels are navigable, the runs will be high, turbulent, and dangerous for amateurs. Newcomers must make sure that an expert is in command or plan on sprouting gills.

Runs on the Tuolumne River should be run with an expert guide at the helm. Contact any of the following outfitters to coordinate your trip:

- ★ **All Outdoors Whitewater Rafting** (800/247-2387, www.aorafting.com)
- ★ **ARTA River Trips** (800/323-2782, www.arta.org)
- ★ **Sierra Mac River Trips** (800/457-2580, www.sierramac.com)
- ★ **Outdoor Adventure River Specialists** (OARS, 855/294-1660, www.oars.com)
- ★ **Whitewater Voyages** (800/400-7238, www.whitewatervoyages.com)
- ★ **Zephyr Whitewater Expeditions** (800/431-3636, www.zrafting.com)

△ *rafting on the Tuolumne River*

△ *diving into Rainbow Pool*

upbeat note, with the knowledge that you have experienced firsthand one of life's most exhilarating adventures.

THE UPPER T: CHERRY CREEK TO MERAL POOL

Pro rafters call the **Upper Tuolumne River** the "Upper T," and some consider this the most challenging technical run in the United States. The run ranges nine miles from Cherry Creek to Meral Pool, and it peaks at Class V+, just a half step from certain death. The Upper Tuolumne is composed of long, nearly continuous rapids, with several Class V rapids, broken only by short pools and with virtually no spots to rest and catch your breath. This run is for experts only. Do not attempt it at high flows.

From the put-in at Cherry Creek, the trip starts with more than one mile of Class IV rapids. Just as you start getting accustomed to the thrills, the excitement cranks up a notch with several Class V drops, including Corkscrew, Jawbone, Mushroom, Cat-

apult, and Miracle Mile. Any of these can popcorn you from the boat if you don't have a good hold. There will be times when you are so wet, you won't be able to tell when you're in the raft and when you're in the river.

At about mile 7 you'll hit Flat Rock Falls, a Class V-VI drop. In high water, you can buy the farm on this one—best to portage here and at Lumsden Falls. Once you get back in the boat, wind out the run with several more Class IV rapids over the course of 1.5 miles to the take-out at Meral Pool.

SWIMMING IN RAINBOW POOL

Rainbow Pool is one of the prettiest swimming holes in California. The beautiful waterfall is fed by the South Fork of the Tuolumne and pours over a small brink into a granite bowl perfect for swimming. When you first arrive, walk to the far side of the pool to take a photo of the waterfall (bring a tripod for a gorgeous timed exposure). Then, walk in from the far side of the pool where the water is temperate and shallow; it gets colder and deeper the closer you get to the waterfall. After your body has adjusted to the chilly temperature, emerge from the pool and hike the short distance up to the brink. Take a deep breath and make the leap! The short leap from the brink into the pool is a rite of passage for everyone. The water is refreshing and just cold enough on a hot summer day to give you a happy jolt. If you bring your children, be sure to take a video of them making the leap—priceless.

Rainbow Pool is 13.5 miles east of Groveland along Highway 120. Turn right (south) onto Forest Road 1N07 (signed for Rainbow Pool) and drive 0.2 mile to the day-use parking area (parking is limited).

Trip notes: There are vault toilets at the day-use area, but no garbage cans; please pack out all trash.

BEST OVERNIGHT: LUMSDEN

With its proximity to Meral Pool, **Lumsden Campground** (Lumsden Rd., free) is one of the best access points for white-water rafting on the Tuolumne River. The campground is set at an elevation of 1,500 feet across from the Tuolumne River. There are eight sites for tents only. Picnic tables and fire grills are provided, and vault toilets are available. There is no drinking water, and river water must be purified before use. Garbage must be packed out. Leashed pets are permitted. Reservations are not accepted; sites are first-come, first-served. Open year-round.

Note: The access road is steep and bumpy and can be washed out during heavy spring rains.

WHERE TO EAT

The Groveland Hotel was built in 1849 and still retains the vintage feel of the gold rush. The hotel is home to the **Provisions Taproom** (18767 Main St., Groveland, 209/962–4000, www.

groveland.com, 7am-9pm daily), a restaurant with 10 beers on tap, a selection of more than 20 bourbons, and the best-stocked wine cellar around. A short list of menu items includes paninis, homemade pasta, fermented veggies, and cheese boards. The woodsy Bourbon Bar is a tribute to Mark Twain, and it feels like he might have tipped back a drink here last night. The hotel comes with 18 rooms, including the legend of a ghost named Lyle in Room 15.

DRIVING DIRECTIONS

The town of Groveland (Hwy. 120) is a gateway to Yosemite and provides convenient access to the put-ins, take-outs, and campgrounds along the Tuolumne River.

To reach Meral Pool and Lumsden Campground: From Groveland, take Highway 120 east for 7.5 miles to Ferretti Road. Turn left on Ferretti Road and drive 1.1 miles to Forest Road 1N10 (Lumsden Road). Make a sharp right and drive 5 miles to the campground, on the left. The Meral Pool take-out/put-in is a short distance downstream from the campground.

To reach Ward's Ferry: From Groveland, take Highway 120 west for 0.5 mile to Deer Flat Road. Turn right on Deer Flat Road and drive 1.5 miles to Wards Ferry Road. Turn right and drive 5.7 miles to the Wards Ferry Bridge. Cross the bridge and look for a dirt road on the right. Turn right and drive a short distance to the take-out.

To reach Cherry Valley: From Groveland, take Highway 120 east for 13.8 miles to Cherry Lake Road/Forest Road 1N07. Turn left on Cherry Lake Road and drive 4 miles; the road enters the national forest. Bear right to continue on Forest Road 1N07 and drive 6.8 miles (downcanyon) to the bridge near the powerhouse. Cross the bridge and continue 1.5 miles to an unsigned paved road on the left. Turn left and drive to the put-in downstream of the powerhouse.

*O*n the "Main T" from Meral Pool to Ward's Ferry, you'll face about 50 significant rapids over 18 river miles. The odds of getting popcorned are about 1 in 100, which means that your number is coming up sooner or later. We call it "Joining the Tuolumne River Swimming Team, Freestyle Event."

On one cold spring trip, I was wearing a dry-suit, life vest, and a helmet when we took the wrong line down a rapid, got hit by a side current, and popcorned. Into the drink we went. As you sail through a rapid, your life vest pops you to the surface where you take a deep breath of air before the river hydraulics pull you back under. Breathing becomes all about timing. Eventually the rapid kicks you out into a tailout or an eddy where you can dog-paddle over to the side. Some feel trepidation over the prospects of getting dumped in the river, while others are paralyzed by fear. But, once you get past it, you'll discover it is more exhilarating than anything else. After all, you just "joined the team."

Side note: My PBS special, *The Mighty T: The Tuolumne River: From Glacier to Golden Gate,* won an Emmy for Health, Science, and Environment from the National Academy of Television and Sciences. It is available for online streaming (www.pbs.org/video/kvie-viewfinder-mighty-t-tuolumne-river) and for purchase from Jim Schlosser at Barbary Coast Productions (415/258-9505, barbarycoastprod@comcast.net, with a 4K DVD).

△ *rafting the Tuolumne River*

On the John Muir Trail (JMT), you have a foothold in the sky. The 211-mile trail officially starts at the highest point in the contiguous United States, 14,505-foot Mount Whitney, then ventures north across a land spiked by 13,000-foot granite spires, untouched sapphire lakes, and canyons that drop as if they were the edge of the earth. After 12,000-foot passes and Ansel Adams-worthy panoramas, you eventually arrive at the showpiece of the world, Yosemite Valley.

Highlights include the Mount Whitney Wilderness, John Muir Wilderness, Kings Canyon National Park, crossing the ice cut at Forester Pass, topping Muir Pass at Muir Hut, the incredible pyramid-like ridgeline near Selden Pass, crossing the headwaters of Rush Creek, and finally dropping down over Donohue Pass to Lyell Fork, into Tuolumne Meadows, and descending 22 miles to Yosemite Valley.

It usually takes most thru-hikers about three weeks to complete, including side trips for resupplies. Most hike it south to north, and that's the way I've always done it. Yet it's possible to get a taste of the trail over a long weekend. The following section hikes can get you there. But for the full flavor, plan a long stretch (one week to 11 days), and you might get to tackle Mount Whitney, too.

The best time to hike the trail is in summer, when the snow levels are at their lowest and the river crossings are safest. This period ranges from late June to a precious few weeks in August. On the Sierra Crest, it's common to get early snowfall in September, and in clear weather, very cold nights. So the trail is limited to those with all-weather mountaineering skills. When I hiked the JMT during September's first snowfall, I was lucky that that the snow lasted just a

▽ Thousand Island Lake

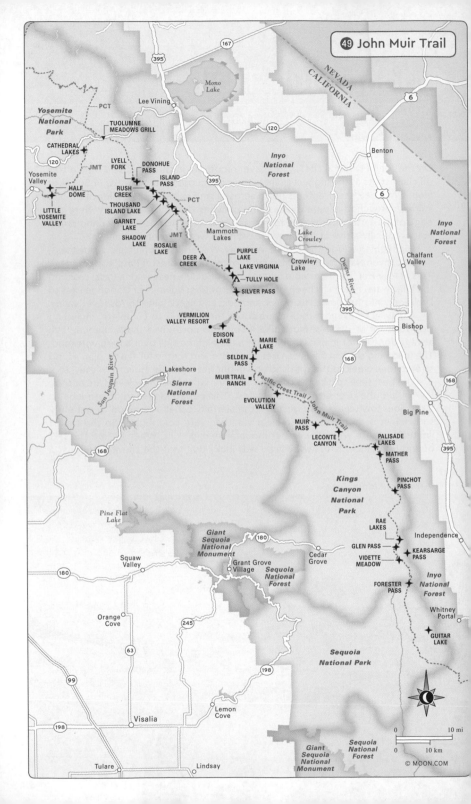

△ John Muir Trail

△ Tom hiking the John Muir Trail

day or so, so it wasn't a show-stopper. It can feel like you're walking in the footsteps of Muir himself.

WHITNEY PORTAL TO LAKE EDISON

(112 miles one-way, 11 days)

From your first steps at Whitney Portal, you might sense that you are walking in the footsteps of giants like John Muir, Josiah Whitney, and William Brewer. They were the first to traverse this landscape and chronicle what they saw and experienced. The landscape looks much the same today as it did then.

The JMT technically starts at the **Whitney Summit** (see #50. *Mount Whitney*). From Whitney Portal, you climb more than 6,100 feet over the course of 11 miles to reach Whitney's summit at 14,505 feet. (I like to add a day going up Whitney to get acclimated, then spend the second night at Guitar Lake, below.)

As you descend Mount Whitney, you can see **Guitar Lake** (5.5 miles) far below for almost the entire route

as you start the northward trek on the John Muir Trail. The trail plunges 3,100 feet to get there.

From Guitar Lake, the JMT drops into Sequoia National Park, then climbs above timberline as it nears 13,180-foot **Forester Pass** (9.2 miles from Guitar Lake) for a day's worth of hiking. This is the highest point on the Pacific Crest Trail (which technically bypasses the spur to the Whitney Summit). The trail is narrow and steep for about a mile, cut into a high vertical slab of rock, with a series of switchbacks. At a key moment near the top, you have to cross the "ice cut," an iced-filled crevice. A slip here is perilous. In early summer, the surface hardens overnight. Some hikers wear Yaktrax or pull out an ice axe just for this crossing.

Pro tip: If you camp at the foot of Forester, make the climb in the morning. Then you can camp at the far north end of Vidette Meadow.

Once through Forester Pass, the trail heads north into the John Muir Wilderness along Bubbs Creek, with great wildflowers at **Vidette Meadow** (4.5 miles from Forester).

△ *Rae Lakes*

Pro tip: Resupply by exiting out at Kearsarge Pass.

From the JMT/Kearsarge Pass junction (4.3 miles from Bubbs Creek), it's 4.8 miles up and over 11,978-foot **Glen Pass,** a spectacular, boulder-strewn ridge with great views to the north into Kings Canyon. Finally you pop out on top, then the trail plunges below to **Rae Lakes** (2 miles from Glen Pass), with pristine meadows and fantastic shoreline campsites (one-night limit).

From Rae Lakes, descend to Woods Creek (3 miles) and cross a wooden bridge. From Woods Creek, it is a long and steady 3,638-foot climb over 7.1 miles to **Pinchot Pass** (12,130 feet). This area is known for afternoon thunderstorms (and lightning strikes) and heavy rain in late July and early August. The JMT heads along the upper **Kings River** for a long, steady ascent over 12,100-foot **Mather Pass** (9.5 miles from Pinchot).

The wonders continue as you hike along **Palisade Lakes** (2.5 miles from Mather), then down into **LeConte Canyon** (10.7 miles from Palisade Lakes), followed by an endless climb above tree line up to 11,965-foot **Muir**

Pass (7.3 miles from LeConte). Snow-fields are common in early summer, which can make this a difficult pass, especially if your boots posthole through the snow. The area near Muir Pass is extremely stark—nothing but granite, ice, and a few small turquoise lakes—crowned by the stone Muir Hut at the pass, where hikers can duck in and hide from sudden afternoon thunderstorms and lightning.

The views astound as the trail drops into **Evolution Valley** (12.3 miles from Muir Pass). It's like a trip back in time, when all was pure and primary, yet incredibly lush and beautiful. Leaving Kings Canyon National Park, the trail follows the headwaters of the **San Joaquin River** into the Sierra National Forest. The trail bottoms out at 7,890 feet, where the air feels thick and muggy, before rising steeply switchback after switchback as it enters the John Muir Wilderness.

Pro tip: Resupply at **Muir Trail Ranch** (P.O. Box 176, Lakeshore, www. muirtrailranch.com).

Finally, you're atop 10,900-foot **Selden Pass** (14.8 miles from Evolution Valley), where you can take in

△ *Mather Pass*

an incredible view of rows of surrounding mountaintops that resemble the Great Pyramids. From there, it's an easy descent to **Marie Lakes** (1 mile), which has a pretty campsite and excellent trout fishing near the lake's outlet.

The final push of this section is the climb up Bear Mountain and then down a toe-jamming stretch to a junction at Mono Creek. Make a left turn and continue 3 miles to **Edison Lake** (12.8 miles from Marie Lakes), where a boat taxi to the tiny **Vermillion Valley Resort** (559/259-4000, http://edison-lake.com) is available, a good place to have a food stash waiting. Enjoy your first shower, then gorge at the small restaurant.

LAKE EDISON TO REDS MEADOW

(34.6 miles one-way, 3 days)

The world is not perfect, but the scenery from Silver Pass comes close. At 10,900 feet, you scan a bare, high-granite landscape sprinkled with alpine lakes. Just north of the pass are five

small lakes: Chief, Papoose, Warrior, Squaw, and Lake of the Lone Indian. These lakes are the highlight of this 38-mile section of the John Muir Trail.

From the Mono Creek junction at Edison Lake (see above), the JMT leads north toward **Silver Pass** (6.6 miles), climbing along Silver Pass Creek much of the way. (There's a stream crossing before Silver Pass that can be dangerous in high runoff. Check conditions in heavy snow years.) Top Silver Pass at 10,900 feet, then enjoy a 5-mile descent that is followed by a quick 400-foot climb over 1 mile to overnight at **Tully Hole** (9,250 feet).

It is 22 miles from Tully Hole north to Reds Meadow, with campsites available at **Deer Creek, Lake Virginia,** and **Purple Lake** along the route. Head up to Red Cones and then make a steady descent toward Devils Postpile National Monument and **Reds Meadow,** where a café, a backpacker campground, and showers are waiting; most hikers pick up a food stash here. Others may time their trip to spend the night at Agnew Meadows (7.8 miles away) instead.

INSIDER'S TIP

Here's how I break out my overnights on the trail from **Whitney Portal to Lake Edison.** I try to set up camp so that I face the climbs first thing in the morning, when I'm fresh.

1) Whitney Portal
2) Guitar Lake
3) Vidette Meadow or Icicle Lake (This is what I call an unnamed lake located at the foot of the climb to Forester Pass. An ice field feeds its far side.)
4) Rae Lakes
5) Kings River
6) Palisade Lakes
7) LeConte Canyon
8) Evolution Valley
9) San Joaquin River in the Sierra National Forest
10) Marie Lakes
11) Edison Lake

AGNEW MEADOWS TO TUOLUMNE MEADOWS

(28 miles one-way, 3 days)

This section of the JMT features breathtaking views of the Minarets, many glacial-cut lakes, and the wondrous descent into Yosemite. The JMT starts by leaving Reds Meadow. The trail heads into the most beautiful section of Inyo National Forest and the Ansel Adams Wilderness, passing Rosalie, Shadow, Garnet, and **Thousand Island Lakes** (15.6 miles from Reds Meadow, 7.8 miles from Agnew Meadows). The background setting of Banner Peak and Mount Ritter is spectacular, and you'll want to overnight here. (As I filled my water bottle one evening, I swear I felt the ghosts of past trail legends watching over me.)

From Thousand Island Lake, the JMT makes a fair climb over Island Pass (10,200 feet), then drops down into the headwaters of **Rush Creek,** where emerald-green flows swirl and pour over boulders like a wild fountain. It's only 3.2 miles from Thousand Island Lakes, but I always stop here (and sometimes camp) because this is one of the prettiest backcountry streams anywhere, plus it has good trout fishing.

From Rush Creek the trail ascends steadily, though nothing too challenging. Soon you're back above tree line

△ *Thousand Island Lakes*

at 11,056-foot **Donohue Pass** (3.4 miles from Rush Creek), the southern wilderness border of Yosemite National Park. (At a trail lunch here, I saw an awesome rockslide on the far wall.)

At Donohue Pass, the trail becomes quite blocky, and you'll rock-hop your way down to the headwaters of Lyell Fork, a pretzel-like stream that meanders through meadows before becoming the Tuolumne River. The trail is nearly flat for more than 4 miles along **Lyell Fork.** Camp at Lyell Fork, at the head of the valley, then hike out to get lunch at **Tuolumne Meadows Grill** (Tioga Rd., 8am-8pm daily summer only). The adjoining store offers another resupply point.

TUOLUMNE MEADOWS TO YOSEMITE VALLEY

(22 miles one-way, 2 days)

After having hiked the JMT from Whitney to Tuolumne Meadows, your first glimpse of Yosemite Valley will seem like a privileged view into heaven. The trip starts at Tuolumne Meadows with a tromp past **Cathedral Lakes** (3.1 miles).

Pro tip: The best overnight option is to camp at Cathedral Lakes, then summit **Half Dome** (permit required) the next day. Descend and then camp at Little Yosemite. It's magic. Apply for the Half Dome permit lottery online (www.recreation.gov) by 9pm Sunday, March 31. The lottery takes place in mid-April.

From Cathedral Lakes, the trail makes a relatively short 500-foot climb over Cathedral Pass, skirts Tresidder Peak, and then descends through pristine Long Meadow. After passing Sunrise Trail Camp, the trail picks up little Sunrise Creek and follows it all the way down to **Little Yosemite Valley** (13.1 miles), where there's a popular trail camp. Due to its proximity to Half Dome, the Little Yosemite Valley Trail Camp is often crowded.

From Little Yosemite, you only have 5 miles left. The JMT is routed along the Merced River, and in 1 mile, you'll reach Liberty Cap, then the brink of Nevada Fall. Then down, down you go. The trail often turns into giant granite steps as it descends past Emerald Pool to Vernal Fall, another spectacular waterfall. Vernal Fall is just 1.7 miles from the end of the trail at Happy Isles. Here the trail turns to asphalt and you will pass hundreds of day-hiking tourists coming from the other direction. The last few steps reach Happy Isles (and a shuttle bus station), where you can sit and take it all in.

PERMITS

You only need one permit to hike the John Muir Trail: from the agency that oversees the respective starting trailhead. If you're starting from Whitney Portal, you need a permit from the **Inyo National Forest** (760/873-2483, www.fs.usda.gov/inyo). All permits in the Inyo National Forest are issued through the **Eastern Sierra Visitor Center** (U.S. 395, 2 miles south of Lone Pine, 760/876-6200, 8am-5pm daily May-Nov.). If you're starting from Happy Isles in Yosemite Valley, you need a permit from **Yosemite National Park** (www.nps.gov/yose). That's the end of the easy part. Now here's the hard part: The trailhead permits for the JMT are in high demand. So you'll need to do some detective work in order to snag one.

A **permit lottery** (www.recreation.gov, fee) is held for backpacking trips that start from the Whitney Portal Trailhead. If you want to hike the JMT from Whitney Portal to Yosemite Valley, you must enter the permit lottery. Permit applications to enter the lottery are accepted February 1-March 15. If you win a permit, that permit is good for the entire trail, including the section through Yosemite National Park.

Pro tip: When completing the online permit application, you must put in for the Whitney Portal overnight permits and select "exiting via Mt. Whitney-Trail Crest Exit." That gets you in the game.

△ *bristlecone pine in the Inyo National Forest*

The odds of winning a permit vary greatly depending on the dates of your trip and size of your group. Those with small groups who depart on Tuesday or Wednesday early or late in the season have a good chance of getting a permit. Avoid planning your trip during the first weekend in August—it's the most popular departure week of the year, and your odds of scoring a permit decrease to as low as 1 or 2 percent (according to lottery statistics). The overall odds of drawing a permit are 37 percent out of 16,000 applicants.

Permit option: If you fail to draw a permit in the lottery, another option is to start your hike instead from the **Horseshoe Meadow Trailhead,** south of the town of Lone Pine. It much easier to snag this permit from the Inyo National Forest (760/873–2483, www.fs.usda.gov/inyo). From Horseshoe Meadow at 10,000 feet, the route hits the Pacific Crest Trail at Cotton-wood Pass (3.8 miles), then ventures north past Soldier Lake Basin before climbing over Guyot Pass and down to Crabtree Meadows (17.5 miles), where you meet a junction with the JMT.

WHERE TO EAT

The longest stretch of the John Muir Trail with no access to food or a cold beer is the 112-mile section from Whitney Portal to Lake Edison. One time on the JMT, Michael Furniss and a pal entered with a food stash at mid-trail at Dusy Basin (on a spur trail above the headwaters of the Kings River), and that's how they dealt with it. Other times, we would cover that 112 miles with a single food stash and then resupply at Edison Lake via Mono Creek (a 3-mile spur off the JMT with a boat shuttle). It might sound weird, but after drinking the purest water in the world for 10 days, that first taste of cold beer at **Vermillion Valley Resort** (559/259–4000, http://edisonlake.com, hours vary June-mid-Oct.) actually tasted strange, even bad. We had no such difficulties with the bacon cheeseburger and crispy (requested) french fries. And did I mention, another beer? Heh, heh, heh. Yep. By the second one, it didn't taste so strange anymore.

DRIVING DIRECTIONS

From US 395 in the Eastern Sierra, drive to the town of Lone Pine and take Whitney Portal Road 13 miles west to Whitney Portal and the trailhead for Mount Whitney.

For directions to Agnew Meadows and Reds Meadow, see #44. *Devils Postpile National Monument.*

For directions to Tuolumne Meadows, see #47. *Tuolumne Meadows.*

CAMPFIRE STORIES

The first time I hiked the John Muir Trail, I brought too much stuff and my pack was too heavy. As I was pounding down from Forester Pass en route to Bubbs Creek, I felt something pop in my right ankle. A dizzy wooziness swept over me. With the weight of the pack and pressure of the long hike, it turned out that a bone spur from a previous ankle injury had broken off. Yet I'd already been paid and outfitted to write a series about the JMT, and so there was no option but to continue ahead.

I wrapped the ankle with an Ace bandage, and with a stout limb that Foonski trimmed up for me, set up a brace that extended from my hip past my ankle to the ground. For the next 17 days, I made it work. The last 2 days, coming down from Half Dome, the ankle swelled up roughly twice its normal size, but I staggered my way down to the end at Happy Isles in Yosemite Valley.

The next day, I went straight to Stanford Sports Medicine Clinic and met with Fred Behling, the orthopedic surgeon for the 49ers. Once the swelling went down a week later, Dr. Behling operated and removed a cluster of broken chunks of bone. In a follow-up visit, Fred was sitting there with a silly grin. "Good news, Tom, we fixed you up good," he said. "But let me tell you, it was ugly in there. You say you just walked the John Muir Trail with that thing?" He looked aside to make sure no one else could hear him and grinned again. "Nobody could walk 200 miles with an ankle broken up like that." Then, after a pause, he added, "Don't worry. I won't tell anybody. It's OK. I understand. I always read your fish report."

△ *baseball game on John Muir Pass*

Climb the mountains and get their good tidings. Nature's peace will flow into you as sunshine flows into trees. The winds will blow their own freshness into you, and the storms their energies, while cares will drop off like autumn leaves.

—John Muir, *The Atlantic Monthly*, 1898 (www.theatlantic.com)

For many, it is a rite of passage to climb Mount Whitney, the highest peak in the contiguous United States. The reward is gaining that 14,505-foot perch, where you can take in the same views as John Muir, William Brewer, Josiah Whitney, and countless others who have scaled this peak.

In the Eastern Sierra, the ridgeline of Mount Whitney resembles a row of jagged teeth. The trail to Whitney Summit is cut below these wolf-like teeth in notches where you can peer down from your boots nearly 10,000 feet over 15 miles toward the Owens Valley. Atop the summit, the view north across the Sierra peaks is an experience that can't be replicated. You are standing in the footsteps of John Muir (and at the official start of the John Muir Trail), and the sense of history is profound.

This trip starts months before you strap your boots on. A permit is required for both day hikes and overnights. Nail down your hiking dates, then apply to the permit lottery. Permit acquired, you must train for this trek with some serious high-altitude aerobics. Do that and you will be ready for Mount Whitney and all the challenges, answers, and wonders it provides.

▽ *Mount Whitney Trail*

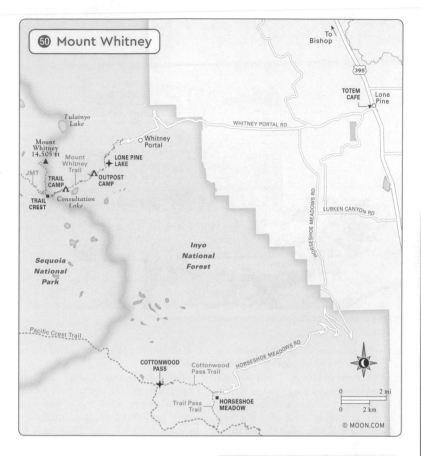

50 Mount Whitney

Most climb Mount Whitney in summer, when the snow levels are lowest on the trail. You'll climb whenever your permit says you can, though, so check trail conditions with the U.S. Forest Service in advance of your date.

HIKE MOUNT WHITNEY

(22 miles, 15 hours or 2–3 days)

The hike from Whitney Portal begins at an elevation of 8,374 feet and continues 11 miles (one-way) to the summit with an elevation gain of 6,131 feet. The deranged few try to do it in one day, 22 miles round-trip at high altitude with no acclimation and potential dehydration. The consequences of doing so can be severe and include hypoxia (low oxygen in the blood),

△ *climbing Mount Whitney*

△ *Trail Crest sign at 13,600 feet on Mount Whitney*

altitude sickness, and high-altitude edema. You may find yourself praying for the ghost of Muir to bring you an oxygen tank. Plan instead to break this hike up over 2–3 days and spend the first day getting acclimated to the elevation, camping midway to and from the summit. You'll feel better and will enjoy it more.

From Whitney Portal, the trail starts out flat and easy, with a slight grade, amid sparse forest, and you'll quickly fall into a rhythm. (Hikers new to high-altitude climbs should try not to go too far too fast in the first two hours. Conserve your resources.) The first mile or so is pretty straightforward: The trail arcs in a half circle, crosses North Fork Pine Creek, then reaches the first set of switchbacks. As you start to climb, you will pass the spur for little **Lone Pine Lake** (2.4 miles, 9,960 feet). Then comes another round of switchbacks that lead to **Outpost Camp** (3.8 miles, 10,400 feet) near Mirror Lake. From Outpost Camp, it's 7.2 miles to Whitney Summit with a climb of 4,105 feet. Many hikers stop and camp here to get acclimated to

the altitude before continuing on to the summit.

Beyond Outpost Camp, the trail emerges from tree line to pass Mirror Lake. At night, a full moon can cast a dull gray light on the high-granite walls of 12,300-foot Thor Peak to the north. (I call it "Moby Dick Rock" because climbing Whitney can make you feel like Ahab chasing the mighty whale.) You then reach **Trail Camp** (6 miles), at 12,000 feet, another place to camp and get acclimated. Many hikers vulnerable to mountain sickness often start feeling the altitude here; drink plenty of water and take ibuprofen.

From Trail Camp, you approach Wotan's Throne, where you'll face 96 switchbacks that climb about 1,500 feet to **Trail Crest** (signed at 13,600 feet). As you pop out on top of Trail Crest, the first view emerges to the north: miles of peaks and canyons. The trail then climbs 905 feet over 2.5 miles on the spur to the summit. There are no steep grades, but the oxygen is so thin that many hikers start to wheeze. Pass Mount Muir (14,019 feet), just above the "wolf teeth" and their

🐾 INSIDER'S TIP

If you want to climb Mount Whitney, you must arrive prepared in mind, body, soul, and gear:

★ Understand that you're committing to a climb of 6,131 feet over 11 miles one-way (22 miles round-trip).
★ Nail down your hike dates. Select weekdays in the shoulder seasons (late May-early June and mid-September-early October, with potentially challenging conditions) and hike with small groups so that you have the best chance of winning a permit.
★ Enter your permit application in the lottery in early February.
★ Train for sustained aerobics at high altitudes. If arriving from a low elevation, do not attempt to hike quickly to 10,000 feet and above, even if extremely fit.
★ Stay hydrated by drinking lots of water, and wear a wide-brimmed hat, sunglasses, and sunscreen to minimize sun exposure.
★ Make sure your socks, insoles, and boots fit perfectly.
★ Be prepared to rely solely on yourself for food, weather protection, camping gear, and clothing, including boots and gloves.
★ All solid human waste must be packed out. Pick up the free "human waste pack-out kit" from the Eastern Sierra Interagency Visitor Center.
★ Respect the climb. You are hiking in the shadow of giants—John Muir, Josiah Whitney, and William Brewer—and, in doing so, are walking through a gateway into a historical wilderness.

notches, and the Wheeler Needle to emerge on the summit.

As you gain the Whitney Summit, the trail is as faint as air, and the sense of accomplishment is overwhelmed by a sense of place and history. A rock hut sits perched on the summit (protection from thunderstorms or a well-aimed lightning bolt), and a metal box next to the hut has a trail book for you to sign and chronicle your presence. Take in the surrounding landscape: Rows of mountain peaks line the north for miles across the horizon, and the entire Great Western Divide is visible to the west. The surrounding blocks of giant rock look as though they were sculpted with a giant hammer and chisel. It's possible you are sitting on the same rock as the trailblazing legends of 150 years ago. If it feels like you are on top of the world, that's because you are.

Permits

To hike Mount Whitney, you must enter a **permit lottery** (www.recreation.gov, fee) for the Whitney Portal Trailhead. Applications are accepted February 1-March 15 of each year. You can also apply for a day-hiking permit or an overnight permit, which allows you to camp at trail camps. Day hikers without permits are not allowed past the trailhead at Whitney Portal.

The odds of winning the lottery vary greatly depending on your start date and the size of your group. Those with small groups departing on a Tuesday or Wednesday early (or late) in the hiking season have a good chance of getting a permit. For those with large groups or hiking on peak weekends in summer, chances are poor.

Option: Horseshoe Meadow

If you fail to win a permit out of Whitney Portal, opt to hike instead from the trailhead at **Horseshoe Meadow** (59.4 miles round-trip), located 30 miles south of the town of Lone Pine. Located on the flank of Mount Whitney, the Horseshoe Meadow Trailhead (10,000 feet) climbs 1,200 feet over 3.8 miles to meet the PCT at **Cottonwood Pass** (11,200 feet), then ventures 17.5 miles north past Rock Creek and Guyot Pass to Crabtree Meadows.

From Crabtree Meadows (11,500 elevation), look for the Whitney Summit in a notch in the Sierra Crest. It is a hike of 3.8 miles from Crabtree Meadows to Guitar Lake, a meadow at the foot of Mount Whitney. You then climb 3,000 feet over the course of 5.5 miles (one-way) to the summit.

A permit from **Inyo National Forest** (760/873-2483, www.fs.usda.gov/inyo) is required. All permits are issued in person at the **Eastern Sierra Visitor Center** (U.S. 395, 2 miles south of Lone Pine, 760/876-6200, www.fs.usda.gov/inyo, 8am-5pm daily May-Nov.).

BEST OVERNIGHT: WHITNEY PORTAL

The campground at Whitney Portal has 43 sites for tents or RVs (no hookups) and three group sites. Picnic tables, food lockers, and fire grills are provided, and drinking water and flush toilets are available. Leashed pets are permitted. **Reservations** (877/444-6777, www.recreation.gov, fee) are accepted. There's a one-night limit for walk-in sites and a seven-day stay limit for the group site. Open late May-mid-October.

The **Whitney Trailhead Walk-In** campsite has 10 walk-in sites for tents only; reach it by hiking in 0.25 mile. Picnic tables and fire grills are provided, and drinking water and vault toilets are available. Garbage must be packed out. Leashed pets are permitted. Reservations are not accepted; sites are first-come, first-served. Open mid-May-late October.

WHERE TO EAT

During each trip to Whitney, I base myself at Lone Pine so that my group can gorge on a giant breakfast before heading out to the trailhead. It's tradition that we always end up at the **Totem Café** (131 S. Main St., Lone Pine, 760/876-1120, 7am-9:30pm daily), a woodsy place with vintage outdoor artifacts, including an old grizzly bear trap on the wall. We order the omelets or a breakfast burrito with crispy (always ask) hash browns. Many northbound PCT hikers also break off from the trail at Horseshoe Meadow, then catch a ride into Lone Pine to head straight for the "The Totem."

DRIVING DIRECTIONS

To reach the Mount Whitney trailhead from Lone Pine and U.S. 395, head west on Whitney Portal Road for approximately 13 miles to Whitney Portal and the trailhead for the Mount Whitney Trail. A small camper's store is near the trailhead.

Yosemite National Park | www.nps.gov/yose

The Pacific Crest Trail (PCT) is the world's greatest hike. The trail starts at California's border with Mexico and extends 2,650 miles north, passing through Oregon and Washington, to the Canadian border.

This section hike of the PCT traverses a hiker's paradise, with glacial-cut peaks, long-distance views, pristine lakes, streams and meadows, wildflowers, and wildlife. Your first steps on this trek start from one of the best and most popular trailheads: Tuolumne Meadows in Yosemite National Park. In less than a day, you'll enter Yosemite's least-traveled region, near its northern boundary, with pristine wilderness streams, lakes, and canyons. Over the next 142.3 miles, the Pacific Crest Trail will guide you to Echo Lake near U.S. 50 and South Lake Tahoe.

My son Jeremy hiked the entire PCT over five and a half months. While he loved the section that doubles as the JMT, he said that the moment he left the crowds behind in Yosemite, the peace he yearns for in the wild returned.

I've always done this trek in two weeks (or sometimes 12 days on-trail), plus driving time for a shuttle vehicle at each end. That's an average of just under 13 miles per day at 2 miles per hour, an average of 6.5 hours on-trail per day, plus an hour of breaks for snacks and lunches. That's doable for most folks, right?

Don't have two weeks to spare? No problem. In summer, it's possible to section-hike this stretch of the PCT instead. From one trailhead to the next, you can spend as little as one day to more than a week out on the trail with plenty left to explore for your next trip.

▽ *along the Pacific Crest Trail*

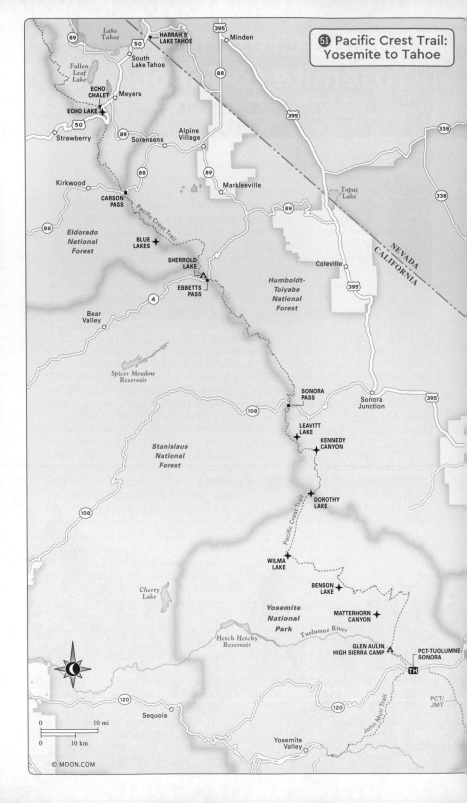

Lake Tahoe

89

50

HARRAH'S LAKE TAHOE

395

Minden

Fallen Leaf Lake

South Lake Tahoe

88

ECHO CHALET

Meyers

ECHO LAKE

50

Strawberry

89

Sorensens

Alpine Village

89

Markleeville

395

338

Kirkwood

88

CARSON PASS

Pacific Crest Trail

Topaz Lake

89

Eldorado National Forest

BLUE LAKES

SHERROLD LAKE

EBBETTS PASS

4

Bear Valley

Coleville

NEVADA

CALIFORNIA

338

395

Humboldt-Toiyabe National Forest

Spicer Meadow Reservoir

108

SONORA PASS

Sonora Junction

395

Stanislaus National Forest

LEAVITT LAKE

KENNEDY CANYON

108

DOROTHY LAKE

Pacific Crest Trail

Cherry Lake

WILMA LAKE

BENSON LAKE

Yosemite National Park

MATTERHORN CANYON

Hetch Hetchy Reservoir

Tuolumne River

GLEN AULIN HIGH SIERRA CAMP

PCT-TUOLUMNE-SONORA

TH

120

Sequoia

PCT/ JMT

John Muir Trail

0   10 mi

0   10 km

Yosemite Valley

120

© MOON.COM

△ *Sonora Pass*

TUOLUMNE MEADOWS TO SONORA PASS

(67 miles one-way, 8 days)

You'll want a week off for this stretch of the trail, with three days to cross from Tuolumne Meadows to Dorothy Lake Pass and another five days for the section from Dorothy Lake Pass to Sonora Pass. Plan on an average of 9–10 miles per day or break it down as follows:

1. Tuolumne Meadows Trailhead to Glen Aulin/Cold Canyon: 5.5 miles
2. Matterhorn Canyon: 10.4 miles
3. Benson Lake: 9.6 miles
4. Wilma Lake: 10.7 miles
5. Dorothy Lake: 9 miles
6. Kennedy Canyon: 9.5 miles
7. Leavitt Peak: 6.8 miles
8. Sonora Pass: 5.2 miles

From the Lembert Dome Trailhead (Tioga Pass Rd., summer only), across the road from the Tuolumne Meadows Campground, the PCT follows the Tuolumne River west for four miles. The trail heads gently downhill to **Glen Aulin**, where you get a great view of Tuolumne Falls. When you cross the bridge at the base of the falls and hike up Cold Canyon, you'll leave everybody else behind.

Once you head up Cold Canyon and venture north toward Tahoe, you have arrived at some of least-used sections of trail in Yosemite National Park. Over the next three days, you'll hike up and down canyons, one after the other, with breathtaking views and long, demanding climbs. Highlights include **Matterhorn Canyon** (at 15.8 miles), **Benson Lake** (at 25.5 miles), the largest white-sand beach in the Sierra Nevada, at **Wilma Lake** (at 36.1 miles), and **Dorothy Lake** (at 45.1 miles), with panoramic views to north.

You cross out of the park at Dorothy Lake Pass and leave Yosemite behind, entering Humboldt-Toiyabe National Forest. The landscape changes to deep canyons and high ridges all the way to Sonora Pass.

Pass through **Kennedy Canyon** and, from the 10,870-foot crest above **Leavitt Lake**, descend 1,250 feet over 2 miles to **Sonora Pass** at 9,623 feet. Switchbacks ease the grade most of the way. At Highway 108, cross the

△ *Benson Lake*

road and walk about 100 yards west to a large day-use parking area. If you can, try to arrange for a shuttle (or a friend with a car).

One year, my mentor, Ed Dunckel, was waiting for our group with a barbecue and a cooler. We feasted on rib-eye steaks, shish kebobs with peppers, onions, and shrimp, Coronas with lime, and even ice-cold oranges. He was the ultimate friend, mentor, and trail angel.

SONORA PASS TO EBBETTS PASS

(30.8 miles one-way, 3 days)

From the trailhead at Sonora Pass (Hwy. 108, closed in winter), climb four miles (about an hour or two) over Wolf Creek Gap at 10,300 feet. The trail then drops down along pretty Wolf Creek and into Carson Canyon. This is the start of the **Carson-Ice-berg Wilderness** (Stanislaus National Forest, www.fs.usda.gov, no permit), a swath of paradise with few people. The Sierra riparian zones here are lined with colorful wildflowers. Good overnights are along the East Carson River and Wolf Creek.

The PCT climbs out of Carson Canyon around Boulder Peak and then down and up two more canyons. All the while, you keep crossing creeks filled with natural gardens. The trail eventually climbs a ridge (about 26 miles from Sonora Pass), then heads steeply down to **Ebbetts Pass** (Hwy. 4, closed in winter). Unlike at Sonora Pass, there is nowhere to stop for water or take a break.

Exit here or pick up the trail (an old dirt road) and climb 0.6 mile up then down into a small basin at little **Sherrold Lake,** near the edge of the Mokelumne Wilderness. This is a good place to set up camp.

Permits: Overnight trips in the Mokelumne Wilderness (Eldorado National Forest, www.fs.usda.gov) require a valid wilderness permit year-round. A campfire permit is required for all open fires (including camp stoves).

EBBETTS PASS TO BLUE LAKES

(17.7 miles one-way, 1 day)

From Ebbetts Pass (Hwy. 4, closed in winter), head north across a series of fantastic volcanic formations in the Mokelumne Wilderness (Humboldt-Toiyabe National Forest). This part of the trail is easy, without a lot of "climb, descend, repeats," and 15-mile days come easy. In dry years, the lack of available water can be a concern; the best place to tank up is at Eagle Creek, below Reynold Peak (9,690 feet).

The trail rises along a stark, windblown, and sandy ridge, with excellent views of the **Blue Lakes;** there is no water along the trail until near Lost Lake. You'll cross several dirt roads on this stretch of trail, but the going is easy—I think this is one of the fastest sections of the PCT in the central Sierra.

There are campgrounds along the Blue Lakes, though you may have to share them with pickup truck campers that drive in on the dirt road. On the ridge above Blue Lakes, there's a mountain peak called "The Nipple." For a few hours, we kept mistaking other mountains for it ("There it is!" Nope.). But when you see it, it is an "ah-ha" moment.

BLUE LAKES TO CARSON PASS

(12 miles one-way, 1 day)

Sometimes you just have to grind it out. The climb from Blue Lakes over Elephant Back to Carson Pass is one of those times, a long, grueling pull. The trip from Blue Lakes Road starts easily enough, with a dirt road often in view and adding a bit of early angst to the affair (most PCT hikers yearn for less civilization). As you hike, you keep wondering when the climb will start.

Well, eventually it does, and the long, steady march takes a couple of hours. After topping Elephant Back, the route drops down to Carson Pass at a rest stop on Highway 88. To the shock of first-time hikers, there is no water to fill your pack. (Desperate? Try to catch a hitch down the hill to Caples Lake Resort.)

From Carson Pass, it's another hour of hiking (about 2.7 miles) north to reach the next trickle of water, a tiny creek that feeds into the **Upper Truckee River.** These headwaters offer an idyllic place to camp (and fill your water bottles).

CARSON PASS TO ECHO LAKE

(15.8 miles one-way, 1–2 days)

The hike from Carson Pass (Hwy. 88, closed in winter) starts with a trek over a mountain rim with a nice view to the west of Caples Lake, then drops 2.7 miles into the headwaters of the Truckee River (fill your water bottles). There is also good camping in this high mountain valley near the Upper Truckee River.

Looking north, Lake Tahoe suddenly comes into view, and a high meadow surrounded by a thin forest greets you—this is Meiss Country. With the return of this pristine landscape, all is right with the world again. Your destination, Echo Lake (and your shuttle car), is within one day's hiking time.

Knowing this, you will be amazed at how inspired (and fast) you suddenly become on this section of trail. It's very pretty, weaving through lush canyons and along creeks, eventually reaching beautiful and tiny Showers Lake (at 2.5 miles). Here the trail seems to drop off into never-never land, as it descends quickly and steeply toward Tahoe. Contentment reigns.

However, when you reach Little Norway (at 8.9 miles) near U.S. 50, reality sets in. Cars are everywhere and the trail suddenly becomes a grind amid cabins and vacation properties. There's one last hill to climb, a half hour of genuine frustration—after all, you're ready for your reward—and then the PCT drops quickly to the parking lot for **Echo Lake** (in 1.5 miles).

Dump your pack and head straight for **Echo Lake Chalet** (9900 Echo Lakes Rd., Echo Lake, (530) 659-7207, 8am-5:30pm daily summer). On one PCT trip, my buddy Latif Burdick got himself a lime bar as his bonus reward.

Though I never would have imagined it before that day, I nabbed one too. I've got to say, that lime bar hit it out of the park.

PERMITS

To thru-hike this section, the only permit you need is a trailhead permit from Tuolumne Meadows (exit the PCT via Cold Canyon). The **Yosemite Conservancy** (www.yosemiteconservancy.org, fee) partners with Yosemite National Park to provide trailhead permits on a quota system. To apply online, click on "Wilderness Permits" and select a date for Tuolumne Meadows exiting Glen Aulin to Cold Canyon.

The key is timing. Permits become available by lottery 168 days in advance of the start of your hike. (So if you want to start hiking on June 30, the first date you can enter for a trailhead permit is January 12.) There is a daily quota for each trailhead: 60 percent of the permit quotas are filled in advanced online; the remaining 40 percent are available first-come, first-served. Most quotas are filled on summer weekends; if you select a Tuesday or Wednesday early or late in the season, your odds of winning a permit increase.

Permits must be picked up in person at least 24 hours in advance at the **Tuolumne Meadows Wilderness Center** (off Tioga Rd., hours vary May-mid-Oct.).

WHERE TO EAT

Once you cross Highway 88 at Carson Pass (see *Carson Pass to Echo Lake*), you are only about 16 miles from your shuttle vehicle at Echo Lake. I always continue north 2.7 miles to camp at the headwaters of the Upper Truckee River. The next morning, I complete the 12.9-mile hike, pick up my car at Echo Lake, and then drive straight to South Lake Tahoe for the best all-you-can-eat buffet on the 19th floor of **Harrah's Lake Tahoe** (15 U.S. 50, Stateline, NV, 775/588–6611, $40). It isn't cheap, but the iced tubs filled with all-you-can-eat shrimp and crab is every PCT hiker's fantasy. Plus, the view of Lake Tahoe is spectacular, and you didn't even have to climb a mountain to see it.

DRIVING DIRECTIONS

To reach Tuolumne Meadows: From the west, take Highway 120 east through Groveland and drive 24 miles to the Big Oak Flat entrance for Yosemite National Park. Pay the park entrance fee and continue south on Big Oak Flat Road (Highway 120) for 7.7 miles to Crane Flat. Turn left onto Tioga Road (Highway 120, summer only) and drive about 40 miles east past Tenaya Lake to Tuolumne Meadows.

From Yosemite Valley, exit via Northside Drive and drive 4.8 miles (stay right) to a fork. Continue onto El Portal Road and drive 0.9 mile to Big Oak Flat Road (signed for Highway 120/Tioga Road). Turn right and drive 9.5 miles to Crane Flat and the junction with Tioga Road. Turn right onto Tioga Road and drive about 40 miles east past Tenaya Lake to Tuolumne Meadows.

To reach Echo Lake: From Placerville, take U.S. 50 east for 45 miles toward South Lake Tahoe and Echo Summit. Pass the Sierra at Tahoe Ski Resort (on the right) and continue 1.8 miles east to Johnson Pass Road (look for a brown Sno-Park sign). Turn left and drive 0.6 mile north to Echo Lakes Road. Turn left and drive 0.8 mile to the parking lot.

From South Lake Tahoe, at the junction of U.S. 50 and Highway 89, follow U.S. 50 south for about 4.5 miles through Meyers. Continue 5.5 miles west to the turnoff signed for Echo Lakes on the right (1 mile west of Echo Summit). Turn right and drive 0.6 mile to Echo Lakes Road. Turn left and drive 0.8 mile to parking lot.

CAMPFIRE STORIES

A Zen outlook on hiking means that if you make a wrong turn, you are simply forced to do more of the exact thing you set out to do. Thus, a wrong turn is a stroke of good fortune. While on the PCT, between Yosemite and Tahoe (south of Ebbetts Pass), a new member of our crew broke a team rule: At every unsigned junction, always wait for the team and then consult. He didn't and it took us miles off course.

The eager hiker was about a half mile ahead and, not waiting, took a wrong turn. We then gave chase. The sideways venture took us down a canyon for miles before we finally caught up with him. When we looked around, we found ourselves surrounded by flora more lush and brilliant than most exotic gardens. Called Paradise Valley on the map, it was about two miles long with a small stream through the center. Lupine, violet daisies, and corn lilies bloomed along the stream for miles. Hiking through here felt as if we were disappearing into a tunnel of flowers with a tumbling brook and the serenade of meadowlarks for background music.

We had lost 2,000 feet of elevation, and the return hike back up to the PCT cost us nearly a day off our schedule. At camp that night, we reviewed some of the dumbest wrong turns we've ever made over the years and we all agreed, "How could we have ever been so lucky?"

△ *backpackers on the Pacific Crest Trail*

㊾ Mitchell Peak

559/338–2251 | Sequoia National Monument and Jennie Lakes Wilderness | www.fs.usda.gov/sequoia

When I lie in my sleeping bag at night and think of the greatest mountaintop views in the hemisphere, the vision of Mitchell Peak always appears, along with Whitney, Tallac, and Eddy.

Mitchell Peak rises 10,365 feet in the Sierras and provides a lookout across 100 miles of the Sierra Crest: from Mount Whitney to the Palisades and beyond to the nearby Great Western Divide and the rim of Kings Canyon.

A bonus for hikers is that Mitchell Peak is often overlooked. The trailhead is outside the more well-trafficked Sequoia-Kings Canyon National Park, located instead in Sequoia National Monument with access through the Jennie Lakes Wilderness.

The primitive Big Meadow Campground is a mile from the Marvin Pass Trailhead to Mitchell Peak and provides a good base. For better accommodations and facilities, nearby Grant Grove has a store, dining, lodging, and my favorite grove of giant sequoias nearby.

Put it all together for the trip of a lifetime.

▽ *view from Mitchell Peak*

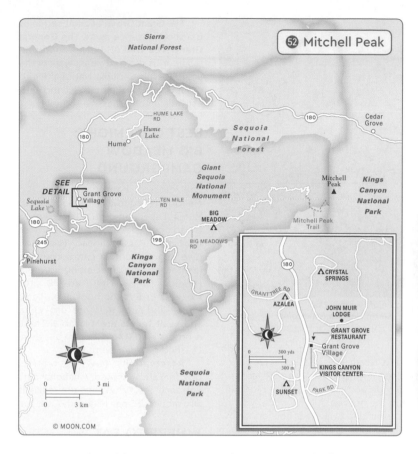

Sequoia
National Forest

52 Mitchell Peak

HUME LAKE
RD

Hume
Lake

180

Hume

Sequoia
National
Forest

Cedar
Grove

180

SEE
DETAIL

Grant Grove
Village

Sequoia
Lake

180

245

Pinehurst

Giant
Sequoia
National
Monument

TEN MILE
RD

198

BIG
MEADOW

BIG MEADOWS
RD

Kings
Canyon
National
Park

Mitchell
Peak

Mitchell Peak
Trail

Mitchell Peak
Trail

Kings
Canyon
National
Park

CRYSTAL
SPRINGS

180

GRANT TREE RD

AZALEA

JOHN MUIR
LODGE

GRANT GROVE
RESTAURANT

Grant Grove
Village

KINGS CANYON
VISITOR CENTER

SUNSET

PARK RD

0   300 yds

0   300 m

Sequoia
National
Park

0   3 mi

0   3 km

© MOON.COM

BEST ACTIVITY: HIKE MITCHELL PEAK

You hike to the top of **Mitchell Peak** (5.2 miles round-trip, 3 hours) for one reason: The panoramic view of the Sierra Crest.

The fun begins with a drive along the rough access road to the Marvin Pass Trailhead (high-clearance vehicles, four-wheel drive advised) at 8,400 feet elevation in Sequoia National Monument. (A free, voluntary registration card for overnight use is available at the trailhead.)

For a hike that tops out with such a sensational view, most of the trail is routed through forest. From the start, it's a steady climb of just under 2,000 feet to reach the top. In the first 1.3

miles, you'll gain 700 feet to reach a junction at Marvin Pass (9,100 feet). Turn left and hike less than a mile to another junction signed to the left for Mitchell Peak. The trail, still in forest, heads up a shaded draw to arc west before climbing steeply; switchbacks aid the grade. Suddenly you hit tree line, arriving at a monolithic field of giant boulders. The trail ends, but the trek is not over. Work your way over the huge boulders for roughly 200 yards. After scrambling over the rocky blocks to make the final summit, you emerge with a full frontal of the Sierra Crest.

To see the landmarks of the Sierra all at once is a surreal moment—everything from the Great Western Divide to the Sierra Crest, and from Sugarloaf

△ *wildflowers in the Sierra Nevada Mountains*

Valley below to the distinctive Middle and North Palisades at 14,248 feet. Look north and you'll see the Monarch Divide and Mount Goddard looming on the horizon. All the while, you are surrounded by a sea of conifers below. It feels like standing on the top of a granite island. Spread your arms and the entire Sierra Nevada is within the scope of your reach.

VISIT GRANT GROVE

Grant Grove Village (Hwy. 180 at Generals Hwy.) is home to the **Kings Canyon Visitor Center** (83918 Hwy. 180 E, 559/565–4307, 8am-5pm daily May-Nov., 9am-4:30pm daily Nov.-May), the Grant Grove Restaurant and store, as well as lodging at **John Muir Lodge** (866/565–6343, www.jmlodge.com) and the **Grant Grove Cabins** (877/436-9615 or 866/807–3598, www.visitsequoia.com). Nearby campgrounds include **Azalea** (110 sites, year-round, fee), **Sunset** (159 sites, summer only, fee), and **Crystal Springs** (49 sites, summer only, fee). All campgrounds are first-come, first-served.

The Grant Grove of giant sequoias is a short distance away. The **General Grant Tree Trail** (0.6 mile round-trip, 0.5 hour) is the trademark walk of the area. It rivals Sequoia National Park's Giant Forest for the prettiest and easiest walk among massive sequoias.

BEST OVERNIGHT: BIG MEADOW CAMPGROUND

The closest campground is Big Meadow (Sequoia National Forest, Hume Lake Ranger District, www.fs.usda.gov), located one mile from the Marvin Pass Trailhead. This primitive, high-mountain campground is located at 7,600 feet along little Big Meadow Creek. There are 38 sites for tents or RVs (no hookups). Picnic tables and fire grills are provided, and vault toilets are available. There is no drinking water; bring your own. Leashed pets are permitted.

Reservations (www.recreation.gov, fee) are accepted. A national park entrance fee (www.nps.gov/seki) is also required. Open May-early October.

WHERE TO EAT

The **Grant Grove Restaurant** (Grant Grove Village, Hwy. 180, 559/335–5500, www.visitsequoia.com, 7am-10am, 11:30am-4pm, 5pm-9pm daily summer, 7:30am-10:30am, 11:30am-3pm, 5pm-8pm daily winter) is the only game in town. This is where everyone in the nearby cabins or campgrounds ends up eating sooner or later. For lunch, try the Reuben; if you're into sauerkraut and corned beef, this is one of the few places you can get one. Most diners opt for burgers at lunch or dinner.

DRIVING DIRECTIONS

From Fresno, take Highway 180 east for 52 miles to the **Big Stump Entrance Station** (fee) for Kings Canyon National Park. Continue straight (east) for 1.5 miles to the junction with Generals

There's no place quite like the **Sequoia High Sierra Camp** (866/654-2877, www.sequoiahighsierracamp.com, open mid-June-mid-Sept., $250/night). You can make a world-class backpacking trek during the day (say, hike to Mitchell Peak) without ending the evening with a freeze-dried dinner and sleeping on the ground.

Instead, your day is crowned by a gourmet dinner with wine or beer available. You can then take an actual hot shower and go to sleep in a bed in a tent cabin. (For a guy like me, with so many nights on the ground, this seems unbelievable). The Sequoia High Sierra Camp is located at 8,500 feet about 0.5 mile from the Marvin Pass Trailhead and the route to Mitchell Peak. The luxury is first-class, yet the location has a wild feel and is off the radar. The air tastes sweet and crisp, and at night there are a million stars overhead. It's hard to believe something of this quality even exists.

△ *tent cabin in Sequoia High Sierra Camp*

Highway (Highway 198). To reach the visitor services at Grant Grove, continue straight on Highway 180 for 1.5 miles.

To reach the Marvin Pass Trailhead, turn right on Generals Highway (Highway 198) and drive 7 miles south toward Sequoia National Park. At Forest Road 14S11 (signed Big Meadows Horse Corral), turn left and drive 10.5 miles east on the narrow road to Forest Road 13S12 (signed Marvin Pass Trailhead). Turn right onto the dirt road and drive 2.8 miles to the end of the road. A trailhead is adjacent to the parking area.

Note: The final three miles is along a rough road; high-clearance vehicles are required, and four-wheel drive is helpful.

Acknowledgements

Thanks to **Denese Stienstra,** my wife and partner afield. We hike about 1,500 miles a year, bike about half that, and are always on the lookout for the best out-of-the way restaurants. She took many of the photographs in this book. I also appreciate that my sons, **Jeremy** and **Kris,** still go out on adventures with me, whether fishing, hiking, or wildlife tracking.

My running mate from the old days, **Jeffrey Patty,** joined me for my first trip on the John Muir Trail. On a high river ford on Blue Creek in Klamath Wilderness, I got washed away and Jeff, a mountain at 6-foot-5, was downstream. He grabbed my hand, fished me out, and saved my life. Jeffrey took the photos on that trip. Thanks to **Rena** and **Michael Patty** for permission to use them.

Brother **Rambob** has always had my back across thousands of trail miles, and in a canoe flip at an icy lake in Oregon, jumped in and helped me get to shore. Yep, saved my life that day, too. The stories, eh?

Michael Furniss has been right there, too. A great photographer, he captured the images from Fern Canyon, the view of Lake Tahoe from the summit of Mount Tallac, and the title page photo, where I'm checking out the map on the Pacific Crest Trail at the foot of the Soldier Lake Basin.

I'm indebted to **Paul Sakuma,** who always seems to show up when I need him most. He took the photo of me and my dog Rebel, at the time 17. Paul's wife, **Patty Au Sakuma,** was willing to share her amazing family story and connection on a visit with her to Angel Island.

Giancarlo Thomae is the biologist who introduced me to the sport of sea kayaking to see humpback whales in Monterey Bay. He's also a world-class wildlife photographer who provided images for this book.

Chris Carr of Shasta Mountain Guides captured the summit photo of Mount Shasta.

Bob Marshall got the shot of me trekking up Green Butte Ridge.

Scott Peden of the Sempervirens Fund created the extended-time photo of Berry Creek Falls. Every spring, I still try to hike there as a birthday present to myself.

Steve Goodall is the great wildlife photographer at Los Vaqueros. **Marc Crumpler** got the stellar image of Los Vaqueros and one of my favorite wild horse photos.

My pal **Tony Rowell** captured a magic moment with his extended-time night photo of the streaking meteor over Mount Whitney.

I've always depended on **Nate Rangel** of Raft California and **Marty McDonnell** of Sierra Mac Rivers for white-water intel and river photos.

Josh Helling is the photographer who caught the moment in time when I climbed the Lyell Glacier in Yosemite. It was my mentor **Gary Bechtel** who encouraged and supported that trek.

I wanted a pretty color photo of the Minarets and field scout **Lara Kaylor** told me she had just the shot.

My buddies **Jeremy Keyston, Tom Hedtke, Bob Simms, Doug Laughlin,** and **Ed Rice** put up with all the photos and video I shoot when they're trying to catch a fish.

On the Lost Coast Trail, **Sandra Miles,** with the King Range/ Bureau of Land Management, provided irreplaceable advice.

In 1980, **Will Hearst** took a huge long shot and hired me for a 13-week tryout at the *San Francisco Chronicle*. At the time, I was the youngest columnist at a major newspaper in America. In the 40 years since, editors have put up with my roamin' and a-ramblin' all over creation to communicate the outdoor experience. I am grateful.

Sports editors **Charles Cooper, Glen Schwarz, Larry Yant** and **Al Saracevic** never tried to rein me in (well, not much, anyway). Editors **Phil Bronstein, Ward Bushee,** and **Audrey Cooper** were at times mystified by behavior that made no sense to anybody but myself, but they still let me do my thing. I am grateful.

Over the years, I've been fortunate to hang with public figures **Waylon Jennings, Dusty Baker, George Seifert,** and **Elvin Bishop.** They are among my heroes and now I am proud to call them friends. They approach each day as a unique gift; the results, in turn, are just as unique.

My mom, **Eleanor,** and dad, **Robert Sr.,** introduced our family to the outdoor experience and taught us to always do the right thing. I never forget that.

My current truck has more than 400,000 miles. Who knows where we will end up next? Enjoy your weekends. See you out there!

—Tom Stienstra

Index

MOON NATIONAL PARKS

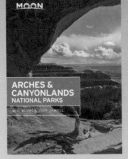

In these books:

- Full coverage of gateway cities and towns
- Itineraries from one day to multiple weeks
- Advice on where to stay (or camp) in and around the parks

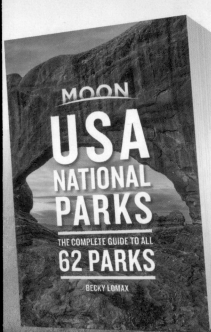

MOON ROAD TRIP GUIDES

MOON
BLUE RIDGE PARKWAY
Road Trip

INCLUDING SHENANDOAH & GREAT SMOKY
MOUNTAINS NATIONAL PARKS

JASON FRYE

MOON
CALIFORNIA
Road Trip

SAN FRANCISCO, YOSEMITE, LAS VEGAS,
GRAND CANYON, LOS ANGELES,
& THE PACIFIC COAST HIGHWAY

STUART THORNTON

MOON
NASHVILLE TO NEW ORLEANS
Road Trip

NATCHEZ TRACE PARKWAY • MEMPHIS •
TUPELO • MISSISSIPPI BLUES TRAIL

MARGARET LITTMAN

MOON
NEW ENGLAND
Road Trip

BOSTON, ACADIA NATIONAL PARK, WHITE
MOUNTAINS, BERKSHIRES, NEWPORT, AND CAPE COD

JEN ROSE SMITH

MOON
NORTHERN CALIFORNIA
Road Trip

DRIVES ALONG THE COAST, REDWOODS, AND MOUNTAINS
WITH THE BEST STOPS ALONG THE WAY

STUART THORNTON & KAYLA ANDERSON

MOON
PACIFIC COAST HIGHWAY
Road Trip

CALIFORNIA,
OREGON & WASHINGTON

IAN ANDERSON

MOON
PACIFIC NORTHWEST
Road Trip

SEATTLE, VANCOUVER, VICTORIA,
THE OLYMPIC PENINSULA, PORTLAND,
THE OREGON COAST & MOUNT RAINIER

ALLISON WILLIAMS

MOON
ROUTE 66
Road Trip

JESSICA DUNHAM

MOON
SOUTH FLORIDA & THE KEYS
Road Trip

WITH MIAMI, WALT DISNEY WORLD, TAMPA &
THE EVERGLADES

JASON FERGUSON

Share your adventures using **#travelwithmoon**

Road Trip USA

Criss-cross the country on classic two-lane highways with the latest edition of Road Trip USA!

Moon Drive & Hike

Get on the road and into the great outdoors with this new series.

These guides are built to help you explore legendary routes at your own pace. Explore the best trail towns, day hikes, weekend getaways, and road trips in between.

Photo Credits

Title page © Michael Furniss
Page 4 © Kailyn Enriquez | Dreamstime.com; pages 6-7 © Tom & Denese Stienstra; pages 8-9 © Tom & Denese Stienstra; page 10 © Jeffrey Patty; page 12 © (top left) Tom & Denese Stienstra, (top right) Chris Carr, (bottom) Pancaketom | Dreamstime.com; page 13 © Lukas Bischoff | Dreamstime.com; page 14 © John Chao/NPS; page 15 © (top left) Florianbernard13 | Dreamstime.com, (top right) Snyfer | Dreamstime.com, (bottom) Alex Zyuzikov; page 16 © (top left) Scott Peden, (top right) Lizziemaher | Dreamstime.com, (bottom) Tom & Denese Stienstra; page 17 © (top left) Kathy Bunton/Delta Kayak; (top right) Hotshot Imaging, (bottom) Tom & Denese Stienstra; page 18 © Donyanedomam | Dreamstime.com; page 19 © (top left) Tom & Denese Stienstra, (top right) Tom & Denese Stienstra, (bottom) Steve Goodall; page 20 © Tom & Denese Stienstra; page 21 © (top left) Radkol | Dreamstime.com, (top right) Tom & Denese Stienstra, (bottom) Giancarlo Thomae; page 22 © Tony Rowell

Chapter 1: page 23 ©Trevor Ducken | Dreamstime.com; page 25 © John Chao/NPS; page 27 © Daniel Ruiz; page 28 © John Chao/NPS; page 29 © Tom Stienstra, © San Francisco Chronicle/Hearst; page 30 © Christina Felschen | Dreamstime.com; page 33 © Christina Felschen | Dreamstime.com; page 34 © James Sakaguchi | Dreamstime.com; page 35 © Aruns911 | Dreamstime.com; page 36 © S. Olson /NPS; page 38 © (left) Michael Furniss, (right) NPS; page 39 © Photog_67 | Dreamstime.com; page 40 © Tom & Denese Stienstra; page 41 © John Chao/NPS; page 43 © (left) NPS, (right) Tom & Denese Stienstra; page 45 © Tom & Denese Stienstra

Chapter 2: page 47 © CampPhoto | istockphoto.com; page 48 © Tom & Denese Stienstra; page 50 © Tom & Denese Stienstra; page 51 © Tom & Denese Stienstra; page 52 © Tom & Denese Stienstra; page 53 © Tom & Denese Stienstra; page 56 © Tom & Denese Stienstra; page 57 Jibewarrior | Dreamstime.com; page 59 © Lindsay Sanders | Dreamstime.com; page 60 © Tom & Denese Stienstra; page 62 Bob Marshall; page 64 © Chris Carr; page 66 © Jennifer A. Walz | Dreamstime.com; page 67 © Tom & Denese Stienstra; page 68 © Tom & Denese Stienstra; page 72 © Tom & Denese Stienstra

Chapter 3: page 73 © Michael Rubin | Dreamstime.com; page 75 © Marc Crumpler; page 77 © Tom & Denese Stienstra; page 78 © Tom Stienstra; page 79 © Tom Stienstra; page 80 © BOUCHET francie | Shutterstock.com; page 83 © OldskoolDesign | Shutterstock.com; page 84 © Alisa_Ch | Shutterstock.com; page 85 © Tom & Denese Stienstra; page 86 Tom Stienstra, © San Francisco Chronicle/Hearst; page 89 © Mike Brake | Dreamstime.com; page 90 © Tom & Denese Stienstra; page 91 © Zrfphoto | Dreamstime.com; page 95 © powerofforever | iStock photo; page 96 © Tom & Denese Stienstra; page 99 © Brian Kushner | Dreamstime.com

Chapter 4: page 101 © Pius Lee | Dreamstime.com; page 102 © Michael Overstreet | Shutterstock.com; page 106 © Tom & Denese Stienstra, © San Francisco Chronicle/Hearst; page 107 © Chris Labasco | Dreamstime.com; page 109 © Brian Sak | Dreamstime.com; page 111 © Donnie Shackleford | Dreamstime.com; page 112 © Tom & Denese Stienstra; page 114 © Tom & Denese Stienstra; page 116 © Ethan Daniels | Dreamstime.com; page 117 © Velvetfish | iStock Photo; page 119 © Velvetfish | iStock Photo

Chapter 5: page 121 © Kathy Bunton/Delta Kayak; page 122 © Larry Crain | iStock Photo; page 125 © Larry Crain | iStock Photo; page 126 © courtesy Bob Simms; page 127 © Chon Kit Leong | Dreamstime.com; page 129 Nancy Hoyt Belcher / Alamy Stock Photo; page 131 © Nirian | iStock Photo; page 132 © jmoor17 | iStock Photo; page 134 © Brian Sak | Dreamstime.com; page 135 © jmoor17 | iStock Photo; page 136 © Mike Brake | Dreamstime.

page 287 © OARS; page 289 © OARS; page 290 © Luciavegaphotography | Dreamstime. com; page 292 © Jerry Snyder | Forest Service; page 293 © Lara Kaylor; page 295 © (left) Jeffrey Patty, (right) Jeffrey Patty; page 296 © Pancaketom | Dreamstime.com; page 297 © Jeffrey Kreulen | Dreamstime.com; page 298 © Jerry S | Dreamstime.com; page 300 © Cecilio Ricardo; page 301 © Jeffrey Patty; page 302 © Andrew Cox | Forest Service; page 303 © Jeffrey Patty; page 304 © Pancaketom | Dreamstime.com; page 307 © Tom & Denese Stienstra; page 309 © Patrick Poendl | Dreamstime.com; page 310 © Stevehymon | Dreamstime.com; page 313 © Clay Shannon | Dreamstime.com; page 314 © Tom & Denese Stienstra; page 316 © Nicholas Motto | Dreamstime.com; page 317 © Burr Snyder/Sequoia High Sierra Camp

Acknowledgments, page 322: top left, Trevor Slaymaker; top center, Jeffrey Patty; top right, Tom & Denese Stienstra; second down left, Jeffrey Patty; second down right, Marc Cretarola; Third down left, Siv Hermistad; third down right, Jeffrey Patty; bottom left, Dave Farrell; bottom right, Tom & Denese Stienstra

MAP SYMBOLS

═══	Expressway	○	City/Town	✗	Airport	⚓	Golf Course
───	Primary Road	◉	State Capital	✗	Airfield	🅿	Parking Area
⋯⋯	Secondary Road	⊛	National Capital	▲	Mountain	▂	Archaeological Site
▫▫▫	Unpaved Road	❶	Adventures	✦	Unique Natural Feature	⚑	Church
-----------	Trail	★	Point of Interest			🝙	Gas Station
⋯⋯⋯	Ferry	•	Accommodation	⚐	Waterfall	⬭	Glacier
▪━▪━	Railroad	▼	Restaurant/Bar	⚑	Park	▩	Mangrove
▒▒▒	Pedestrian Walkway	■	Other Location	🆃🅷	Trailhead	▱	Reef
▥▥▥	Stairs	Λ	Campground	🎿	Skiing Area	▱	Swamp

CONVERSION TABLES

$°C = (°F - 32) / 1.8$
$°F = (°C \times 1.8) + 32$

1 inch = 2.54 centimeters (cm)
1 foot = 0.304 meters (m)
1 yard = 0.914 meters
1 mile = 1.6093 kilometers (km)
1 km = 0.6214 miles
1 fathom = 1.8288 m
1 chain = 20.1168 m
1 furlong = 201.168 m
1 acre = 0.4047 hectares
1 sq km = 100 hectares
1 sq mile = 2.59 square km
1 ounce = 28.35 grams
1 pound = 0.4536 kilograms
1 short ton = 0.90718 metric ton
1 short ton = 2,000 pounds
1 long ton = 1.016 metric tons
1 long ton = 2,240 pounds
1 metric ton = 1,000 kilograms
1 quart = 0.94635 liters
1 US gallon = 3.7854 liters
1 Imperial gallon = 4.5459 liters
1 nautical mile = 1.852 km

°FAHRENHEIT	°CELSIUS	
230	110	
220		
210	100	WATER BOILS
200		
190	90	
180	80	
170		
160	70	
150		
140	60	
130		
120	50	
110		
100	40	
90	30	
80		
70	20	
60		
50	10	
40		
30	0	WATER FREEZES
20		
10	-10	
0		
-10	-20	
-20	-30	
-30		
-40	-40	

INCH: 0 1 2 3 4

CM: 0 1 2 3 4 5 6 7 8 9 10

52 WEEKEND ADVENTURES IN NORTHERN CALIFORNIA
Avalon Travel
Hachette Book Group
1700 Fourth Street
Berkeley, CA 94710, USA
www.moon.com

Editor: Sabrina Young
Copy Editor: Ann Seifert
Graphics and Production Coordinator: Ravina Schneider
Cover Design: Kimberly Glyder Design
Interior Design: Tabitha Lahr
Moon Logo: Tim McGrath
Map Editor: Kat Bennett
Cartographer: John Culp
Indexer: Greg Jewett

ISBN-13 978-1-64049-934-8

Printing History
1st Edition — September 2020
5 4 3 2